HOW TO BE I

How do we advance? As individuals, families, and businesses? As societies, nations, and a species? In a world where it's said there is nothing new under the sun, we humans are remarkably resourceful at creating new things. The key to innovation is understanding, but not just by using facts, data, and casual observations. Progress demands the profound and useful understanding of a person or a thing, a situation or an issue. And profound and useful understanding that truly effects change is that most elusive of phenomena: insight.

How To Be Insightful provides a novel and deeply practical framework that anyone can use to generate more powerful and impactful insights from the increasing volumes of data we all face every day, whatever we do. The framework – the STEP Prism of Insight – has been developed through decades of both practice and training, and the book includes many exercises designed to help strengthen and develop readers' insight muscles. The book explains the history, psychology, and neuroscience of insight and includes snapshots of insight from international experts in many different fields – psychology and neuroscience, music and acting, forensic science and market research.

Sam Knowles is a data storyteller with 30 years' experience helping businesses communicate with more impact. A classicist with a psychology doctorate, he helps organisations to talk "Human". He's the author of *Narrative by Numbers* (2018) from Routledge.

"Many books which claim to be about generating insight are really about managing evidence. This book puts the individual in insight and helps the reader understand how insight can be personally created."

Jane Frost, CBE, Chief Executive Officer,
The Market Research Society

"Insight is the lifeblood of great marketing. But the really disruptive insights that springboard into great creative and commercial success can be frustratingly elusive. Sam has plotted a path to help us all to uncover those big insights that will power breakthrough thinking."

Mark Evans, Managing Director,
Marketing & Digital, Direct Line Group

"In the insights business, data or casual observations often masquerade as insights. But genuine, data-driven insights that help shape decisions about the future are much rarer. The model at the heart of Sam's book will help reverse this imbalance in insightful thinking."

Matt Painter, Managing Director,
Corporate Reputation, Ipsos MORI

"When an idea is rooted in true insights, it will always be more effective and deliver a better result. Sam Knowles' framework and model for generating these kind of insights more reliably is something I would urge people to take a look at, whatever kind creative or communications challenge you may be faced with."

Andy Porteous, Chief Strategy Officer,
Mavens of London

"Sam is that all too rare creature – a numbers guy who communicates in plain English. As well as a storyteller, he is a compelling writer and his latest book will not only be of immense practical use for those looking to enhance the quality and frequency of insights. It's also quite fascinating."

Karsten Shaw, Director of Analytics, Populus

"Combining his experience in academic research and brand marketing, Dr Sam Knowles believes everyone has the power to be insightful. *How To Be Insightful* inspires readers to unlock their curiosity and unleash their insight potential, to reap the benefits of the data-led age."

Annalise Coady, President, EMEA, W2O Group

"Insight is one of the fundamental particles of the craft of successful marketing. Sam takes his typical forensic approach to this topic and creates a practical way of applying his wisdom in the workplace – great stuff!"

Sean Gogarty, Former Global Divisional CEO,
Unilever; founder of Verummundi

"Anyone who knows Sam will not be surprised that he has written a book to help understand understanding. From Greek philosophy to modern neuroscience, he explores the physics and metaphysics of eureka moments. At the heart of every insight is a curious mind, and this timely and important book sprang from a very curious mind indeed."

Thomas Stoeckle, Adjunct Professor, University of Florida

"A clear and practical guide that 'does exactly what it says on the tin' – providing fresh and informative background on the history and science of insight; but most importantly hands-on tips and techniques, explained through real-world examples, for how to be insightful."

Richard Cox, Chairman, Mullen Lowe Salt

"In today's data-rich-insight-poor world, Sam Knowles shines an insightful light on the challenge of exactly how to generate insight; an easy read and eminently usable."

Andrew Challier, Chief Client Officer, Ebiquity

"Insight is at the heart of human understanding – and Sam gives us a practical guide on how to understand the things humans often can't say, don't say, or won't say."

Karnvir Mundrey, Host, The Future of
Branded Content & PR podcast

"Sam has a real knack of being able to distinguish insights that are blindingly compelling from those which are just genuinely interesting. *How To Be Insightful* is a real treat, both practically and historically, in helping us identify how being more intuitive in the way we examine the world can help us develop better ideas for our clients and their brands."

Ian Jenkins, Global Head of Strategy,
Insight & Intelligence, Intrinsic Insight

"In a world where all your competitors have access to much of the same data and information, competitive advantage relies on a superior ability to search, identify, and use insights to establish a deeper meaning and engagement for your brand and business. Sam's brilliant new book is both inspiring and practical in giving you a critical edge."

Simon Thong, Founder Director, Revel

HOW TO BE INSIGHTFUL

Unlocking the Superpower that Drives Innovation

SAM KNOWLES

Routledge
Taylor & Francis Group

LONDON AND NEW YORK

First published 2020
by Routledge
2 Park Square, Milton Park, Abingdon, Oxon OX14 4RN

and by Routledge
52 Vanderbilt Avenue, New York, NY 10017

Routledge is an imprint of the Taylor & Francis Group, an informa business

British Library Cataloguing-in-Publication Data
A catalogue record for this book is available from the British Library

Library of Congress Cataloging-in-Publication Data
Names: Knowles, Sam, author.
Title: How to be insightful : unlocking the superpower that drives
    innovation / Sam Knowles.
Description: Milton Park, Abingdon, Oxon ; New York, NY : Routledge,
    2020. | Includes bibliographical references and index. |
Identifiers: LCCN 2019055047 (print) | LCCN 2019055048 (ebook) |
    ISBN 9780367261702 (hardback) | ISBN 9780367261719 (paperback) |
    ISBN 9780429291807 (ebook)
Subjects: LCSH: Insight. | Technological innovations.
Classification: LCC BF449.5 .K59 2020 (print) | LCC BF449.5 (ebook) |
    DDC 153.4—dc23
LC record available at https://lccn.loc.gov/2019055047
LC ebook record available at https://lccn.loc.gov/2019055048

ISBN: 978-0-367-26170-2 (hbk)
ISBN: 978-0-367-26171-9 (pbk)
ISBN: 978-0-429-29180-7 (ebk)

Typeset in Joanna Sans
by Apex CoVantage, LLC

CONTENTS

ACKNOWLEDGEMENTS AND INSPIRATIONS

The eighth instalment of the Star Wars triple trilogy, *The Last Jedi*, begins a couple of days after Episode VII, *The Force Awakens*, ends. The second season of *Killing Eve* begins just 30 seconds after the first has ended. This is becoming increasingly fashionable in sequels.

How To Be Insightful is very definitely the sequel to *Narrative by Numbers*, published (thanks **Judith**, **Rebecca**, and **Sophie**) by Routledge in spring 2018. In my George Lucas-like envisioning of this series of books, I'd originally intended *How To Be Insightful* to come first. But it took my friend and *Elisabeth's Lists* author, **Lulah Ellender**, to point out that I needed to write *Narrative by Numbers* before I could move over here into insightsville. I'd been struggling with the neuroscience of insight – now so elegantly sorted out by Messrs Kounios, Beeman, and Mlodinow, as you'll read in Chapter 4 – but was buzzing about a lecture I'd just given on data storytelling at the University of Greenwich. Thanks for your insight, Lulah. And thanks also to course director **Nicky Garsten** for that annual gig in SE10. I wouldn't have had the insight and spark to create *Narrative by Numbers* – and to do so first – without you both.

So if you put down my first book just half an hour ago, here's a Star Wars episode VII into VIII style segue into this new one. You'll recall we were at the memorial service of Asa Briggs, the pioneering vice chancellor of Sussex University, where I learned statistics in the early 2000s as a student retread. It was at Briggs' memorial service that my hodgepodge of education (master's in classics, master's and doctorate in psychology) made sense as the lens through which story and analytics could be yoked together. This was the same Asa Briggs who in his last book outed my father **Kenneth Guy Jack Charles Knowles** as having worked at Bletchley Park, a secret Kenneth kept from his family to his death in 1988. Kenneth was a deeply insightful man, able to see connections that others couldn't. He could do the "Where's Wally/Waldo?" thing apparently at will and *The Guardian* crossword in a regulation 29 minutes, though his bizarre upbringing in affluent Edwardian London did mean he lacked a little insight when it came to his own romantic life. I say that as the grateful last child (of a baker's half dozen) from his fourth of five wives.

But a decent part of what I know about mashing up analytics and story I owe to my old man. His own trajectory – and one that inspired me, 60 years on – was Mods and Greats at Oxford in the late 1920s/ early 1930s, Bletchley Park during the war, and co-founding the Institute of Economics and Statistics back at Oxford in the late 1940s. *Narrative by Numbers'* official publication date was staged to fall on Kenneth's 110th birthday, and there's more about all of these stories in the commemorative blog at http://insightagents.co.uk/happy-birthday-dad/. Thanks for the memories and all those late night, post–Chandos Arms, Madeira-fuelled conversations, Dad. They're the origin of my insatiable curiosity, a critical dimension in being insightful.

I developed the model at the heart of this book – the STEP Prism of Insight™ (no less) – back in 2015. I've used it as the basis for insight training since then and started to sketch out the structure for this book a year or so later. So, *How To Be Insightful* presents no difficult second album syndrome. Not something that could be said of the fictitious progressive rock band Victims of Circumstance that my oldest and best friend **Peter Russian** and I created and graffitied on the walls of Buckinghamshire in the summer of 1984. We had difficult first single syndrome, but we learned how to run a very effective whispering campaign long before that was A Thing. Thanks for the insights and insightful reading of so much of my writing over the years, Pete, including early sections of this book. You were perhaps a bit harsh on the lyrics of our EP *The Peace of Nicias, 421BC*, though. A great song *and* ancient history A-level revision in the same set of words? Who could ask for more?

To my closest of close family – my wife, life, and business partner, **Saskia**, my splendid son **Max** (officially a better footballer and guitarist than I could ever be, and now a better photographer, too): thanks for putting up with me, particularly when I'm writing. I broke the back of this book in a cottage in Chichester in spring 2019 while Max was on year ten work experience nearby.

I can give no thanks whatsoever to the builders with whom we shared our lives during the gestation period of some of this book, save the fact that their lack of empathy and understanding of human motivations and behaviour taught me bucket loads about what insight most definitely is not. Our architects, meanwhile, were a different leather thing altogether.

And never, of course, forgetting **Tony the Cat**, named in honour of Tony Soprano, doyen of my Instagram feed for many years, who sadly purred and nuzzled his last during the editing process thanks to dodgy kidneys, but the nicest, gentlest, most insightful animal I ever did meet.

To you all, thanks for the inspiration. The mistakes – as ever – are the sub-editor's. Or perhaps, in our ever-more AI world, the sub-editor's algorithms.

PREFACE

"You never really understand a person until you consider things from his point of view . . . until you climb into his skin and walk around in it."
Atticus Finch to Scout in **To Kill a Mockingbird**

"A PROFOUND UNDERSTANDING OF A PERSON, THING, SITUATION, OR ISSUE"

How do we advance? As individuals, families, and businesses? As societies, nations, and a species? In a world where there is nothing new under the sun, we humans are remarkably resourceful at creating new things – for good and for ill. From the iPhone to Brexit, from Repeal the Eighth to smart toilets, from Skolstrejk för klimatet to the "impossible" vegan burgers that "bleed" beetroot juice. Innovation truly is a universal human superpower.

The key to innovation and progress is understanding. But not just facts, data, and casual observations. These are all useful building blocks towards understanding, but they aren't what I mean by understanding. What I mean is profound and deep understanding of a person, a thing, a situation, or an issue that we can use to help us advance. This for me is the very definition of insight, but insight is also that often slippery, ill-thought-through, cognitive construct that can and should underpin all novelty. With all the good ideas apparently already dreamt up and taken, the only way to create something new is to take a little bit of this and a little bit of that (old stuff), put it in the blender of our subconscious minds, and be ready to capture the new combinations that surface in our conscious awareness. The act of creation, as Arthur Koestler put it in his classic 1964 treatise of that name on the subject, is an act of "bisociation": blending elements drawn from hitherto unconnected matrices to create a new matrix.

Many people claim that they're not creative. This is particularly true of those who work in the creative, media, and communications industries, those responsible for developing and running campaigns to persuade people to think or behave differently. For a function often lampooned and caricatured as "the colouring-in department", there's often staggeringly low self-belief among its inhabitants about how creative they actually are. But it's also a frequent refrain of those who work in apparently more mundane, less "creative" job roles, from finance to procurement, from supply chain management to human capital management.

"Only creative people can be creative" comes the retort. In the media world, creativity has long been ghettoised to be the sole province of cre-atives, as if the suits (account managers), planners, and growing legions of data analytics folks are somehow not creative or able to innovate. I'm not talking about creative accountancy and tax dodging (though that does come from bringing different worlds and data sets together in the way I do approve of – it's just the motives and outcome that are ethically question-able). I'm talking about performing that uniquely human skill of crashing together stimulus, information, and data from multiple sources and creating something new. To those who claim not to be creative – or say they find it hard to generate the insights they need to unlock creativity – I blow a loud, 360-degree raspberry and offer you this considered response: "Phooey!"

Schools and universities teach us a lot of things, but outside philoso-phy, mathematics, and some aspects of psychology, the track record of educators passing on metacognitive skills – thinking skills about how to think – is shockingly poor. Yes, secondary schools around the world offer classes in critical thinking, but because the system and education depart-ments and therefore schools and teachers don't take these seriously – because, ultimately, there's often no formal qualification to instruct and earn – the lessons too often dissolve into animal noises and armpit farts.

It doesn't get much better when we get out into the world of work. Training may have developed beyond "Excel skills 101" and "How to keep a meeting short" into EQ and empathy. But courses on thinking about thinking? Training on how to be insightful? All too often it feels too difficult or challenging or abstract.

No more. Having unearthed, magpied, and refashioned a simple model that gives the structure and headspace to help anyone and everyone to become more insightful, I want to share it with the world. It's a simple model with four key pieces of advice for anyone trying to solve any problem which requires fresh insight: be curious (**Sweat**), deliberately remove yourself from trying to address the challenge at hand (**Timeout**), recognise what insight feels like to you when it comes (**Eureka**), and share it with the world early (**Prove**). I've taken the first letter from each of the four steps – S-T-E-P – and called the model the STEP Prism of Insight.

Since 2015 I've trained hundreds of people in the UK, Europe, and North America using the STEP Prism of Insight, and the results are encouraging. The overwhelming majority of delegates to my courses feel more confident and competent at generating and articulating better, richer – ultimately more insightful – insights. Not just immediately after the course as they fill in feedback forms, but six, 12 months later when I return to their offices to train colleagues. They know what insight is and they know how to make it more likely they'll find one. At work, in bed, in the shower, on a run.

The model is unashamedly simple, just as looking into the actual workings of the mind – the world's most powerful supercomputer – is precisely the opposite: opaque and resistant to introspection. But because it works, and because I'm a man on a mission to provide actionable tools people can adopt into their everyday ways of working, *How To Be Insightful* is full of practical advice and techniques. Just like *Narrative by Numbers* before it – the logical prequel to this book – *How To Be Insightful* is designed to help everyone unlock the superpower that truly does drive innovation.

This is true **for those who work in marketing services** – where I've lurked for more than 30 years. Advertising, market research, PR, digital media, and communications agencies, where practitioners are charged by clients to respond with insight to creative briefs. Where they're required to develop evidence-based, data-driven campaigns with a profound understanding of customer needs, rooted in fundamental human truths.

It's true **for those who run established business**, whose worlds are being rocked by young and digital, upstart start-ups that cut out the middleman and threaten to make the old ways of working irrelevant. They need to disrupt the disruptors with their disintermediating ways or else face extinction. While the model could never claim to be a universal panacea to disruption, being more insightful is one critical way of ensuring long-term survival.

It's true for **those who work in new product development and innovation** in – frankly – any sector, those people and teams who are required to create new variants of existing products. Or completely new product lines altogether. The approach to generating insights detailed in this book is as relevant for app developers as it is for academics, for fast-moving consumer goods brand and product managers as it is for financiers.

It's true for **those who work in strategy, planning, or insight** roles in any organisation, responsible for using research and intelligence to drive company performance and so outflank the competition. No insights – no genuine, actionable, data-driven insights – no point in even turning up.

And it's true for **those who work in the market research and intelligence industry**. Faced with mountains of data and thousands of cross-tabulations, researchers are charged by their clients to make sense of the numbers, data, and statistics. To extract meaning and implications and deliver proper insights that drive change within their clients' businesses is an honour and a privilege.

Thanks to *How To Be Insightful* and the STEP Prism of Insight, all of these roles just got a little bit easier. Join me on a tour through the history, psychology, and neuroscience of insight. You'll learn to put just that little bit of scaffolding around how you think about thinking. Along the way, you'll find a hidden superpower inside you that truly does drive innovation. And that superpower allows you "climb into the skin" of others and walk around, as Atticus Finch tells Scout in *To Kill a Mockingbird*.

To support this book and its mission to help the world's data-driven storytellers become more impactful yet, we've created a website called www.howtobeinsightful.com – come and say hi and join the community. We're building a living online archive of everyone's favourite tools and techniques in each part of the STEP Prism of Insight. It would be great to hear what you do for Sweat, Timeout, Eureka, and Prove.

Thank you, as ever, for your consideration.

1

WHAT IS INSIGHT?

"The Guide says there is an art to flying", said Ford, "or rather a knack. The knack lies in learning how to throw yourself at the ground and miss."
Douglas Adams, *Life, the Universe and Everything*

SWIMMING THROUGH THE MIST

Between May and September every year, I swim. Slowly, methodically, rhythmically. I do most of my swimming in the UK's oldest outdoor lido, the splendid and thriving Pells Pool in Lewes, East Sussex. It's just finished its 158th continuous season at time of writing. I don't really go in for wild swimming, and Pells isn't that cold – especially since they swapped out the leaky Victorian lead pipes for new plastic ones about ten years ago.

Every time I swim in the Pells, it's the same. Eleven laps of very basic breast stroke. Not bobbing up and down, under and over the water with my face and head like the David Wilkies and Duncan Goodhews of my childhood Olympic memories. Just forward propulsion and 65 to 70 strokes to haul my frame through the 50 yards of the pool. No wet suit. No flippers. No moulded hand scoops. Not even one of those bone-shaped wedges between the thighs that triathletes-in-training favour.

Total immersion and total concentration in spring-fed water does something apparently very positive to my mind. Every cell of skin wet, body temperature lowered, and no goal other than to complete 550 yards in between 15 or 20 minutes (I told you I was slow). By focusing on nothing other than the act of being and moving in the water, I free my subconscious mind to do its thing. To shuffle the elements and components of solutions to the challenges I'm facing and to throw them out in novel configurations. To discard many of the more fanciful and whimsical solutions along the way without me even knowing that two had been added to two to make nine, pi, or the square root of 75. And then – just occasionally – to allow a more promising solution to pop into consciousness and say, "Well, what do you think?"

It's an act of monotonous repetition, ploughing up and down the azure waters of Pells, navigating a straight line by following a darker-blue rubber lane marking screwed to the floor of the pool. But it's also an act of distraction so powerful and so effective I sometimes think it ought to be prescribed. Don't get me wrong. I don't go swimming *in order to* solve problems; to surface the deep or profound understanding of the challenge I'm facing. But the very act of giving one's attention to being in the very moment of a routine swim commands sufficient conscious, attentional resources to allow problem-solving to go on beneath the surface – beneath the conscious waves of my mind, if you will. And that dedication of conscious capacity to something as mundane as swimming – staying afloat, breathing, counting the laps, not drowning – is apparently enough to liberate the more cognitive, problem-solving, interconnected webs of neurons to get to work.

Now this insight problem solving often isn't (necessarily) instantaneous or immediate. It's not as if I get out of the water, towel myself down, and the answer presents itself fully articulated and irrefutable. It's very rarely like Zoltar, the end-of-pier fortune telling machine in the Tom Hanks' movie, *Big*, presenting a card saying, "Your Wish is Granted".[1] Solving problems, generating profound insights into the hidden or inner "why" of the challenges we face in our business and personal lives, isn't like that. It's not that linear, that logical, that reducible to a predictable formula. Insight problems are not the same as analytical problems, which yield to time input.

As we'll see in the course of this book, there's no simple trick to suddenly becoming or being more insightful. Sorry to disappoint you so early.

You may well experience a eureka moment, a blinding flash of inspiration that seems too obvious and yet so right. But that concrete sense of certainty which often accompanies insights and breakthrough thoughts can also be a slow dawning realisation over a period of hours, days, or weeks, as you and your subconscious mind align the planets or get enough of the jigsaw pieces into place to convince you – and others – that you're really onto something.

The breakthrough for me that follows swims in the Pells can indeed come all at once – of course it can. But it often comes much later, too. The very real advantage of swimming is that it gets you into a sense of flow and mindless mindfulness that makes you more receptive to the shuffled memories and doodles dealt in the margins of your brain. By deliberately focusing on nothing – by absorbing your conscious problem-solving mind with anything but the problem at hand – paradoxically you make the act of creating, finding, and recognising a solution to crack it that much more likely. And even more than any other form of exercise, swimming cannot be done with a phone in hand. Getting distracted by the ping of a notification – perhaps an invitation to play yet another game of Words With Friends from that fiendish competitor, Themigou – is not possible in a pool.

In the third instalment of his *Hitchhiker's Guide to the Galaxy* trilogy – a trilogy that ended up with five books during his lifetime – the crowned prince of writer's block Douglas Adams reveals the secret to flying. "The Guide says there is an art to flying", seasoned space traveller Ford Prefect tells ingénu astronaut and Earthling, Arthur Dent, "or rather a knack. The knack lies in learning how to throw yourself at the ground and miss." For me, this is the perfect description of what swimming does for me beyond physical exercise – and many others I've talked to about the metaphysical and transcendent benefits of this and other forms of exercise. As I've shown in *Narrative by Numbers*, it's very dangerous to generalise from the particular with a very small "n" (particularly an n of 1). This is the trap of which the worst example is Peter Cook and Dudley Moore's Derek and Clive with their sketch about Uncle Bert; "Well, I've got an Uncle Bert and he's worse . . ." But bear with me. This is important.

If you deliberately distract yourself from the insight problem you're trying to solve, you give your subconscious mind more opportunity to work on alternative answers to questions, run them through the filter of ridiculousness ("Is this daft or not?"), and allow those that seem to pass muster through for conscious consideration. Ford Prefect's prescription for flying suggests that, if you think about humanoid creatures actually flying – including yourself – then you'll inevitably crash face down into the ground, obey the laws of gravity, and hurt yourself. And, of course, not fly. But if you "throw yourself at the ground and miss" – if you think about anything other than the fact that you're trying to fly, and continue to distract yourself from that ludicrous thought – then fly you can.

Arthur Dent suffers an inevitable series of failures as he attempts to learn how to put flying out of his mind and therefore be able to fly, grazing different parts of his body with increasingly painful consequences. As his antihero seeks to move from what life coaches call "conscious incompetence" and on to "conscious competence",[2] Adams takes the reader on a journey during which it seems likely Arthur will never learn to fly. Until, not trying and not thinking about it anymore, he trips on a step and suddenly finds himself hovering, then ascending, and ultimately soaring above the trees. It's a joyous passage of writing.

Swimming is like that for me. And it's not just me and it's not just swimming. I find running and sometimes cycling – all done slowly, like an ultra-slow triathlete – achieve the same thing. And so, too, do many of

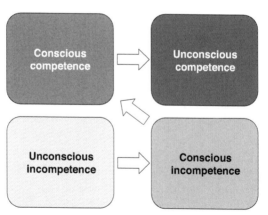

Figure 1.1 From unconscious incompetence to unconscious competence

the most insightful thinkers I've met and worked with. Running is perhaps the most effective of all diversionary tactics, the perfect means of taking timeout from the challenges we need to solve, taking us away from the insights we need to generate and unlock to make progress, to innovate, to move forward. I've scarcely met a planner – that breed of data-driven problem-solvers most often charged in marketing and advertising agencies with coming up with insights into consumer motivation – who doesn't run. And also who doesn't attribute or associate the act of running to the development of some of their best and most profound insights.

That act of self-propulsion in running, of one foot in front of the other, of changing heart rate and breathing rate and body temperature, of it being just you and your body that are doing the exercise and no other equipment involved – that's priceless. All of these factors appear to have a profound impact on diverting the conscious mind from the task at hand, of allowing the unconscious to work away at it, and for solutions to arrive as if from nowhere in a flash or over days, weeks, or months.

There's no meaningful experimental literature on why and how timeout does this, but it is clear that timeout– from seasoned and effective practitioners – is one of the keys to unlocking genuinely insightful thinking. To soaring, like Arthur Dent, high above the trees. To seeing the forest from the trees. To having a profound and deep understanding of someone or something. To joining together previously acquired facts or observations about the state of the world into something new and so shining a light on the problem we're trying to solve. There's more – much more – to insight and insightful thinking than just distraction and timeout. But because timeout is the most startling element of the model of insight presented in this book – some call it a palace revolution – it's as good a place as any to start.

GETTING OUR DEFINITIONS IN A ROW

Insight is a very useful thing, but it's an abstract, thinky thing, and therefore often slippery and hard to nail down. But as this book is about insight and how to be insightful, we need a set of good, strong, early definitions to point us in the right direction. There will be different definitions and interpretations of insight as we go – when we speak to actors and musicians, psychologists and psychiatrists, forensic scientists and market researchers. But let's start as we mean to go on, giving a clear and definitive definition of insight.

For me, **insight is a profound and useful understanding of a person, a thing, a situation, or an issue**. An insight is a nugget of data-driven, evidence-based certainty. An insight helps us to understand and think about an issue differently, more completely, with – to be circular for a second – more insight. This sense of profound understanding means that an insight is also well defined as "the why behind the what", the implication of a situation, and an ability to see the full picture. In business and in life more generally, insights help to answer the more meaningful "So what?" questions.

The physicist Leonard Mlodinow – with whom we'll spend a good slug of time with in Chapter 3 when we consider the neuroscience of insight – teases apart ideas and insights in this way in his book *Elastic*:

> In the science of thinking, however, "idea" usually refers to something simpler, the complexity of which can be contained in a single thought, and that pops suddenly into our consciousness. An "insight" is defined as an idea (of that sort) that represents an original and fruitful way of understanding an issue or approaching a problem.[3]

That is a nice and neat, helpfully precise distinction.

I've been running training courses in insight and how to be insightful since 2015, having in that year first codified the model we'll explore in the second half of this book, the STEP Prism of Insight. When I wrote this chapter, I'd just delivered my 42nd STEP Prism course – a rather pleasing number for Douglas Adams fans.[4] One of the first exercises I get delegates to do – often as homework in advance of the course – is to give me their raw, unfiltered definition of what insight means to them. I like them to define insight without recourse to media – particularly Google (which returns a very passable dictionary definition of "the capacity to gain an accurate and deep understanding of someone or something" in response to the search string "define: insight"). And one of the best definitions in all my 42 courses – with more than 450 delegates to date – has been "the ability to see round corners". Thanks Aoife. And you'll remember producing this definition of insight spontaneously.

I prefer to have my insight training delegates tell me what they think insight is unprompted for much the same reason that James O'Brien – that rarest of creatures: a liberal talk-show host – dedicates one of the 15 hours he broadcasts on London's LBC Radio to knowledge that is not sought out online. Every Thursday from noon to 1pm, O'Brien forbids listeners from Googling the answers to other listeners' questions on his very popular Mystery Hour.[5] He does this because he wants to celebrate deep and often profound knowledge already acquired, not to allow people to search for an answer and take credit for someone else's knowledge. In an age when it's possible to find out almost anything – even with a ham-fisted search query riddled with typos – raw, unfiltered responses often give us a better understanding of where current knowledge lies.

Like Ford Prefect's prescription for humanoid flight, Aoife's definition of insight as "seeing around corners" is of course impossible. At least without a series of mirrors and a lot of preparation. But its metaphorical power is brilliant. If we were to have the ability to see around corners, we'd be able to solve problems we didn't even know were coming. In exactly the same way, with a deep and accurate understanding of the challenges we're looking to solve in our lives – particularly in our jobs, but also in our relationships – with insight we're able to come up with more useful, better-informed solutions, solutions that are much more likely to succeed.

More than just understanding, insights also allow us to do something – to take action – with renewed purpose and more understanding than we had before we developed the insight or someone revealed and explained the insight to us. When in possession of the why behind the what, we have an edge. Our thinking is transformed, and work and life feels somehow easier and more straightforward. We move – as a Californian former boss used to say about the power and value of insights – from "So what?" to "Now what?" At the time, he wanted me to change the title on my business card from "Head of Strategic Planning" – a role entirely predicated on the ability to bring together multiple data sources and find insights – to "Mr So What? Now What?" In my very English way, I politely demurred until my boss lost interest. At the time, I thought I'd need a whole book to explain why I'd suddenly taken on this new, poseur's title. Well here – at last – it is, Tim.

Ten years ago and more, in a different job, I worked alongside a great advertising planner from whom I learned a huge amount about insight. At the time, Mike Teasdale ran the planning department for Lowe & Partners advertising (now Mullen Lowe), with a particular focus on Lowe's big global client, Unilever. Mike had the unenviable task of coordinating a team of almost 90 Lowe planners writing advertising briefs for and with Unilever brand teams around the world. For food, home care, and personal care products, Mike's team and their clients produced around 300 advertising briefs a year. And on each of the standardised, templated briefing forms, the second, all-important question asked, "What insight drives this brief?"

Often, the first drafts of these briefing templates featured insights that weren't insights. They said things like "Mums like tea" or "People are eating meals differently from how their parents did". These generally needed a lot of work. At other times, the box was filled with something much closer to a genuine insight. I recall one that began, "When it comes to foods, what's nutritious is often not pleasurable, and what's pleasurable often isn't nutritious. But it doesn't have to be this way". In one of our frequent conversations about insight over the years, Mike defined insight to me as "a glimpse inside the mind of the target audience, shining a light on a possible solution to the problem we have defined. Insight increases the chances of creative breakthrough, makes the creative process less random, and incites behaviour change."

The line "shining a light on a possible solution to the problem we have defined" is telling. In a separate interview, the founder of market research agency Firefish, Jem Fawcus (see pages 25–29), reminded me of "the only joke in market research", from the great advertising planner Jeremy Bullmore. The joke goes, "Why is insight like a fridge?" <DRUM ROLL; BEAT.> "Because when you look into it, a light comes on."

Mike's three points that "insight increases the chances of creative breakthrough, makes the creative process less random, and incites behaviour change" are also important in what insight is and what insight does. (As well as what it isn't and doesn't do). They emphasise that insight is about progress, about using data-driven understanding to do something new.

And this makes insight relevant not just in marketing services, the sometimes esoteric world I've inhabited for more than 30 years.

It makes it relevant in business more generally – solving problems in innovation and in new product or service development. By becoming well informed and gaining a deep understanding of more than one product or service category, you can develop genuinely innovative offerings that meet hitherto unmet, unimagined needs. This can happen with food – from the McFlurry's blend of milkshakes and chocolate bars to the whole fusion food movement. It can happen with technology – most of Steve Jobs' second stint at Apple saw him combining technologies to create new categories, most particularly with the iPod, iPhone, and iPad. Just watch the rather folksy launch keynote for the iPod to hear Jobs smash the geeky "MP3/MP4/WAV" music format industry norms of the time by encouraging audience to "take your entire music collection with you in your back pocket" – a truly compelling insight if ever there was one.[6] And it can happen in financial services, with the development of products such as mortgages for parents and children together. Until the global phenomenon of housing shortages in major cities – combined with unaffordable property prices for first-time buyers – mortgages were usually designed and sold in rigid and singular life stages.

It makes it relevant in academia, and particularly in cross-disciplinary collaboration. Fifteen years ago, as I came towards the end of my PhD in experimental psychology at Sussex, I toyed with the idea of becoming a full-time academic; why I didn't is another story for another time. One institution I was drawn to almost magnetically was the Medical Research Council–funded Cognition and Brain Sciences Unit at Cambridge.[7] The MRC Unit does fascinating, extraordinary, applicable work in many overlapping sectors, including mood, language, perception, attention, and memory; memory was my thing. But it wasn't the quality or the breadth of work that attracted me. It was the policy on morning coffee and afternoon tea.

You see, the MRC Unit has a rule and the rule is this. If you're in the building, if you're not running a time-sensitive experiment, if you're not teaching, or you're not on ungettoutable university business, you have to attend morning coffee and afternoon tea. To be fair, you can drink whatever beverage you fancy at either break, but at 10.45–11.15am and

3.15–3.45pm, you are required to put down tools, gather in the common room, share beverages (and often biscuits and cakes), and talk to others outside your immediate area of specialism.

This policy is all good social engineering, of course, and encourages colleagues who don't work together to meet and talk. It enables those of very different levels of experience to talk about what they're doing and what problems they're facing. And it facilitates discussions between researchers in very different disciplines of narrow subject areas that otherwise wouldn't take place. All thanks to the promise of hot drinks and crunchy or crumbly treats.

The consequence of this experiment in social engineering isn't expanding waistlines and illicit affairs – at least no more so than in any other workplace with a shared meeting and eating space. The consequence is more collaborations between areas of research not naturally thought to be compatible and accelerated problem-solving and insight generation by the hive mind application of more than the sum of the parts to the challenges aired and discussed over tea or coffee.

And it makes it relevant in politics and public life more broadly. At time of writing – and doubtless long after publication, reprinting, and the second edition – UK politics has ground to a complete halt thanks to the internecine, self-inflicted civil war of Brexit that's tearing the families, political parties, and indeed the whole United Kingdom apart. One of the defining characteristics of the whole Brexit omnishambles has been the profound lack of genuine insight by most of the leading protagonists in the debate and an overreliance on entrenched dogma based on isolated data points and casual observations. Unusually for such a toxic and unresolvable quagmire, Brexit is actually helpful in gaining further clarity of some further dimensions and defining characteristics of what insight both isn't and what it is.

WHY DATA AND OBSERVATIONS JUST AREN'T ENOUGH

One of the frustrations that our friend Mike Teasdale faced daily with his near century of Lowe planners was that many of the insights presented as such on Unilever client briefing templates weren't, in fact, insights.

This is not specific to the one advertising agency or the one client, albeit the client had many, many different brands and briefs. Nor is marketing especially guilty of putting forward non-insights as insights compared with other functions of business. That said, as a function that succeeds or fails on the strength of its insights, it does tend to be rather more obvious here than in finance or procurement, say.

Throughout the campaign for the EU referendum in 2015 and 2016, the Remain campaign used many different data points, research reports, and statistics to make the case for staying in the EU. Remain deployed data from many different, authoritative sources, including HM Treasury, the Bank of England, and the Confederation of British Industry. Leave, by contrast, used one single number – "£350m a week to the NHS" – which became the defining earworm of the campaign. Remain used lots of data once, while Leave used one data point ad nauseam. You may recall that Leave dubbed Remain "Project Fear" because of all the data it present to voters, both directly and via the media.

What cognitive psychology 101 tells us is that if you try to persuade people of your argument by declaring and repeating simple facts or data at them, you're bound to fail. The very act of stating and repeating facts which support my-side arguments make those who are sceptical or opposed to your position dig in and become more entrenched in their opposition to those arguments. Using facts in an attempt to persuade fails on two counts: (i) its lack of empathy (and we'll come back to that, more than once) and (ii) its misunderstanding of how we make decisions. Intriguingly, psychological literature has even now started referring to "the Project Fear Phenomenon" as a recognised thing.

It is now generally agreed that humans make decisions based on emotions. We use what cognitive psychologist Daniel Kahneman categorised as System 1 thinking in the book that summarised his life's work, *Thinking, Fast and Slow*. System 1 thinking makes use of our quicker, evolutionarily ancient reptilian or limbic brain systems, which are triggered and swayed by emotions. Decision-making is mediated by a complex of structures including the brain's emotional barometer, the amygdalae, two almond-shaped structures, one in either hemisphere. The amygdala determines the 4Fs of emotional behaviour – fight, flight, freeze, or fornicate. It determines whether we should try to kill (and potentially eat) the stimulus that presents itself in front of us, run away from it or stand stock still (and so avoid being attacked or becoming dinner ourselves), or mate with it and so carry on our line for the next generation. We share the limbic system with many other species, including all mammals, birds, and reptiles. And because we make decisions emotionally, facts (and data) are not enough to win arguments, even in more rational and cognitive creatures like humans.

Kahneman shows that the role of factual information in decision-making is in fact to help us rationalise and justify the decisions we make. For this we use our white and grey matter – brain areas and structures that make us distinctively human and that we don't share in full with even the higher apes. This more cognitive process is mediated using so-called System 2 thinking. Facts matter here, but only for post hoc justifications of the emotional decisions we've already made. System 2 thinking is slower, more deliberative, more energy intensive. It's a luxury only humans have evolved to use.

Data and facts matter in narrative – of course they do. They matter even more in a so-called post-truth, fake news world, whatever the Goves and Trumps may claim. It's also really important how you present facts and data – in what way, in what volume, and to what effect. How to tell powerful and purposeful stories with data and statistics, blending the rational and the emotional, is the focus of my previous book. And it's why I wrote it first. Building data-driven, evidence-based stories – using data as your starting point – is a step on the journey to being genuinely insightful. It's a necessary step, but it's very definitely not sufficient. Facts help build insights, but facts most definitely are not insights.

APPLYING INSIGHT TO COMMUNICATIONS AND CAMPAIGNS

In our age of information glut, all sorts of organisations are faced with more data than many of them know what do with or can cope with. The sheer volumes of data that surround businesses, charities, universities, and governments threaten to overwhelm them. If they don't have strategies for extracting meaning from data, they run the very real risk of confusing data with insights. This manifests itself inside organisations – commercial, not-for-profit, and third sector – every day. In seeking to move others to action, colleagues present raw data, summaries of data, and screen shots from dashboards that aggregate data as if they were insights. Colleagues tell colleagues that "The data are telling us x, therefore we should do y"; agencies are advising clients to move to action with similar appeals to data-driven logic. But data isn't insight, however smartly a dashboard may attempt to dress it up. And decisions about the behaviours and motivations of current or prospective customers shouldn't be based on data and data alone.

One step up from data and on the journey to insights is the observation. "Mums like tea" falls into this category. So too – as Jem Fawcus says in our interview – do statements like "Millennials are drinking more craft beer", "People are snacking differently", and "Women don't like how they are depicted by the beauty industry". Observations like these are often more than just casual observations or presentations of a promising fact or two. Observations like these can be the conclusion or culmination of in-depth, cross-cultural research in many markets, apparently bringing together key findings into higher order truths.

Let's consider the last observation: "Women don't like how they are depicted by the beauty industry". It's a statement of fact, which beauty brand Dove used as one of the foundation stones of its Campaign for Real Beauty. But to move from an observation to an insight, it needs to do more than just be stated as fact. To be a profound understanding and move people to action, facts and observations need to be explained in the context of other facts and observations, and this context needs to have a consequence which establishes the basis for action. In the case of real women and the beauty industry, we can move from facts and observations to insight in this way:

"Women don't like how they are depicted by the beauty industry" BECAUSE "most women don't have (size zero) figures like those that dominate the media" AND AS A RESULT "they suffer from low self-esteem". Now that is an insight. It uses data about what women think, explains why they think in this way, and connects these two factual observations to a clear outcome. This expression justifies and legitimises Dove's stance against the beauty industry and sets the scene for the brand's Campaign for Real Beauty, now in its 15th year and driving innovation, increased profit, and growth in the category for the past decade. It's true that the campaign took a few years to connect its insight to new product formulations, and it's true that the campaign had an annus horribilis in 2017 with three misfiring campaigns (body-shaped bottles, a Facebook campaign suggesting that lighter skin was more desirable than darker skin, and campaigning against breast feeding). But as an example of a successful, insight-rich campaign, Dove wrote the rulebook.

From this example – and there are other examples included in Table 1.1 – we can tease out a helpful equation of insight that lets us know whether we have a data point, a casual observation, or a full-blown insight. And the equation is this:

[STATEMENT 1] because of [STATEMENT 2] creates [USEFUL CONSEQUENCE]

Now this isn't – of course – the universal equation for creating an insight. There are plenty of ways to express an insight, and not all insights have to be – or can be – presented like this. But I find it to be pretty useful and attractive. And the principal reason I find it to be useful is that it categorically prevents the chance that what you present as insight is a simple statement of fact. Or a casual observation. It's a worked-through thought with built-in deep understanding. An insight.

In this prescription, which is fact- and/or data-driven, there's an explicit – often causal – linkage between the data observed, and together the facts (or data points) have a useful consequence. And it's that useful consequence that gives brands, companies, or organisations the legitimacy to campaign for or against something; to stand for or against something; to provide a solution to the challenge identified. This, therefore, gives them legitimacy and permission to take part in the conversation. It makes their contribution relevant and understandable, and it gives that contribution what Susan Blackmore first identified as memetic potential.[8] In less academic language – though memes are pretty commonplace

Table 1.1 The building blocks of insight

CAMPAIGN	[STATEMENT 1]	"because of"	[STATEMENT 2]	"which creates"	[CONSEQUENCE]
Sport England *This Girl Can*	85% of women fear being judged by others when they exercise		The presentation of sport and exercise in the media as the preserve of honed athletes		A gender exercise gap, with 1.6 m fewer women than men taking regular exercise
Gillette *The Best a Man Can Be*	Men's attitudes to gender, the roles that gender plays in society and sexuality are now outdated		The rapid spread of campaigns vs sexual harassment (#metoo) and pro-equality (#seeher)		Many men don't know how to navigate a world where masculinity is seen as toxic
KFC *FCK*	KFC ran out of chicken in hundreds of UK restaurants. That's right. KFC with no chicken		The failure of a new supplier to meet contractual obligations. No flagship product = crisis		Loss of trade, loss of face, or an opportunity for self-effacing, knowing apology
Persil/Skip *Dirt Is Good*	Since the 1920s, laundry ads told off mums if their kids' clothes weren't "whiter than white"		The perception that parenthood is more about protection from unseen evil than development		A generation of children who rarely go outside and don't grow via experimentation

(Continued)

Table 1.1 (Continued)

CAMPAIGN	[STATEMENT 1]	"because of"	[STATEMENT 2]	"which creates"	[CONSEQUENCE]
Always *Like a Girl*	Girls' self-esteem drops twice as fast as boys' during puberty		Gender stereotypes label some activities as male and heroic while others are weak and girly		The perception that being a girl and being raised as a girl is second best
John Lewis *Excitable Edgar* *(Christmas ads)*	Buying presents for family and friends that are well received is a perennial challenge		We've got stuck in a rut buying the same old things every year: socks, talc, soap-on-a-rope		Christmas has lost its magic and sparkle, making present buying a chore
Nike *Just Do It 2018* *"Dream Crazy"*	We limit our aspirations of what we can achieve in sport because of our mindset		Society constantly tells us how far we can go based on our origins and our circumstances		Unfulfilled potential of those who could've been a Williams or a Kaepernick but weren't
Stabilo *Highlight the* *Remarkable*	National and global historical narratives often don't tell the story of what really happened		History has traditionally been written by men, about men, for the next generation of men		Women's role in history has been understated. It's time to rewrite history

these days, thanks to social media – it gives the brand's insight-driven talking points genuine talkability and shareability.

There are links to all of these campaigns in the endnotes of this chapter.[9] For those not familiar with them, do check out the links and read/watch them in parallel with the short commentary on each one, either immediately below or in the sections indicated. The insights underpinning the campaigns are segmented and analyzed in Table 1.1.

Sport England/This Girl Can: Sport England used real women, really exercising to banish the myth that others judge you negatively when they see you exercising. You might see flushed cheeks, hair out of place, sweat, running make-up, wobbly bellies and backsides, and hideous Lycra. Women are right to think that others judge them when they see them exercising. But they judge them entirely positively and think "I should do that." Sport England's three campaigns have helped to close the gender exercise gap: 1.6 m more women exercise than did before the campaign broke, and 250,000 of these women now exercise every week. See Chapter 9 when we introduce the Insight Spotting Framework.

Gillette/The Best a Man Can Be: this example is an example of an insight that led a brand to run a campaign which was fundamentally out of character and counterproductive. For 30 years, Gillette had – many argued – contributed to the culture of toxic masculinity by appealing to its customers to be more manly and like the idealised male models in its global "The Best a Man Can Get" campaign. With a rapidly changing gender narrative, the #metoo, #timesup, and #seeher movements spreading like wildfire and changing attitudes and beliefs at a societal level, Gillette felt it couldn't miss out. With a subtle twist on its endline and a fundamental (and didactic) shift in the behaviour of the men in its ads, Gillette attempted to ride this wave.

While the brand should be (and was) applauded for spotting and attempting to roll with the Zeitgeist, independent analysis of what the campaign says and what the brand does reveals that it is completely out of character and an example of "Don't do what I do, do what I say". Two former, very senior Unilever marketers – Simon Thong and Sean Gogarty – have recently formed a super-smart research and insights business for brands called Ice Sight (www.ice-sight.com). In a no-punches-pulled analysis,[10] they concluded that the campaign was a waste of time and money because it made the brand behave out of character. An insight can be a true insight, but it needs to be an insight that's in sync with the history, heritage, and fundamental character of the brand. Using one of the most approachable applications of archetypes currently on offer in the world of commercial communications – and there are several practitioners in this space – Ice Sight showed that consumers see the brand's archetype as the Hero, while the ad's archetype is the Caregiver. The ad has given the brand a dose of schizophrenia or at best multiple personality disorder.

KFC/FCK: crises for quick service restaurants don't come much bigger than the one KFC faced in 2017. Having made changes in its supply chain that meant that hundreds of its UK restaurants had, erm, no chicken, KFC was faced with a choice. It could play it by the crisis management rulebook and be corporate, considered, and cautious. Or it could rip up the rulebook and use its established cheeky tone of voice to apologise (with the odd swear, a great pun on its company name in acronym form), hold its hands up and say things weren't good enough, and set the stage for a triumphant return. Thankfully, it chose the path less travelled.

Persil/Skip/Dirt Is Good: Unilever capitalised on a growing body of academic research which showed that, with the best of intentions, parents were actually stifling their kids' development by trying to keep them out of harm's way. It also changed the laundry category norms by declaring that "Dirt Is Good", overturning 85 years of orthodoxy that had made dirt the enemy and castigated parents (in reality, mums) if their children's clothes weren't spotless and whiter than white. In so doing, Persil carved itself a legitimate voice in the parenting debate and went to fund, open, and run more than 1,000 outdoor playgrounds around the world. Parents of course could rely on the brand to get kids' clothes clean. But they could also rely on them to provide environments in which they could get dirty and explore.

Always/Like a Girl: sanitary protection hasn't always been a reliable attention-grabber, but Procter & Gamble found its voice with "Like a Girl". It managed to move its communication from the confidence consumers had always experienced with its products functionally into emotional self-confidence. Capitalising on evidence showing that girls' self-confidence drops twice as fast as boys' during puberty – at just the moment when girls are forming often decades-long attachments to sanitary protection products – Always took on the gender stereotypes that label some activities as male and heroic while others are weak and girly by showing just the opposite. In this way, the brand was able to shake the perception that being – and being raised – a girl is in any sense second best. In a different way and for different reasons, it's a motif that Lewes Football Club has taken on with its @EqualityFC principles, which mean it is the world's only football club to pay its men's and women's teams the same and give them the same playing budget. (Note: I recuse myself from further debate on the club, as a foundational shareholder of the community-owned club, which is also known as "the Barcelona of the South Downs".)

John Lewis/Excitable Edgar: the series of John Lewis Christmas ads – all about brand and what John Lewis stands for, never about products – was a bold switch of direction for a retailer in the wake of the 2007–2009 global recession. But its dramatisation of what "thoughtful gifting" at Christmas means has won more national and global awards for creativity – and more importantly marketing effectiveness; bang for buck and return on investment – than any other retailer in the past decade, and probably ever. Single-handedly, John Lewis has helped bring magic and sparkle back into buying Christmas presents. And sparked a whole new phenomenon of Christmas advertising.

Nike/Just Do It/Dream Crazy: the foundational insight of Nike as a business is "if you have a body, you are an athlete". With Colin "take the knee" Kaepernick as the brand's and the ad's sage and guide, Dream Crazy was a high-risk campaign that paid dividends – literally – when it encouraged everybody, of whatever gender, sexual orientation, physical ability, and origin, to strive not just to be that platitude of the life coach ("the best version of yourself you possibly can be") but to be the very best in the world.

Stabilo/Highlight the Remarkable: can a highlighter pen really be insightful? Apparently yes, from this 2018 campaign. Everyone knows the phrase "Behind every great man is a great woman". What Stabilo showed – in a so-clever-its-simple demonstration of the product in action – is that many moments in history have been mistold. Rather than the man always being the hero and the woman his sidekick, the truth is that all too often women were upstaged, and their actions and successes not even mentioned. Stabilo chose to highlight (literally and figuratively) remarkable women and their untold stories in a powerful and award-winning set of print ads.

This whistle-stop tour, viewing various campaigns through insight-coloured specs, should give you a good sense and understanding of what I believe good insights to be and how they can be deployed to build more powerful, purposeful stories that are in character with the storyteller. Before we close out this first, definitional chapter, there are a couple of characteristics of insight we need to consider: insight as empathy and insight as a statement of the bleeding obvious.

INSIGHT AS EMPATHY

Let's go back to Dove's Campaign for Real Beauty, the campaign that changed the narrative of the beauty industry and how it talks to and about women. We were talking about it before we were so rudely interrupted by the insight equation and the eight mini-case studies. There are a couple other rules and principles of good insight that Dove's campaign makes clear. And the first is that a genuine insight is often an expression or a manifestation of empathy. Empathy is that fundamental human ability to put oneself in the mind of another, to see the world from their point of view. Here's what Jamil Zaki, author of *The War for Kindness: Building Empathy in a Fractured World*, says:

> *Empathy evolved as one of humans' vital survival skills. Over millennia, we changed to make connecting easier. Our testosterone levels dropped, our faces softened, and we became less aggressive. We developed larger eye whites than other primates, so we could easily track one another's gaze, and intricate facial muscles that allowed us to better express emotion. Our brains developed to give us a more precise understanding of each other's thoughts and feelings. As a result, we developed vast empathic abilities. We can travel into the minds of not just friends and neighbors but also enemies, strangers, and even imaginary people in films or novels.[11]*

In the case of Dove, the data that gave it a tantalising glimpse inside the minds of the women it wanted to engage with came from a cross-cultural study the brand ran in 20 markets around the world. The consistent message coming back from women in very different countries and cultures – from China to Brazil, from Russia to Indonesia – was that the traditional beauty industry had squashed their self-esteem. For just 2% of women in all markets use the word "beautiful" to describe themselves.

The way that beauty has been portrayed in fashion and cosmetics marketing the world over for decades – using stereotypical models of very limited body size, shape, and age – has helped to whittle away at self-confidence. With this insight – this deep and profound understanding of how women think and behave – Dove had permission and the legitimacy to tackle the beauty industry from within. From a position of empathy, it could use (in its language) "real types not stereotypes" and use real women – "women like me" – to front its campaigns and market its products.

So, if we go back to our original definition of insight as "a profound understanding of a person, a thing, a situation, or an issue", we can see that a central element of insight is empathy – the ability to put yourself into the shoes, the mind, the mindset of those you're looking to influence. As we'll see from many different sectors, empathy is central to insight.

As a coda to this section, I need to draw attention to the recent publication by Andrew Tenzer, the Director of Group Insight at Reach, the biggest news publisher in the UK. Tenzer uses a combination of native wit and experimental psychology to demonstrate quite unequivocally that those who work in marketing services are in fact no more empathetic than "the man on the Clapham omnibus", to steal Greek historian Moses Finley's memorable phrase. That's right. Tenzer shows in his excellent, closely argued report *The Empathy Delusion* that the very profession mandated by its clients to get inside the minds of their current and potential customers – a profession that prides itself on its empathy – has no more insight into insight, no more empathy, than anyone else. In addition to the pleasure that delicious irony always brings, I commend this smart report.[12]

A STATEMENT OF THE BLEEDING OBVIOUS?

The second important criterion of insight that may well have struck you in the examination of campaigns I've argued to be insightful is this. Quite often, an insight can at first glance or realisation appear to be a statement of the bleeding obvious. I don't mean because we're presenting just a couple of unrelated facts or a casual observation where we need an insight. I mean that the expression of understanding appears to be so self-evidently true many others must have had the thought already. A quick Google search should tell you if this is the case or not. You may be surprised.

I've often developed insights for campaigns that I've initially dismissed as being so obvious as to be trivial. Having absorbed myself in all sorts of information about an issue, stepped away from all that input, and allowed my subconscious to reshuffle the old stuff and create something new, a thought has emerged. But that thought has appeared to be almost fatuous or banal in its simplicity, and I've dismissed it, gone back a step or two, and started reading more and talking to others. And the same insight has cropped up again. And again. And again. Once: chance. Twice: hypothesis. Three times: a trend. Must be something worth looking into.

The 18th-century English satirist Alexander Pope defined "true wit" like this.[13]

> True wit is nature to advantage dress'd,
> What oft was thought, but ne'er so well express'd
> Something whose truth convinced at sight we find,
> That gives us back the image of our mind.
> As shades more sweetly recommend the light,
> So modest plainness sets off sprightly wit.

"What oft was thought, but ne'er so well express'd." Brilliant. Pope was saying that poets who create great poetry do so by making brilliant use of what everybody else already knows. As for poetry, so for insights. In fact, not only is it not a bad thing for insights to appear to be a statement of the bleeding obvious. Once you've determined that your insight is a genuinely novel conception of an established state of the world – that it is an empathetic and profound representation of a person, subject, issue, or thing – it's often a defining characteristic of a powerful insight that it does elicit a reaction of "And? Really? Is that all?" Its profundity will shine through when you realise what it allows you to think, do, and say as a result. As the Canadian author of *The Monk Who Sold His Ferrari*, Robin Sharma, puts it, "The secret of innovation is to see what all see but think what none think". Bleeding obvious until you really look and think about it properly.

WHY WE FIND IT HARD TO THINK ABOUT THINKING

One of the reasons people find it hard to talk about and develop genuine, breakthrough insights is that to do so requires them to think about thinking. And that's hard work. Now a fifth of the way through the 21st century, we know a lot about the chemistry and electricity of the brain, its wiring and its plumbing. We've got a good idea about which parts of the brain are at least in part responsible for a wide range of different cognitive and bodily functions. But we have no insight beyond the ingenious metaphors and analogies of psychologists and neuroscientists about how the mind actually works in its entirety; how the same fundamental architecture transmits electrical and chemical signals of excitation and inhibition over the same circuits and yet mediates images, sounds, tastes, touch, smells, emotions, memories, the works.

As those working in the past 70 years in the field of artificial intelligence have come nowhere close to replicating the processing power, complexity, and speed of the human brain, it's very likely not in the ones and zeroes and hexadecimal of computer code. Harvard psychologist Steve Pinker concludes his modestly titled 1997 doorstop *How the Mind Works* that, although each one of us is in possession of the most powerful supercomputer ever likely to be on this planet, we actually lack the cognitive architecture capable of introspecting and understanding how the mind works. Interactions between more than 100 different neurotransmitters govern the functioning of 100 billion neurons and trillions of interconnecting synapses, all held together in a structure bootstrapped and built over billions of years from the ground up.

Many books and writers have shaped my own thinking about thinking – my own metacognition – and one of the most important is the often-impenetrable *The Art of Thought*. Published by one of the first teachers at the London School of Economics, William Wallas, in 1926, this promisingly titled book still holds up remarkably well for its core conception of how insights arise. As we'll see in Chapter 4 and following, Wallas' four-step model is the foundation of the model I'm offering you in this book, albeit radically updated, simplified, and passed through the lens of James Webb Young's 1940 reinterpretation of Wallas' model, *A Technique for Producing Ideas*.

In his book *The Art of Thought*, Wallas considers why thinking about thinking is so hard. An article in *The Times Literary Supplement* for 31 January 1924 commented,

> *We all indulge in the strange pleasant process called thinking, but when it comes to saying even to some on opposite, what we think, then how little we are able to convey! The phantom is through the mind and out of the window before we can lay salt on its tail, or slowly sinking and returning to the profound darkness which it has lit up momentarily with a wandering light.*[14]

The *TLS* author puts it rather more poetically and approachably than Wallas would have put it. Although the structure of his thinking and writing is rigid, clear, and consistent, his prose is often turgid and abstract. That the very author of *The Art of Thought* finds it hard to think about thinking is instructive. In my rationalist's, simplifier's way, it is my ambition to make the process of thinking about how we solve insight problems that little bit more straightforward. I have kept the explanatory model deliberately so simple because this metacognition thing has most people running for the hills.

THE AGENTS OF INSIGHT

Throughout more than 30 years working in marketing communications, I've been struck by the carefree abandon with which even relatively senior figures in the industry have tossed the word insight around. Agency-side – agencies of all different flavours – and client-side. As the Big Data revolution has rolled around and shiny new dashboards have become flavour of the month *Groundhog Day* style, many present just data or summaries of data and label their slides as "insight". They have a couple of conversations in the pub or after their Pilates class and present back their casual observations as if they'd unearthed a profound and deep understanding. Or they use the echo chamber of their liberal media Facebook or Twitter feed and report the opinions they've been served by smart but blindsiding algorithms as if they've found the golden nugget that unlocks understanding. Remember, reliable estimates put UK adland's support of Remain in the EU referendum at more than 90%, so you can imagine the surprised faces staring glumly into decaf soya lattes on the morning of 24 June 2016 in Soho. So much for insight gleaned from social media there.

It's because of this cavalier attitude to insight I've observed since the late 1980s that I'm seeking to redress the balance and get some proper rigour into the insight-generating process, particularly – but not exclusively – in the insight industries. It's why I developed the STEP Prism of Insight model and am happy to share it with the world here. And it's why I called my business Insight Agents, because it is my purpose to offer a combination of this rare, prized, casually tossed about term that is the foundation stone of innovation (that's Insight), and the down-and-dirty, roll-up-your-sleeves practicality of how you get there (agency – doing – hence Agents).

The capacity to unlock the superpower that drives innovation is in us all; it's a defining characteristic of human resourcefulness and creativity. For much of the time, we take it too lightly or – by contrast – think it's too difficult or strategic or clever-clever. What I aim to show here is that it's within everyone's reach if only they stop and actually think about thinking.

INTERVIEW: JEM FAWCUS, FIREFISH

Insightful interview 1 of 8

NAME	Jem Fawcus
ORGANISATION	Firefish – market research
ROLE	Owner & Group CEO

Jem Fawcus has worked in market research for 30 years, man and boy. In 2000, he founded Firefish, today a group of research companies turning over more than £13m. Firefish describe themselves as human strategy partners; "we make sense of the human experience and bring this to the heart of the decision-making process to help brands innovate, communicate and grow." The company works for such brands as Twitter, PayPal, and Magnum.

Insight is at the heart of everything Firefish do, and for Fawcus, insight is very much more than a piece of information or an observation. "It's a description that transforms your understanding of the audience, the issue, the world. It's a statement or nugget of intelligence that makes you think differently and see the world in a different way. Clearly, it's rooted in an observation of someone or something – a person, a product, or a market. But the most important thing is that it makes you think and behave in a different, more appropriate way."

Fawcus believes that, although the market research industry is also often called the insight industry, a lot of its output is little more than casual observations, masquerading or dressed up as insights. "If a brand says to us that their insight is something like 'millennials are drinking more craft beer' or 'people are snacking differently', I sigh a little. Those aren't insights. They don't make me think differently about drinking or snacking. They're not a 'nugget of why' to make you think or act differently. Genuine, transformative insights are relatively rare, and they're not easy to find. Finding them is not in any sense a linear process. They can come from anywhere. They may appear or they may not. And although they don't respond to timelines or linear inputs, they do come from a combination of hard work – taking in lots of information and stimulus – and creative thinking."

The starting point for Fawcus is to be clear about what you're looking for and why. Have your own (or steal someone else's) definition of insight and don't accept substitutes or pale imitations. "It really helps if you look at the problem you're trying to solve from lots of different angles, through lots of different lenses – a cultural lens, an individual behaviour lens, an individual experience lens, a market lens – and then bring all those perspectives together, triangulating them into an insight. When you start out, you can't know which data sources will give you what you need, but you can be sure that the more rounded a view you get of a subject, the more likely you are to find an insight."

One way Firefish often look at a brief – for example what is going to drive the future of healthy snacking – is to apply a big cultural lens to the problem at hand. For instance, the world is becoming less binary, less black and white. Boundaries are blurring. This is true of gender (he, she, they), the fluidity of sexuality (gay, straight, bi, LGBTQ+), of politics (no left or right, no Leave or Remain, but shades in between), no more online vs offline but both. The same is true of food. The meals vs snacks distinction is becoming blurred as cultural influences spread – tapas, Pinxtos, small plates, grazing. In this case, snacking isn't a discrete behaviour; it needs to fit into the broader perspective of blurring boundaries.

To seek out and validate insights, the Firefish team spend a lot of time doing the traditional research things – like observing people in their actual behaviours and environments (ethnography) and talking to them – though they tend to do these things in unusual ways. Or with unusual groups of people. "If you want to know about the future of online or cashless banking," observes Fawcus, "of course you'd talk to people who currently pay with their phones. But you'd also talk to the homeless, who often have neither money nor internet access." He winces at the names some researchers give their observational processes, with "consumer safari" being the one that raises his eyebrows highest.

Other data sources can include social media data, purchasing patterns, and online search trends. Fawcus believes that anecdotes matter or can give clues, and it helps to keep an open mind, in the way that Mr Online Shopping Algorithm himself, Amazon's Jeff Bezos, observed when he said, "When the data and the anecdotes conflict, I always go for the anecdotes." What matters is anything that can give you that "nugget of why".

In his introduction to *The Signal and the Noise*, 538 blog chief Nate Silver says, "The numbers have no way of speaking for themselves. We speak for them. We imbue them with meaning." It's such an important thought that David Spiegelhalter used it to open his 2019 book, *The Art of Statistics: Learning from Data*. And it's a principle with which Fawcus is entirely aligned.

Although Fawcus is at pains to emphasise that you can't predict or force insights into the world, he's clear of what individuals and teams need to do in order to "reorder observations, facts, data, information, to produce the necessary explanation of the world". It takes mental energy, creativity, passion, and an enquiring mind. Curiosity is critical, as is the ability to sift through noise around the signal to find a simple thread that explains a certain behaviour or attitude.

"Having immersed yourself in information from all angles, you often think to yourself, 'How can I possibly make sense of all this?' You see ideas contradicting themselves, it's 2am, the client's coming in for a breakfast meeting, you're about to cry . . . and then . . . and then there's this mental leap, fuelled by passion and tenacity and the lines get less blurred and a ruthless clarity comes upon you and you can reduce the challenge you've been working down to just brilliant simplicity. That's the moment of insight. Gut instinct, intuition, and experience can get you close, but insight comes from genuine empathy and understanding of the audience you're trying to reach."

Talking of experience, although experience of what insights are and how to articulate them matter, experience of a product, category, or issue isn't necessarily helpful. Fawcus believes that fresh perspective and naivety – asking naïve questions – can help. You won't make the same old established mistakes or come to the same conclusions that those who've tried and failed before you have made. He cites recent developments in the financial services industry. Innovations in mortgage products for parents *and* children to pay together, for instance, have been driven by naïve experts – those naïve in the mortgage market, but expert in the fact that the world is no longer binary or black and white.

"I've also often observed that insights are retrofitted, especially in the creative and brand world," says Fawcus. "It's perfectly legitimate to work back to an insight from a great creative or product idea that you know will work. Brands pay agencies like mine to help build their brands and be commercially successful, based on a deep understanding of current and potential customers. From that perspective, an insight is only as good as the marketing strategy that comes out of it and the results that generates.

If you have to retrofit an insight to a product or campaign, so long as it works, that's not cheating."

Fawcus believes that the explosion in available data – and the tools to crunch and visualise genuinely big data sets – have helped bring more information but not necessarily more insight into the research sector. He's intrigued that some of the biggest social media businesses, who appear to have so much insight into how to get people to behave in certain ways (with likes, views, and shares), should nevertheless have so little insight into the impact of the very same products on people's lives (from gerrymandering elections to harming teenagers' self-esteem – and worse.)

To close, Fawcus restates and refines his core definition of insight: "It's fundamentally a description of a human behaviour or attitude which combines observation and meaning – the what and the why – to give a new way of thinking about and understanding the issue." Properly insightful stuff.

NOTES

1 www.youtube.com/watch?v=FQ0sHPD5JMg; https://www.imdb.com/title/tt0094737/

2 Paul Curtis & Warren Philip (1973). *The Dynamics of Life Skills Coaching.* Training Research and Development Station, Department of Manpower and Immigration.

3 Leonard Mlodinow (2018). *Elastic: Flexible Thinking in a Constantly Changing World.* Allen Lane, p. 138.

4 In *The Hitchhiker's Guide to the Galaxy,* 42 is the answer to the ultimate question of "Life, the Universe, and Everything". It took a supercomputer named Deep Thought seven-and-a-half million years to calculate the answer.

5 James O'Brien's Mystery Hour podcast on iTunes https://podcasts.apple.com/gb/podcast/james-obriens-mystery-hour/id666751844. See also James' approach to dealing with illiberal, uninformed phone-in guests on his talk radio shows in his 2018 book, *How to Be Right . . . In a World Gone Wrong.*

6 The whole event bears rewatching, but if you're pushed for time, the 90 seconds from 2' 22" onwards will make the point, www.youtube.com/watch?v=kN0SVBCJqLs

7 http://www.mrc-cbu.cam.ac.uk

8 Susan Blackmore (2000). *The Meme Machine.* Oxford University Press.

9   Sport England: http://bit.ly/2YLS48w, Gillette https://gillette.com/en-us/the-best-men-can-be, KFC http://bit.ly/2wdl23J, Persil/Skip www.dirtisgood.com/home.html, Always http://bit.ly/2K1NUFh, John Lewis http://bit.ly/2VPbYxk, Nike http://bit.ly/2WugRk0, and Stabilo http://bit.ly/2X5ck4n

10 Sean Gogarty (13 May 2019). The real impact and effectiveness of Gillette's "#metoo" ad http://bit.ly/2Vtak48

11 Jamil Zaki (2019). Can We Revive Empathy in Our Selfish World? *Nautilus* http://bit.ly/2wFme0Z

12 The report can be downloaded from http://bit.ly/2NOJ6Vr

13 Alexander Pope (1711). *An Essay on Criticism*. CreateSpace.

14 Graham Wallas (1926). *The Art of Thought*, p. 24.

2

THE HISTORY AND PSYCHOLOGY OF INSIGHT

"[T]here has always been, since the dawn of civilisation, an unformulated 'mystery' of thought which has been 'explained' by no science."
Graham Wallas, *The Art of Thought*

STARTING WITH WHY

This book is designed to be a deeply practical primer. Its purpose is to introduce and make readers familiar with a framework and a set of tools that allow them to have – and be aware that they are having – genuinely breakthrough ideas. Almost always, these insights will be innovative concepts that recombine old stuff together into new. If they're genuine insights, they'll enable us to solve the challenges we face in our personal, intellectual, and professional lives. And so I've written this book to show how, by investing a little time and effort, anyone can be insightful – more often, more predictably, and more usefully.

The approach championed here is less about knowing how we got here and much more about how to get where we want to go. It doesn't demand an intimate knowledge of the history, psychology, and neuroscience of insight. You could easily benefit from the model without knowing any of the more detailed theory that underpins it, and I only ever scratch the surface of these topics with delegates on my insight training courses. There's only so much theory you can include in a half-day workshop because learning outcomes need to be real, practical, and actionable. If people are prepared to take time out from their day jobs for training, they want to be able to put theory into practice straightaway, and I respect that.

As we build towards the model that's at the heart of the book – turn to Chapter 4 if you can't wait to get started – I do think it's worth looking at each of these themes in turn in a little more detail. The fundamental offer here is that it pays to be metacognitive, to think about thinking in order to enhance the experience and outcomes of one's own thinking. As an insight nerd, I'm fascinated by all things insight and am naturally filled with the evangelist's zeal to share everything I've discovered about the topic on the road to building the STEP Prism of Insight.

I genuinely believe that if you've invested the resources necessary to get a copy of this book and the time to have read up to here already, you're secretly pretty interested in the subject, too. What's more, my promise to you is that by delving deeper into the history, psychology, and neuroscience of insight, you'll set yourself on course to becoming an insight ninja. So buckle up and enjoy the (brief) ride and be prepared to broaden your perspective on insight. By satisfying your curiosity, you will fill the hopper of your subconscious mind with new stimuli that will – without doubt – come in handy for a problem you have to solve two days, two years, or two decades from now. And you can't get much more delightfully metacognitive than that.

"WAY, WAY BACK MANY CENTURIES AGO . . ."

Our view of ancient, classical Greek society is biased, partial, and mediated. Most of the literary and philosophical output of the classical era comes from fifth and fourth century BC Athens. The city was an intellectual and democratic hotbed . . . provided you were a free man, neither a woman nor a slave, as most of the inhabitants of the city were. The apparently very civilised culture provided citizens – free men – with the luxury of time and resources to explore, discuss, and start to codify answers to questions of the meaning of life for the first time. That's not to dismiss the very fine thinking and writing of the age which went on to shape and direct Western thought and the enlightenment, from Socrates' declaration of his own ignorance and his gadfly-like inquiries, to his pupil Plato's extensive body of work, and in turn *his* pupil Aristotle[1] and his corpus of work, most of which has survived antiquity. It's just to reflect that philosophical enquiry and introspection was limited to a rarefied few, floating on the back of the wealth of a city made rich by exploitation of many other cities and Aegean islands in exchange for peace. But that's another story.

The Greeks (as they so often did) had a word for it. Actually, they had several words for it. At a fundamental level, the product of thought for the Greeks was defined as *idéa* (whence the English word idea). Liddell & Scott – the most comprehensive Greek-English dictionary – defines *idéa* as "form", "the look or semblance of a thing, as opposed to its reality". The word *idéa* comes from the verb *idêin*, to see. The metaphorical, metacognitive Greeks viewed thought as a process that generated mental representations of things – physical but also metaphysical; concepts like courage, just as much as physical things like owls, crested helmets, and statues of the gods.

Throughout his Socratic dialogues, Plato works towards his theory of forms, which reaches its most comprehensive expression in *The Republic*. The theory proposes that each fundamental characteristic – beauty, truth, loyalty – exists in a perfect, pure, unadulterated form. These forms exist independent of the physical world. When we observe someone who is beautiful, truthful, or loyal, these physical manifestations are only a shadow or an echo of the forms. *Idéa* is distinct from *sophía* ("wisdom") and both *epistēmē* and *gnōsis* ("knowledge"). Wisdom is the state of having acquired knowledge, such that one can appreciate the forms in their physical manifestations.

Getting closer to insight – which we've defined for our purposes as "a profound or deep understanding" – we have *noēsis*. Noēsis means "knowing", "understanding", or "intelligence"; the act of understanding, the process of using one's mind (*noūs*, whence the English word nous), the act of having an idea, the art of being insightful. Which brings us to Archimedes, a philosopher ("lover of wisdom") from the third century BC

Greek colony of Syracuse on Sicily. Challenged to determine whether a crooked goldsmith had used silver in part to make a gold crown for the king of his city-state, Archimedes is said to have pondered the quandary while in the bath. The bath mattered, because he suddenly realised he could calculate whether the crown was pure gold or part-gold/part-silver by the amount of water it displaced. Thrilled by his discovery, Archimedes apparently couldn't wait to tell the world. He leapt from his bath – not even towelling himself down – and ran naked through the streets of Syracuse shouting *"Heúrēka!"*; "I have found it! I have discovered it!" And what he'd discovered was the fact that the goldsmith was, indeed, crooked.

The original eureka moment, the insight, and the methodology developed in the bath did not survive in the transmission of Archimedes' work, and it may be entirely fictitious anecdotage. But it has strong, memetic potential; it's sticky. As a result, Archimedes has gone down in folk memory at least as the world's first streaking scientist rather than a mathematician on a par with Euclid. But for our thesis, his most famous one-word, one-liner is instructive. Ideas for the Greeks were about seeing forms. Insights are about the process of the mind. Having insights – putting together old stuff to create something new that solves a problem – is about finding or discovery. Ancient Greek didn't have a specific word for the modern concept of the insight, but modern Greek does. In modern Greek, an insight is a *dioratikótēta*, an abstract noun that comes directly from the ancient Greek *dioratikós*, "clear-sighted". And as many attest of the relief that comes with insight – as the fog of mental confusion lifts with the breeze of mental clarity – insight is all about clear-sightedness.

It was more than two millennia before first psychology and then neuroscience enabled us to look inside the mind and brain. And yet, ancient Greek philosophers found poetic but very grounded ways of describing with precision and distinction what science has more recently confirmed and elaborated. Amazing what a combination of imperial ambition, a powerful navy, and extorting gold from weaker states in return for "peace" can achieve. For the Greeks (and particularly the Athenians), this led to a cultural legacy of philosophy, poetry (tragedy, comedy, epic poetry), and architecture. For the Romans, it was state control via religion, from the cult of Augustus to the popes and the Vatican, via the Holy

Roman Empire. For the British empire, it was industrialisation, and for the American empire, digitisation. Yuval Noah Harari has a lot to say about this in the excellent *Sapiens*.

If this book were a history of the philosophy of ideas, we'd now spend a dozen pages looking at how Plato's and Aristotle's ideas helped to shape the enlightenment. We'd look at British, French, and German schools, from Locke and Hume to Descartes and Kant. We'd see how a series of philosophers – sometimes complementary, sometimes confrontational – advanced our understanding of epistemology, the theory of knowledge. But not only is that outside my specific expertise, it's also outside the scope of this book and its declared aim on making its readers more insightful. And there are many excellent books to read on the subject, and nowhere better than A.C. Grayling's recent update of Bertrand Russell's 1946 classic, *The History of Philosophy*. Our interest falls within the realm of epistemology for sure, but it's also grounded and practical. What matters to us in the history and psychology of insight are traces and clues that help us understand with more clarity what insight is and how we can become more insightful ourselves.

ON CHIMPANZEES, SNAKES, AND BENZENE RINGS

Wolfgang Köhler was one of the founders of the German school of Gestalt psychology, which identified that an integrated complete assembly of parts – an organised whole – is greater than the sum of its parts. The Gestalt school was the first in modern psychology to attempt to understand insight. The "sum of the parts" is a helpful metaphor for insight. When our subconscious mind joins together old stuff to make something new, part of the reason we experience the eureka of insight is that we can do more with a deep understanding of an issue than we can with the component parts that contribute to that understanding.

A quick analogy from the physical world: if we have the cogs and springs, gears and weights of a clock – plus hands, a face, and a winding mechanism – they don't help us run a business. But if they are assembled into a working clock that keeps time according to our 24-hour days, each with 60 minutes and each of them with 60 seconds, we can use the clock to run an airline or a restaurant or a factory with three shifts. As with bits of a clock, so with bits of an insight.

Towards the end of the First World War, Köhler published a book called *The Mentality of Apes* in which he demonstrated the existence of insightful behaviour in chimps. When food was put out of reach – too high or behind bars – Köhler observed that the chimps could overcome the challenges set for them. They could do this in a way that was "unwaveringly purposeful", using boxes and sticks. Once they'd solved the problem, they could routinely do so again when faced with the same problem. One of Köhler's peers in Gestalt psychology, Karl Bühler, coined the term *Aha-Erlebnis* to describe what Köhler had observed at the moment of problem-solving among the chimps – including a particularly insightful chimp named Sultan. *Aha-Erlebnis* means "the aha (or eureka) moment", "the moment of sudden insight or realisation". As Gary Klein says in his book *Seeing What Others Don't*:

> If [only] we had an insight Geiger counter, these cues would set it off: a sudden discovery, a jolt of excitement, a combination of ideas that fit tightly together, a feeling of confidence in the new direction.[2]

Klein's metaphorical Geiger counter would have been clicking like it was in Chernobyl or Fukushima in the study of 19th-century German chemist, August Kekulé. In the early 1860s, Kekulé developed a pioneering understanding of the chemical structure of benzene in the time before microscopic, instrumental methods could look into the physical structure of chemical compounds. But he said that the source of his inspiration, which led to his Aha-Erlebnis, was a waking daydream of a snake biting its own tail. The metaphorical image that came to him was the ouroboros of Egyptian and Greek magical tradition.

The history of Kekulé's moment of insight is disputed and subject to no little academic controversy. This is not least because during his lifetime he recounted more than one different daydream which led him to the same conclusion. Writing more than 30 years ago in the *New York Times*, journalist Malcolm Browne suggested that Kekulé's daydreams might have been "merely tales he told to amuse the audience at the 1890 Benzolfest". However, he added that, "Other than robbing popular psychology of one of its favorite anecdotes, the field of psychology would not be affected" if that were the case.[3] What's telling for us are (i) the power of analogy to unlock seemingly intractable problems; (ii) the very real benefits of taking timeout – including apparently aimless daydreaming – from the process of problem-solving; and (iii) the shared experience that solutions to problems can come all at once, triggered by surprising stimuli that apparently have nothing to do with the challenge at hand.

THE GRANDFATHER OF MODERN INSIGHT?

Graham Wallas is an enigmatic and important figure in the history of insight, and his description of how he believed insight occurs underpins the central model of insight generation that lies at the heart of this book. In a very real sense, I'd argue that Wallas should be thought of as the grandfather of modern insight.

Wallas was a socialist and early member of the Fabian Society, joining two years after its foundation in 1884. Though he was also a psychologist, most of his published writings were about politics and society. His publications include 1908's *Human Nature in Politics* and *Great Society* six years later. A rationalist and an atheist from his time at Oxford onwards, Wallas was also an educationalist. First a schoolteacher, he became a university lecturer in 1890 and taught at the recently established London School of Economics from 1895 onwards, an institution he helped to found.

In 1926, Wallas published a thin and sometimes densely written (sometimes almost impenetrably abstract) book with the delightful title *The Art of Thought*. With the vernacular of the time, Wallas' language is often full of abstract, Latinate nouns that make it challenging to understand where he's taking readers and why: preparation – incubation – illumination – verification. The fact that his language is neither snappy nor memorable may explain why his book was out of print for many years.

But at the heart of his book is a four-step model that offers a remarkably good and enduring explanation of the process of insight. This is despite a growing corpus of knowledge in cognitive psychology over the intervening 95 years, and despite the more recent advances in our understanding of how thought happens in the brain. What we've learned since suggests that Wallas was broadly right, though he didn't have the psychological or neuroscientific evidence to support his hypotheses.

Wallas says we solve problems in this way:

1 **Preparation**: the problem is investigated from all directions
2 **Incubation**: not consciously thinking about the problem
3 **Illumination**: the appearance of the happy idea
4 **Verification**: the validity of the idea is tested

Now as discussed, Wallas was a social psychologist. He was particularly interested in the dynamics of societal and political decision-making and influence; how we need his sort today! He was also an early cognitive psychologist, particularly towards the end of both his life and his career. *The Art of Thought* was published just six years before he died. But what Wallas most definitely was not was an experimental psychologist.

As such, Wallas' theories were based on observation – albeit more than casual observation – on reports from both himself and others. But in an age when the brain was both uncharted and unchartable territory, he could neither know what he was looking for in terms of brain activity nor be able to see it in action if he could. Which is why his prescription is all the more remarkable for (a) its description of such an elusive and undescribed phenomenon, and (b) the fact that recent neuroimaging work has served to confirm what were no more than well-informed hunches. We'll come back to how and why in the next chapter.

EVALUATING WALLAS

There are some who believe that Wallas' model of insight generation is too simplistic to describe the processes involved in idea generation or that it doesn't properly account for the experimental evidence provided by psychology. But I don't believe the objections to Wallas' model hole it beneath the waterline. Nor do they undermine the model's usefulness as the basis for helping everyone think about their thinking and solve more problems more reliably.

Introducing his work in *Seeing What Others Don't*, psychologist Gary Klein says that Wallas' model is "still the most common explanation of how insight works . . . still the way most people explain how insight works. It's a very satisfying explanation that has a ring of plausibility" (pp. 17, 20). Klein objects to Wallas using his model to explain success stories only and believes that the "incubation" stage doesn't fit with some of the examples of insight Klein considers in his book. Klein also objects to the illumination stage being a "flash of inspiration" and that it "seems too magical to be satisfying". Very recent neuroscientific evidence refutes Klein's position, as we'll see.

Coming from a more creative point of view, Scott Barry Kaufman and Carolyn Gregoire invite their readers to "Discover the 10 things great artists, writers and innovators do differently" in their 2015 book, *Wired to Create*. As with Klein, so with the current authors: Wallas' is the very first model they consider as a framing concept to explain creativity. Their principal objection is that Wallas' model is too simplistic, reductionist, and simple. "If only the creative process was so tidy", they lament. It is certainly true that it's neat and simple and reductive. It's a model, after all. But to reject it out of hand as a description of how the mind works "because it tells us so little about the mental processes occurring during the act of creation" is a reductionist step too far – particularly when that was never Wallas' intention.

In fact, the characteristics identified by Kaufman and Gregoire as the "Ten Things Highly Creative People Do Differently" map incredibly closely on to Wallas' four steps, thus:

- **Preparation**: 1. Imaginative Play, 2. Passion, 6. Openness to Experience, 9. Turning Adversity into Advantage
- **Incubation**: 3. Daydreaming, 4. Solitude, 7. Mindfulness
- **Illumination**: 5. Intuition, 8. Sensitivity
- **Verification**: 10. Thinking Differently

It's perfectly possible to argue that, far from being a rejection of Wallas' model, Kaufman and Gregoire enrich it. Their "ten things" give further examples and illustrations of quite why Wallas' framework is such a compelling and rounded description of a phenomenon that's always been so reluctant to be described.

All models are abstract descriptions, explanations, and simplifications of the world as we experience it. Provided they're not plainly and materially rendered wrong by later discoveries or experiments – and provided they help to explain and so move our understanding forward – we should make the most of them. I remember when I was learning physics to Year 11 public exam standard (I'm old enough and English enough to have taken an O-level), I was told that to study at a higher level would require unlearning O-level theory and learning a whole new way of looking at the world. In the case of neuroscience, the "lock and key" models of neurotransmitters being released from some neurons and absorbed by receptor sites on others are purely metaphorical and representational. Yet in both cases, the models are designed to explain super-complex processes in a way that is both graspable and practical. And in both cases, they succeed.

What's more, mental processes are stubborn to introspection because, in Harvard Psychologist Steve Pinker's memorable phrase, *The Stuff of Thought* does not yield to the act of thought. In a private correspondence about his 1997 book, the modestly titled *How the Mind Works*, Pinker told me,

> *My thoughts on the remaining mystery of consciousness are laid out in the very last section of the last chapter of the book. I don't know if you'll find them satisfying, because they don't answer the question of where subjective experience comes from, but they do offer a suggestion as to why the question is so puzzling, and for me they complete the picture in an interesting way.*[4]

What he concludes is that we lack the cognitive architecture to understand our own cognitive architecture. Talk about meta!

HOW WE SOLVE INSIGHT PROBLEMS

There are several different theories about how people come to have insights and a number of different, classic tests used to test how insightful a particular individual or cohort may be. These have been very well covered by other authors, and if you're interested, I recommend you read these books once we're done. They include Gary Klein's *Seeing What Others Don't*, Steven Johnson's *Where Good Ideas Come From*, and perhaps best is Kounios and Beeman's *The Eureka Factor*, which we'll return to in the next chapter. I suggest they've been covered best by US academics Kounios and Beeman not because their writing is necessarily better or more fluent than Klein's or Johnson's but because the American duo directly relate the classic tests to what's actually happening in the brain. It's a happy and satisfying marriage between psychology and neuroscience.

It is worth a short detour into both the theories and the tests, however, to give you a taste of how psychology has looked to explore and uncover the slippery phenomenon that is insight. The two dominant theories of insight resolution are known as representational change theory and progress monitoring theory.

Representational change theory suggests that insight problems are tough nuts to crack because, to start out with, we observe the component parts of an insight riddle, deconstruct them into their component parts, and use a combination of both logic and long-term memory to try to work them out. This is where Daniel Kahneman's System 2 thinking kicks in – slow, effortful, and cognitive, and uniquely human. We use our grey matter (the prefrontal cortex) to try to rationalise our way through the challenge at hand. We do this because this strategy often works for us.

The trouble is, with insight problems – problems that require putting together existing pieces of information in new and hitherto untried ways – the strategy that usually works turns out not to. Existing knowledge puts constraints on our ability to solve the task at hand, and this can lead to frustration. But once we see that the usual strategies don't work, we start to relax our constraints. This allows us to bring other, previously acquired knowledge and skills to the challenge – what de Bono and others have called "lateral thinking" or "thinking outside the box". What's more, even with simple problems, when the usual approach has failed, we often start to break the problem down into bitesize chunks. Psychologists call this "chunk decomposition", while business strategists often talk of breaking down Big Hairy Audacious Goals (BHAGs) into manageable, bitesize chunks. They encourage teams to "eat the elephant, one chunk at a time". Isn't business hilarious?

By relaxing constraints and chunking down (though sometimes up) the problem, we change how we represent the task at hand in our working memory, hence the name of this theory of insight resolution: representational change theory. Once thus liberated, insight often follows. The theory suggests that those who are able to do both of these things more quickly will solve insight problems more quickly and are therefore more insightful. These are exactly the sort of techniques – most notably in constraint relaxation – that physicist Leonard Mlodinow champions in his 21st-century survival guide *Elastic: Flexible Thinking in a Constantly Changing World*. Mlodinow describes the impediments or constraints to insight solutions "mental blocks and idea filters".

The other major theory of how we solve insights is known as progress monitoring. This theory suggests that, when we're faced with a problem of any kind – insight or otherwise – we monitor how we're getting on with the task at hand. In the jargon of representational change theory, we look to decompose the task into chunks. With insight problems, it soon becomes apparent that using tried-and-tested problem-solving strategies bears little fruit. And when we're monitoring our progress and find that we're not making much headway, we look for different solutions. But because insight problems are a special kind of problem, only the most elastic of thinkers will deploy the novel, leftfield solutions required to crack them early in the problem-solving process. Progress monitoring theory, therefore, describes both how insight problems are solved *and* why they either take so long to solve or lead people to give up on them before they find a solution.

The two theories exist side by side in the psychological literature. They don't necessarily contradict one another, and they've both been tested by psychologists using the same kind of stimuli and tests. The theories also explain why jokes work (because they violate usual constraints that we bring to comprehension) and why, once we've solved them, insights often feel like statements of the bleeding obvious. It is often a defining characteristic of an insight, well expressed, that it seems to capture something that surely everybody knows. When we've gone to the trouble of relaxing our normal constraints, entertained novel approaches to resolution, and chunked the problem down, we've seen – in the title of Gary Klein's book – what others don't. Unless we suffer insult or injury to our brains or a sudden bout of amnesia, we can't unlearn what we've worked out. Forever more we will be blessed with the Curse of Knowledge.[5]

THREE PSYCHOLOGICAL TESTS OF INSIGHT

When it comes to psychological tests, I've picked the three that are both among the best known and best exemplify what psychologists from recent decades have been looking for. They're also good tests of insightful thinking which – if your teams and colleagues don't know them – you might find useful and interesting in your own.

1. The nine dot problem

Participants are presented with a three-by-three grid of nine dots laid out in a square, three in each row. They're asked to join all nine dots together by drawing just four straight lines, and without taking their pen off the paper. Most people fail at this task. The apparent silhouette of a square constrains them from drawing – quite literally – outside the box. Once liberated from this mental block, the problem is a problem no more.

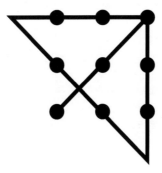

Figure 2.1 The nine dot problem (solved)

2. The alternate uses test

This is a very simple test of fluid (or constrained) thinking. Participants are asked to think of as many different uses of simple, everyday objects as they can. Things like a brick, a shoe, or a napkin. These simple things have regular uses and purposes day to day. The skill of the fluid or elastic thinker is that they can think of more alternate uses for the objects other than building, wearing on your feet, or wiping away traces of soup from your lips. The more uses participants can think of, the less constrained their thinking and the more insightful they are. The test has a long and rich history in the psychology lab, and we'll return to it in more detail – and my development of it – in Chapter 9.

3. Duncker's candle test

We've met the Gestalt school of psychology earlier in the chapter – Köhler and his apes, Bühler and his *Aha-Erlebnis*. Karl Duncker followed in their footsteps, and in 1945 developed the candle test as a means of testing both functional fixedness and insightful thinking. Participants are presented with either the reality or the concept of the following scenario. On a table there's a box of drawing pins (thumb tacks if you live to the west of the Atlantic), a box of matches, and a candle. Next to the table is a corkboard. The challenge is to work out how to attach the candle to the corkboard so that, when lit, it doesn't drop any wax onto the table. Irritatingly, the experimenter has misplaced his candlestick. Or perhaps candlesticks don't exist in his world; maybe they've been outlawed.

Each of the items in the scenario has its regular function. And the solution requires participants to suspend their disbelief about these usual functions, if they are to solve it. In fact, it requires them to excel at the alternate uses test. They need to empty out the box of drawing pins, separate the inner sleeve of the box that was holding the pins from the outer sleeve. Then they light a match, hold it to the bottom of the candle until it starts to melt, and then jam the softened, waxy bottom of the candle to the inside of the box. This turns – through the magic of alternate uses; of lateral thinking; of insight – the inside of the box into a makeshift candleholder. All that remains is to pin the inside of the box that now holds the stuck-on candle to the corkboard, and hey presto! Or rather Aha-Erlebnis! as we should say to a Gestalt psychologist. The candle can now be lit and the wax that doesn't evaporate into the aether will run down the candle and collect in the inside of the box.

There are many other psychological tests of insight, but these are three all-time classics. Others include cryptic crosswords (though there are a whole set of rules involved there which help to break the constraints of how we normally think about words), anagrams, and riddles. For the latest tests, you should probably take out a subscription to either *Puzzler* or *The Journal of Problem Solving*, or perhaps watch boxed sets of past series of John Lloyd's *QI*. You'll find it really Quite Interesting.

A TECHNIQUE FOR PRODUCING IDEAS AMONG THE MADMEN

With these models and tests of insight in mind, let's return to Graham Wallas. If Wallas' model of insight generation is less widely known – and particularly less widely practised – than it should be, I'd argue that this is down to the impenetrable and abstract language he used to explain his model rather than any fundamental fragility in the model itself. The opposite is the case for a very short book that was inspired by *The Art of Thought*. What's more, this second book has – through the medium of advertising practice by one of the world's most successful agencies – helped to popularise Wallas' model, albeit covertly.

James Webb Young was a pioneering figure in advertising in the US. He worked for leading ad agency J. Walter Thompson from 1912 – when he joined as a copywriter – until his retirement in 1964. Young was the first chairman of the US Advertising Council, and from the early 1930s onwards he was professor of business history and advertising at the University of Chicago's school of business. But it is as the author of one of the business world's shortest – but most influential – books that he is best known today. *A Technique for Producing Ideas* blends the work of the Italian sociologist Vilfredo Pareto and Graham Wallas' *The Art of Thought* to create a 48-page booklet that continues to punch well above its weight and pagination.

Chapter titles include "Combining Old Elements" and "Ideas Are New Combinations". The definitive chapter is called "The Mental Digestive Process". Here, Young introduces us to his five-step model, although his step 2 is – I believe – an unnecessary addition to Wallas' framework. For me, it's best thought of as part of the third step.

Here is his model, which he introduces by saying,

This, then, is the whole process or method by which ideas are produced:

> **First**, the gathering of raw materials – both the materials of your immediate problem and the materials which comes from a constant enrichment of your store of general knowledge.
>
> **Second**, the working over of these materials in your mind.
>
> **Third**, the incubating stage, where you let something beside the conscious mind do the work of synthesis.
>
> **Fourth**, the actual birth of the Idea – the "Eureka! I have it!" stage.
>
> And **fifth**, the final shaping and development of the idea to practical usefulness.

(pp. 39–40)

Young doesn't actually cite Wallas as the source and origin of his model in the sparse text, but *The Art of Thought* is the first reference of just three in his bibliography. Young was friendly with Bill Bernbach, one of pioneering post-war madmen of Madison Avenue and one of the founders in 1949 of Doyle Dane Bernbach (DDB). DDB went on to become one of the global powerhouses in advertising. From the 1965 edition of *A Technique for Producing Ideas* onwards, the booklet has included a foreword by Bernbach. In this, he says,

> *James Webb Young . . . is talking about the soul of a piece of communications and not merely the flesh and bones. A chemist can inexpensively put together a human body. What he can't do is spark it with life. Mr Young writes about the creative spark, the ideas, which bring spirit and life to an advertisement. Nothing is more important to the practice of our craft.*

Citing also Bertrand Russell and Albert Einstein, Bernbach highlights the critical importance of "intuition . . . the only path to new insights".

From before he even founded his own agency, Bernbach was a champion of the vital role of insight in building a proposition to move consumers to action. For Bernbach, an ad without genuine insight is like a corpse without a soul. The ability to develop a profound and meaningful understanding of a product, a market, and consumer motivations – the ability to mine for and express genuine insights – is fundamental to the discipline in commercial communications of strategic planning. Strategic planning involves the application of scientific rigour to advertising through intelligent use of data, evidence, and research. In the age of Big Data, it has become increasingly challenging – but also increasingly possible – to use data to build better and better-informed insights. *Narrative by Numbers* shows you how.

Strategic planning as a formal discipline in advertising – alongside creative (developing scripts, copy, and visualisations) and account management (the so-called suit function) – is generally agreed to have been developed in the late 1960s in London. When working for Pritchard Wood, Stanley Pollitt created a planning function for the agency. The function was named account planning three years after that by another pioneer of the evidence-based approach to creating communication, Stephen King of J. Walter Thompson. The story of the birth of planning in advertising is well told in the book *98% Pure Potato* by Tracy Follows and John Griffiths.[6]

What Bernbach's endorsement of Young's book suggests is that the insight-led approach to developing advertising with impact was part of DDB's founding philosophy. This seems to have happened in New York up to 20 years before strategic planning became formally established in London agencies in the late 1960s. Before advertising guru David Ogilvy – a Scotsman in New York – created his eponymous agency in 1948, he trained at the Gallup research company. In his book *Ogilvy on Advertising*, he attributes the success of his campaigns – some of the defining ads of the post-war period, for VW, Schweppes, and Rolls Royce – to meticulous research into consumer habits.[7] Meticulous research from which he mined data-driven insights that unlocked understanding.

This is exactly the same approach that formed the centrepiece of the middle series of the epic AMC TV series *Madmen*, where a psychologist Dr Faye Miller repeatedly added insight and impact to the 1950s ads created by antihero Don Draper. Dr Miller's role was inspired by Ernest Dichter, who was said to be the first to apply motivational research and actual consumer behaviour to marketing. Dichter coined the term "focus group" and features in Vance Packard's seminal 1956 work on the hidden power of advertising, *The Hidden Persuaders*. In partnership with Sandy Sulcer, a copywriter at agency Needham, Harper & Steers in Chicago, Dichter made the case for the tiger – symbolising power and desire – as the core device to promote the Oklahoma Gasoline company, which became Esso and ultimately ExxonMobil. The insights and understanding behind the choice of the tiger held good for many decades.

Often, good, insight-rich ideas arise in several places – businesses, academic institutions, governments – simultaneously, and it's never quite clear if any one individual or team was the sole originator of the idea. Even the most profound idea in the history of science – evolution via natural selection – was likely the work of multiple authors beyond Charles Darwin. They included Darwin's collaborator Alfred Russel Wallace and the zoologists Jean-Baptiste Lamarck and Edward Blyth.

MOVING BEYOND MARKETING

Dave Trott is one of the finest creative talents UK advertising has ever produced. Having trained in New York, he returned to London where he became the boss of copywriting at Gold Greenlees Trott. Now in his early seventies, he writes weekly provocations for the ad industry bible *Campaign*, with beautifully clear prose in distinctive, single-sentence paragraphs. He also produces a book of his thoughts every couple of years, and recent titles have included *One + One = Three*, *Predatory Thinking*, and *Creative Blindness*. If you don't know Dave's insightful work, you need to. In conversation with another legendary London madman a couple of years back, Trott said, "Creativity is our last, legal, unfair advantage – otherwise we're just stylists."[8]

Commercial communication is the world I've inhabited for more than 30 years, and Trott's description of the role and value of insight in advertising shows quite how crucial profound and deep understanding is here. Brands and corporations, charities and governments look to develop campaigns that move people to action: to adopt a habit (cleaning the toilet with bleach, eating smashed avocados on rye bread), to do more of something (buy Coke, eat salad, or take exercise), to do less of something (eat fatty foods, drink alcohol), or to stop doing something altogether (smoking, throwing rubbish out of cars, being in the European Union). Campaigns that are effective in their business and communications objectives are campaigns that understand the motivations and mindset of those they seek to influence. Effective campaigns are campaigns that are driven by insight.

But insight matters in many more industries and many more roles than just marketing and strategic planning. Those individuals and teams that have a reliable approach to generating genuine insights – of developing profound and meaningful understanding of people and things, issues and topics – are more likely to succeed. Insight matters to organisations and companies looking to disrupt a market (think Netflix, Instagram, and Spotify). Meanwhile, those being disrupted by upstart start-ups need insights every bit as much as the disruptors do if they are to survive and not become a footnote in history (think Blockbuster, Kodak, and any number of retailers of physical musical media, from the Virgin Megastore down).

Insight truly is the superpower that unlocks and drives innovation. By truly understanding the market or ecosystem in which your organisation operates, you can develop new products and services, promises and slogans, that will push the buttons of those you look to influence. The emergence of data – particularly Big Data sets – has made it simultaneously more challenging and more possible to develop genuine, data-driven insights that can fuel innovation.

Beyond the challenges of harvesting, cleansing, and analyzing multiple data sets into a single worldview, the Big Data world presents two additional challenges. First, a levelling of the playing field, with both century-old and month-one organisations able to compete on equal terms, provided they have the right talent in place to mine and make sense of data. And second, the pace of change, which is faster than ever and only getting faster. This means that the need for more and better insights – delivered faster, yet still meaningful and able to incite genuine change – is growing. Company lifespans are shrinking. Sixty years ago, the average lifespan of a company listed on the S&P 500 was 61 years, whereas today companies last no more than 18 years. And corporate lifespan is shrinking, too. This means that three-quarters of those companies listed on the stock exchange today will have changed inside the next decade. This is true on stock markets the world over.

It's no wonder companies need insight like never before, which is why this book – and the model at its heart – have never been more necessary. But before we start to play with it in detail, and having considered the history and psychology of insight, we turn now to the neuroscience of insight.

INTERVIEW: STEPHEN JOHNS, ROYAL COLLEGE OF MUSIC

Insightful interview 2 of 8

NAME	Stephen Johns
ORGANISATION	Royal College of Music
ROLE	Artistic Director

Stephen Johns is Artistic Director at the Royal College of Music. In more than 30 years in the classical music industry, mostly as a producer and A&R – artists and repertoire – man, he's worked with many of the world's greatest classical music performers and conductors, including Sir Simon Rattle. His recordings have won numerous awards, including four Grammys.

For Johns, the ability to get inside the mind of the composer of a piece of music is fundamental to how good a performer it is possible to become; the best performers are those that come to develop insight into the intentions of composers without a single verbal clue. Technical competence is a hurdle that has to be mastered first – as a musician is learning their craft – and to begin with, a good performance is about putting fingers on the right keys, blowing or bowing in time, producing the right collections of notes in the right sequence. But a technically correct performance doesn't reveal that a performer has understood the intentions of the composer. It simply shows they can interpret the often abstract and arbitrary notation or tablature with which composers capture and record instructions for playing.

It's like being able to read and understand words and grammar and sentence and even story structure. That doesn't mean a reader understands the motivations of the author or the characters she's reading about. That comes with time, with Gladwell's 10,000 hours, with curiosity and experimentation. For Johns, insight in musical performance and composition is all to do with your "knowledge and experience and upbringing. The wider your grid and terms of reference, the easier it is to assimilate those and take them forward to somewhere more interesting."

In music as elsewhere, Johns sees insight as "the ability to join the dots"; the ability to see the facts arrayed before you, assimilate them, and create something new out of that. The "dots" of music were created hundreds of years ago as a relatively crude set of instructions that transcend linguistic, cultural, and historical boundaries, remaining largely unchanged over centuries. Musicians can perform from a score written by Beethoven or Mozart as actors can read from Shakespeare's folio. And yet a well-trained pair of ears can instantly tell one performer from another and whether they have truly got inside the mind of the composer and understand what was intended – perhaps for the first time. "In a very real sense, it doesn't matter what others have done before – how others have interpreted intentions. Incredible variety is possible in terms of colour, line, pulse, and gesture, all of which can be interpreted from the same, simple, black-and-white dots and dashes on a page. That's insightful."

In musical performance, performers have moments of insight when rehearsing and interpreting the intentions of the composer. The real skill comes in conveying these moments of meaning to an audience such that they – although they may not have the technical skills or experience of the performers – can share in the profound and deep understanding. The notes may be the same as every other time you've heard or played the same piece of music, but it's the resonance that's different.

After three decades working with musicians – representing them, promoting them, and producing award-winning recordings with them – Johns has Gladwell's *Blink*-like capacity to judge whether a performance or recording is good or new or different; if the performer has insight into the composer and composition. This is based on what he's heard before, and so detecting originality in performance. More broadly, Johns believes that the ability to have insights and epiphanies about both musical performance and composition – as a performer, composer, or member of the audience – demands dedication and work at the coalface. It demands curiosity and a relentless fascination filling the hopper of experience and memory.

I was struck by my conversation with Stephen Johns that, although the medium of music is in many senses very different from developing insights about people or things or topics, we use the same neural hardware to make sense of the emotion and impact of music as we do words and concepts and ideas. Music is a way of representing and responding to the world that its creators and performers want to share with others; it just happens to use tone and semibreves, colour and pitch to build its thoughts – rather than letters and words and phonemes and syntax. We interpret the component parts and the whole using the same grey and white, blancmange-like matter. This is true whether we're appreciating the melody of McCartney's *Yesterday* – a much-overused but rather nebulous exemplar of insight, as it was said to have come to him in a dream – or the lyrics.[9] What matters is that those looking to gain understanding from music are always curious – consciously and subconsciously, absorbing content and structure and nuance from a broad canon of art. It is that – in music – that enables us to have insight into "line", the narrative thread of a composition, and the story that the composer is looking to tell.

NOTES

1 My late father Kenneth wrote the world's first book on industrial relations, *Strikes*, in 1952 when he was director of the Institute of Statistics at Oxford. He used footnotes and endnotes for jokes as well as illumination. Here's something that sails between the two. I've used the term "metacognitive" more than once, and I can guarantee I'll use it again before we're done. Seeing Aristotle poke his head over the parapet allows me to wheel out a bit of etymology that's always rather amused me. In ancient Greek, *metá* simply means "after" or "beyond";

a metaphor is something that's "carried beyond" – metaphorically speaking. In English, the prefix has come to indicate concepts that are abstractions behind another. Metadata is one of the most frequently stumbled upon these days. The use of the word meta as a stand-alone was popularised by Douglas Hofstadter in his 1979 *Gödel, Escher, Bach: An Eternal Golden Braid*. He made the first recorded use of the phrase "going meta", meaning taking a debate to a new level of abstraction (aka "going nowhere"). But back in Aristotle's time, things were different and simpler. Aristotle wrote a book about material things that he called *The Physics*. The book he wrote *after The Physics* – about non-material things – was called *The Metaphysics*. Think about that next time a bearded consultant tries to baffle you with all his meta-mansplaining. (*"How did I do, Dad?"*).

2 Gary Klein (2013). *Seeing What Others Don't: The Remarkable Ways We Gain Insights*, Nicholas Brearley Publishing, p. 9.

3 Malcolm W. Browne (1988). The Benzene Ring: Dream Analysis. *The New York Times* https://nyti.ms/2H2n25T

4 How the Mind Works – Steve Pinker email to the current author – little old me! – 25 March 1999.

5 There's a whole lot more on the Curse of Knowledge and how it limits effective data storytelling in Chapter 5 of *Narrative by Numbers*.

6 John Griffiths & Tracy Follows (2016). *98% Pure Potato*. Unbound.

7 David Ogilvy (1985). *Ogilvy on Advertising*. Vintage.

8 "The IPA Podcast: Dave Trott in Conversation" – https://soundcloud.com/the-ipa-podcast/dave-trott-in-conversation

9 For a discussion of the myths and learnings of the story of the creation of *Yesterday*, see David Kadavy's article on his Medium channel, Getting Art Done, *Yesterday* came to Paul McCartney in a dream: Was it a creative miracle? http://bit.ly/32BaH0e

3

THE NEUROSCIENCE OF INSIGHT

"Creativity is not about mental strategies. It's about getting into the right brain state."

John Kounios, *The Eureka Factor*[1]

THE POWER OF ANALOGIES

Gordon Moore, the co-founder of Intel, observed in 1965 that the number of transistors on integrated circuits doubles every two years. Since then, doubling has actually happened every 18 months. Just when you think it isn't possible to squeeze any more transistors onto a chip, Moore's Law proves us wrong. In 1971, the Intel 4004 chip – the first commercially available microprocessor – boasted 2,300 transistors. Its first application was as the beating heart of the Busicom 141-PF calculator, landfill fodder for many decades already. In 2018, Apple's A12X chip was brought to market in the company's latest, ultrafast iPads. The A12X has ten billion transistors.

The impact of Moore's Law on the history of integrated circuit chips from 1971 to 2018 is shown in the chart from Our World in Data[2] (Figure 3.1). Aficionados of *Narrative by Numbers* will not be surprised to learn that to fit 47 years of a geometric progression onto a single chart, the transistor count is presented in a logarithmic scale. Doubling every 18 months over 47 years means that the A12X has more than 4.3 million times as many transistors as the humble Intel 4004. No wonder its

Moore's Law – The number of transistors on integrated circuit chips (1971-2018)

Moore's law describes the empirical regularity that the number of transistors on integrated circuits doubles approximately every two years.
This advancement is important as other aspects of technological progress — such as processing speed or the price of electronic products — are linked to Moore's law.

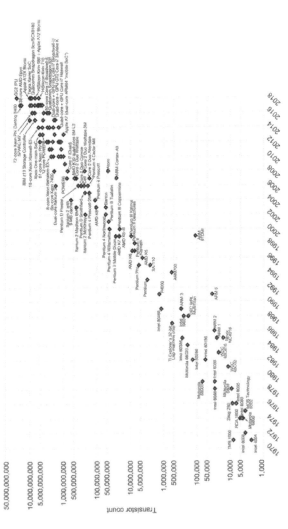

Figure 3.1 Moore's Law

nickname is Bionic. Remember all the fuss about Intel's Pentium in the early to mid-1990s? It might have had two processors on a single chip, but between them they could only muster 3.3 million transistors.

Moore's Law is Silicon Valley's version of the grain of rice conundrum. It goes like this. Locate a chessboard and some rice. Actually, an inexhaustible supply of rice. Put one grain of rice on the first square, two on the second, four on the third and so on. Continue until you reach square 64 on the 8 × 8 matrix of the chessboard. How many grains of rice will you need? Sounds like a relatively innocuous equation: $1 + 2 + 4 + \ldots$. Mathematically it's expressed in this way, where T_{64} is the total number of grains of rice needed, and the powers of two increase for each square (2^0 is 1, $2^1 = 2$, $2^2 = (2*2 = 4)$ etc.):

$$T_{64} = 2^0 + 2^1 + 2^2 + \ldots + 2^{63}$$

The answer, perhaps surprisingly, is 18,446,744,073,709,551,615. Or eighteen quintillion, four hundred and forty six quadrillion, seven hundred and forty-four trillion, seventy three billion, seven hundred and nine million, five and hundred fifty one thousand, six hundred and fifteen. That's enough to feed 100 tons of rice to every human on the planet or a kilo a day for 275 years.[3] Now that's quite a lot of rice. Certainly enough to put an end to world hunger, and more rice than has ever been grown on earth.

I've brought forward these two analogies about chips and rice to put you in the frame of mind to think about the sheer complexity of the human brain. (I'm also very keen on the use – and power – of analogy in insight generation and problem-solving, but we'll come to that when we start working with the STEP Prism of Insight model, in the next five chapters).

THE WORLD'S MOST POWERFUL SUPERCOMPUTER

Moore's Law has only been in operation since the 1960s, and there are only 64 squares on a chessboard. Evolution by natural selection has been at work since life on earth began, some 3.5 billion years ago. Animals go back 590 million years, apes 28 million, humans 2.5 million, and *Homo sapiens* around 120,000. By the time *Homo sapiens* won the humanoid wars about 45,000 years ago, we were pretty similar to how we are now. Maybe hairier, less emotionally intelligent, and not so handy with a smart-phone. But in evolutionary terms, it's not thought we've changed all that much since we saw off the Neanderthals.

The human brain has around 100 billion neurons, each of which can form thousands of links – technically synapses – with other neurons, meaning there are between 100 trillion and a quadrillion synapses in your typical human brain. Neurons are all made of the same kind of material, insulated from each other (except where they join) by myelin; you can think of the myelin sheath on each neuron as being like insulating tape on wires. Neurons transmit signals electrochemically throughout their length, which can be up to several metres. Signals are either excitatory or inhibitory, and so far more than 100 different types of neurotransmitters (dopamine [plea-sure], serotonin [mood], adrenaline [fight or flight]) have been identified.

All of this hardware adds up to the most powerful supercomputer on the planet, with an installed user base of seven-and-a-half billion and rising. The computer comes with a vast array of installed subroutines, programs, and apps, including (Chomsky's) Universal Grammar, which predisposes us to be able to learn to speak and understand language – any language. What's more, the neural network is plastic throughout life, enabling the development of essential skills, vital for survival (walking, talking, and finding a mate). The plasticity of the brain also enables the development of non-essential skills of infinite variety (ultra-marathon run-ning and demagogy, flirting and making jam) and a capacity to develop collectives, companies, and culture.

The human brain is so much more powerful than any computer yet made or realistically conceived, by incalculable orders of magnitude. No computer can cope with vision like a human can, no computer can catch a cricket ball like Ben Stokes in the 2019 World Cup, no computer can develop and express empathy like the Liverpool FC manager, Jürgen Klopp. What's more, no computer can compete with the simultaneous bottom-up and top-down processing of the human brain.

Comparisons and the arms race between the human brain and com-puter technology are ultimately an irrelevance, a comparison of two very different types of problem-solving machines that have evolved and been developed over very different timeframes. We know how computers work because we have designed them, we don't know how brains work with anywhere near the same level of precision.

This is partly because they've evolved over hundreds of millions of years in response to events and stimuli from the environment, to a design manual being written while our ancestors looked after and grew their brains, and to no plan.

It's partly because the brain is so big and complex, with its hundreds of neurotransmitters all interacting, its billions of neurons, and trillions of synapses; we don't know what joins to what and why. As Steve Pinker concludes in *How the Mind Works*, we lack the cognitive architecture to comprehend . . . how the mind works. Trained scientists and statisticians struggle to understand the meaning of five-and-more level interactions (this IF that BUT this NOT that AND this). In the case of neurotransmitters alone, there are often dozens of chains of electrochemicals being released in the brain simultaneously. Yes, dopamine might dominate, but it'll be being fine-tuned by GABA – the master inhibitor of all neurotransmitters, present in two-thirds of all neurons – with a side order of acetylcholine, glutamate, and endorphins. Steve Pinker is right: wrap your cognitive architecture around that and try not to look confused.

And it's partly because all of the brain is made out of the same stuff. Each of the senses is mediated in very different ways yielding very different experiences – sight, sound, touch, taste, smell. And all of these observations are about mechanical manifestations of sensory brain activity, before we get anywhere near the cognitive and metacognitive processes – like insight, what insight is, and how it might arise in the brain.

LOOKING UNDER THE HOOD

When psychology developed as a discipline in European labs in the late 19th and early 20th centuries, there was no available technology to look at and track the electrochemical maelstrom taking place beneath the skull. So resourceful early psychologists started comparing those with brain injuries with those without (neurotypicals).

For many generations, the name Phineas Gage has appeared in abnormal and clinical psychology 101 lectures and textbooks, and the old railroad worker has been around so long he doesn't look like losing his grip anytime soon. When packing explosives with a tamping iron, Gage packed and tamped a bit too hard. The iron caused an explosion, shot up from the ground – red hot – and flew straight through his skull, entering under his left eye and shooting through the top of his head. The heat of the explosion cauterised most of the wound as the rod exited at the hairline, protecting dear Mr Gage from infection. He just had a scaffolding-pole-sized hole in his forehead.

Clearly, an injury of such magnitude shook the unfortunate chap, but amazingly – having lost 10% or more of his grey matter, including most of his left frontal lobe – he survived and could function. Except gradually, after his convalescence, his family and co-workers observed he became "gross, profane, coarse, and vulgar, to such a degree that his society was intolerable to decent people".[4] Although Gage could still talk – and swear – the removal of much of the left frontal lobe rendered him entirely disinhibited, inappropriate, and unable to judge what was right for Victorian American society. More has been written about Gage that any other neurological case study, and if you've ever done even the most basic course in psychology, you'll almost certainly know the name.

At the time, psychology was only starting to emerge and flower as a genuine science, lacking the technology and the shoulders of previous generations of giants on which to stand. Phrenology was popular, and the Gage case only reinforced its popularity. Phrenology is (was; it should be consigned to the annals of historical curiosity, not academic psychology) the study of the shape and size of the skull to indicate and geolocate character traits and mental abilities. Every psychology department has at least one – and probably dozens – of professors in whose offices lives a replica phrenology head, oh-so-ironically propping up books and journals. All sorts of complicated, multifaceted traits are located on these bogus craniums, from aquisivity to caution, imitation to ideality.

What Gage and phrenology suggest – quite correctly – is that certain structures or areas of the brain are – at least in part – responsible for certain mental functions. But what they don't tell us with any real precision is which areas of the brain are solely or uniquely responsible for specific brain functions because that's not how the brain (and so the mind) works. We know that the visual cortex – up to 40% of the brain's volume, at the back of the head – is responsible for vision. But vision isn't one thing. It's light and colour and saturation and hue edges and angles and curves and motion and distance and 2D and 3D and speed of approaching or retreating objects and a whole lot more.

Yes, we can get a sense of which areas of the brain are responsible for some – often quite specific – elements of visual perception. But brain-damaged vs neurotypical patients can only take us so far. In part this is because the brain is so complex that even the simplest functions are mediated through multiple brain areas. It operates – to stretch the computing analogy that's well past breaking point – on a parallel distributed processing model. And in part it's because there's such a limited universe of patients with specific (but limited) brain injuries, attached to neuropsychological research units, willing and able to take part in experiments. Brain lesions and injuries have informed our understanding of the brain and how it works (and doesn't), but studying the impact of brain damage is limited and crude. In the case of phrenology, while the intention may have been right, it's about as scientific as astrology or homoeopathy.

Further clues about brain function come from brain surgery. Most brain surgery involves removing either malignant or benign tumours – cancers – from the brain while causing as little damage as possible to healthy brain tissue. Or *Do No Harm* in the Hippocratically titled memoir by renowned English brain surgeon, Henry Marsh.[5]

In the UK Marsh pioneered a technique of brain surgery which is done under local anaesthetic only, with the patient awake during the procedure. While the brain contains up to a 100 billion neurons, these nerve cells don't carry or cause the sensation of pain. So local anaesthetic only is necessary to ease the pain of cutting through the flesh that covers the skull before sawing through the cranium and removing the minimum amount of bone necessary to have easy access to remove the tumours.

The benefit of this technique, known as awake craniotomy, is that it helps the surgeon know as soon as the act of removing brain matter is starting to have a negative impact on the healthy brain tissue that remains once the tumour has been suctioned out. Marsh and other awake craniotomy surgeons have their patients talk, respond to the presentation of visual stimuli by saying what they're seeing, counting back from 1,000 subtracting seven each time – those kinds of tasks.

The tasks demanded of the patients depend on the location of the tumour. It could be in or around Wernicke's area, at the back of the left temporal and parietal lobes. The cluster of structures in this part of the brain is strongly involved in language comprehension, using the right words, and expressing thoughts. If – after removing the tumour – a patient starts to talk nonsense or mislabel a helicopter as a kangaroo, surgeons know they've gone far enough, remove the suction tool, draw the meninges back over the brain, and glue the skull back in place. If the patient starts to fail to be able to produce speech while a lesion in Broca's area was being removed, again this would be a good time to stop. Broca's is towards the front of the left temporal lobe and is involved in the control of speech production.

Awake craniotomy is used to prevent surgeons removing too much brain tissue, most particularly healthy, still-functioning brain tissue. It's testament to the plasticity of the brain that critical functions such as speech production and comprehension can be rerouted in the event of an invasive tumour or lesion. But there's no point in a surgeon removing a tumour and a bit more brain matter "just to be safe" if the patient ends up unable to talk, walk, or understand their place in the world.

One final point on this topic. If you want to see something truly amazing, here's a YouTube video (http://bit.ly/2yWAQua) of a guitar-playing patient having a brain tumour removed using awake craniotomy . . . while playing a guitar. The surgeon, Sujit Prabhu, describes how the patient, Robert Alvarez, was keen to preserve his ability to sing, remember lyrics, and maintain complete motor function and dexterity. And so he did, while playing *Creep* by Radiohead. Alvarez describes picking up a guitar as like Thor picking up his hammer: "I wanna put it in the air and let the lightning strike it." Ninety percent of the tumour was successfully removed, with the remnants dealt with via radiotherapy. Or perhaps radioheadtherapy.

BRAIN SCANNING TECHNIQUES AND TECHNOLOGIES

Understanding what happens inside the skulls of neurotypical folk has been an area of active study for almost a century. The German psychiatrist Hans Berger invented electroencephalography (EEG), a method of recording electrical activity on the surface of the brain, in the early 1920s. EEG has advanced and developed over the years and is still widely used today in cognitive neuroscience experiments, recording so-called event-related potentials (ERPs). Skullcaps containing dozens of sensors record ERPs, which record which areas on the surface of the brain respond to the presentation of specific stimuli, situations, tasks, or demands.

EEG has since been upgraded but also supplemented by computed tomography (CT), computer-aided tomography (CAT) scanning technology, which uses x-rays to produces 3D images of brain activity. These were followed by positron emission tomography (PET), magnetic resonance imaging (MRI), and functional MRI (fMRI). This allows for more detailed, real-time understanding of blood flow (and so activity) right across the brain, in three dimensions and glorious Technicolor. As first CT, then CAT and PET, then MRI and ultimately fMRI scanners spread across academic research institutions, there was an arms race among psychologists to identify which area of the brain lights up in response to what stimulus or cognitive task. For a while, dazzled by Shiny New Object Syndrome and the shock of the new, many journal editors collectively lowered their critical faculties and were happy to publish any paper that could show the role of brain structures X, Y, and Z in mediating all manner of psychological traits, be they jealousy, a fascination with plush toys, or psychopathy.

All sciences mature, and it is central to the scientific process that subsequent generations learn from the mistakes of those who come before – even if those mistakes were driven by enthusiasm and excitement and a desire to answer fundamental questions. And while we may – *pace* Pinker – lack the cognitive architecture to understand how the mind works, cognitive neuroscience today knows very much more about what's going on in the brain as regards complex mental processes. And that includes insight, and in particular the moment of insight, the eureka moment. It also includes the conditions immediately preceding aha that make your brain more or less likely to experience and capture an insight. Ironically, it's taken a no-nonsense, clear-thinking, straight-talking physicist to explain the state of the art to the world. Enter the hero of this chapter, former Caltech physics professor and one-time scriptwriter for *Star Trek: The Next Generation*, Leonard Mlodinow.

THE NEUROSCIENCE OF INSIGHT

Mlodinow is still – technically – a physicist. His book-jacket bio concludes with the line that he is a "full time writer, while continuing to publish physics papers as a hobby". In addition to the *Star Trek* credits and a career in the gaming industry, he has also co-authored books with both Stephen Hawking and New Age guru Deepak Chopra.

Despite this impressive, polymathic curriculum vitae, it's Mlodinow's most recent book that draws together the evidence on the neuroscience of insight in such a straightforward and compelling way. *Elastic: Flexible Thinking in a Constantly Changing World* (2018) should be required reading for those curious about insight, particularly the seventh chapter, titled "The Origin of Insight". I'll summarise the main arguments here – not least because those 21 pages made everything clear to me and finally joined the dots for me and enabled me to write this chapter and ultimately this book. But also to whet your appetites to want to put in an order for Mlodinow's book straightaway and read it as soon as you can – as soon as you've finished this book, perhaps. I'd also encourage you to absorb his every word so you can benefit from the deeply practical blueprint he sets out to enable more flexible and creative thinking in a world drowning in information overload. Taking the advice from the final chapter, on liberation, and the exhortation "Let's get stoned", depends – of course – on where you live and your attitude to risk. And there are plenty of mind-opening strategies that enable elastic thinking beyond the psychopharmacological, including harnessing the benefits of fatigue and the role of positive mood.

Much of what we know about the neuroscience of insight – which Mlodinow summarises so well – comes from the twin, now collaborative labs of John Kounios and Mark Beeman, professors of psychology at Drexel and Northwestern universities in North America respectively. Kounios and Beeman are also the authors of another set text for readers of this chapter (and this book), 2015's *The Eureka Factor: Creative Insights and the Brain*, an interested lay reader's explanation of what they've discovered about the neuroscience of insight.

What Kounios' and Beeman's individual and joint work has shown for the first time is what happens in the brain – and where – just before and during the process of generating insights. What I find so satisfying is that Kounios and Beeman's work corroborates and validates the STEP Prism of Insight as a model of insight generation. It shows quite how helpful first Wallas' and then Young's and now our model of insight are. To create something new, we need a store of information to recombine (we need both chronically and acutely to Sweat, to be curious). But for insight to happen, we have to allow our subconscious minds to have the time and space to try all sorts of recombinations (we need Timeout, to step away from the challenge at hand). There are things we can do – and we'll cover these in depth in each chapter dealing with each of the four steps – to make it more likely that a wide variety of different recombinations are tried out by the subconscious mind. And then there truly is an aha moment (Eureka). For each of these stages, Kounios and Beeman provide neural correlates of actual activity in the brain, of stimuli acquired through curiosity, left alone, and then integrated together to form something new. For Mlodinow, this is the very essence of elastic, insightful thinking, an "original and fruitful way of understanding an issue or approaching a problem" (p. 138). Of insight. What Kounios and Beeman describe as brain activity at the moment of insight is the fMRI equivalent of Klein's insight Geiger counter that we met earlier. In an equally pre-neuroscientific analysis, Arthur Koestler said in *The Art of Creation* that when we recognise that two previously unrelated matrices are, in fact, compatible, that's when we have a eureka moment.

Using a combination of EEG (Kounios) and fMRI (Beeman) in their experiments, these two researchers have also now identified that just before and at the moment of insight, there are bursts of activity in the right temporal lobe; specifically, this is in the right anterior superior temporal gyrus. There are unconscious – or subconscious – brain states that help to incite the aha moment, each of which can be enhanced to make them more likely. Just before an aha moment, visual areas of the brain dim, making us very briefly less aware of the environment around us and less distracted and distractible. Kounios and Beeman advise that, if you want to have more insights more reliably, you should be in a dark, quiet space.

Being in a good mood also makes insights more likely, because positive moods activate the anterior cingulate in the middle of the front of the cortex. This structure expands the scope of thought, allowing us to entertain longer-shot – less likely – ideas, the very stuff of creativity. And that state can be enhanced by expanding our perspective, so again, the researchers advise going outside (or at least to a high-ceilinged room) to expand our brain's frame of reference and so bring forward more insights. Being too keen or impatient to force out an insight – under pressure from an unreasonable boss or client – can lead to inferior solutions and block our ability to find a new one. So avoid distraction, be happy, and be somewhere big. We'll come back to the importance of bigness in the interview with Baroness Susan Greenfield at the end of this chapter.

Hardware issues and storage capacity aside, Mlodinow shows why computers – so far – have failed to come anywhere close to human levels of cognitive power. He demonstrates that we've designed them to process either bottom-up (building associations or patterns from data points in an unstructured way) or top-down (imposing structured patterns on data and modelling based on how data points fit or conflict with predefined structures). In the case of insight, he shows how "bottom-up processing arises from the complex and relatively 'unsupervised' interaction of millions of neurons and can produce wildly original insights" (p. 46). This contrasts with top-down processing in humans that's channelled by the brain's so-called executive regions and generates, logical, analytical thinking. It's the unsupervised, bottom-up variety that generates insights, new ways of looking at the world, and creativity.

DIDN'T SOMEONE SAY THE MIND IS FLAT?

It's a fascinating process writing a book, and in particular knowing when to stop taking on board new stimuli and when to start writing your own words. You follow leads and references and chains of thought assiduously, and then, when you're satisfied you've covered all relevant angles and have assembled your arguments, you start writing. You start adding your own perspective to what you've discovered, accommodating the wrinkles and nuances you've unearthed, ideally without too much fudging of issues or blurring of boundaries. I'm told by novelists – particularly those who look create a sense of place and time that's not their own – that this is just as true for fiction as non-fiction.

You're making good progress, your thesis (or characters and plot) are coming along nicely, and you're in writerly flow. And then – as if from nowhere – you're sideswiped by a new or different way of looking at the world that's apparently at odds with yours. Suddenly, you stumble upon an article or book or whole school of thought that seems to contradict the very tight and cogent argument you're making. It makes you doubt everything you're writing and undermines your self-confidence. This is exactly what happened to me when over lunch one day I was explaining to a good friend the role of the subconscious mind in generating insights in the background during Timeout. "According to Nick Chater – and I'm sure you've read his brilliant book, *The Mind Is Flat*," said my friend, "there's no such thing as the subconscious mind." I spluttered into my flat white, nodded sagely, panicked inside, and went to the bathroom to order Chater's book by app before we paid the bill.

I devoured the book for the first time in just a couple of days. Then I read it again. And it *is* excellent. It's a great assemblage of all the experimental, behavioural, psychological evidence that – taken together – paints a very compelling picture of what Chater calls "the illusion of depth" and the reality of "the improvised mind".

I can entirely understand Chater's motivation to line up the experimental evidence for the lack of a subconscious mind. Before I found and read his book, I'd idly considered doing something similar some years back, looking to undermine those schools of psychodynamic psychotherapy – particularly Freudian. You know the ones. They maintain that we repress negative experiences, memories, and feelings into our subconscious and that it is the act of repression that leads to psychological pain. I don't believe that (and I choose the word "believe" advisedly, because there are many similarities between Freudian psychotherapy and religion). Indeed, if you've got strong wrists, good eyesight, and time to read the very dense – but very excellent – *Why Freud Was Wrong*, I can't see you doing anything other than agree with me.

Very well argued and evidenced as it is, Chater's book is also very controversial and – to an extent – deliberately contrarian, seeking and advancing my-side arguments and creating definitions that are often partial and unanswered. Several times when I was reading the book, I thought (and wrote, in pencil, in the margins) that some of the evidence he brings forward is indeed more about definitional differences. Is it perhaps more about different ways of describing the phenomena observed, as we try to make sense of mental processes which historically have been so opaque and resistant to examination through introspection?

Chater argues that everything is on the surface and that we react to stimuli as they're presented to us. He's not denying the existence of long-term memory – of course he's not; how could he? – but he does appear to be arguing that nothing happens to memories apart from storage and access. Meantime, the work of Antonio Damasio, Joseph LeDoux and others have shown that memories are very plastic and liable to change once they've been encoded and hardwired. I believe that Chater puts far too great a store on the capacity and capabilities of short-term, working memory and too little on the organisational principles that shape what we pay attention to, what we focus on, what we access, store, retrieve, and ignore. He also proposes that the contradictory nature of all of us – our ability to see the lack of logic in holding mutually contradictory positions on the same topic – has to deny the existence of the subconscious. And – back to Pinker and cognitive architecture – just because we can't understand or get access to something (the subconscious mind) does not mean it's not there.

Having read Chater's challenging book, I went back to Mlodinow to see if there were answers there. I was not disappointed. There was plenty of experimental evidence from the studies he reports and stitches together into a narrative – most notably from Kounios and Beeman – that provide very direct evidence of the subconscious mind in action. When talking of the role and benefit of timeout, Mlodinow reports, "But today we know that quiet brains are not idle brains, that in periods of mental peace, our conscious may be overflowing with activity" (p. 110). Kounios and

Beeman provide experimental evidence of unconscious processing and multiple attempts at recombination, before insights are let through the filter between the subconscious and the conscious mind. They show that "although our conscious experience of the moment of insight is sudden, it comes from a long string of behind-the-scenes events that mirror the processes involved in understanding language, and with a similar division of labor among the right and left hemispheres" (p. 144).

So while I very much enjoyed putting myself outside my comfort zone – one of the core principles of the timeout phase of the STEP Prism of Insight – on balance, I wasn't convinced that Chater had made his case for the lack of a subconscious. I don't deny that we are "astonishingly inventive, ad hoc reasoners, creative metaphor-machines, continually welding together scattered scraps of information into momentarily coherent wholes" (p. 221). But I don't accept he's proved the "ad hoc" and "momentarily coherent" as the only ways in which we do our magical recombinatorial thing, nor that we don't do it outside conscious introspection. A couple of pages before, Chater says, "human intelligence is based on precedents – and the ability to stretch, mash together and re-engineer such precedents to deal with an open-ended and novel world" (p. 217), with which I totally agree. But his assertion one line later – that "the secret of how this is done has yet to be cracked" – is disabused by Mlodinow and his cast of players, including Kounios, Beeman, Crammond, and Radel.

ON THE BENEFITS OF NEURODIVERSITY

The marketing boss of UK insurance market leader Direct Line, Mark Evans is a champion of neurodiversity. Driven by family experience of dyslexia, Evans has written and spoken from conference stages on the benefits of companies embracing neurodiversity.[6] Those who differ from the neurotypical mainstream – including people living with dyslexia, dyscalculia, autism, dyspraxia, and attention deficit hyperactivity disorder (ADHD) – are often excluded from the workforce. Many employers don't know how to work with those who are wired differently and may behave differently from the mainstream. What's more, most companies' recruitment processes and most of the recruitment procedures have been designed – with no malice aforethought – to exclude neurodiverse talent. Those with dyslexia might fail a writing test, dyscalculia a numeracy test, and autism to engage in either eye contact or reciprocal questions and answers.

And yet, many of the most successful, inspiring, and insightful illuminati to have lit up the world are most definitely neurodiverse. As Evans points out, "Steve Jobs, Jamie Oliver, Steven Spielberg, and Richard Branson were/are dyslexic and Charles Darwin, Sir Isaac Newton, and Albert Einstein were autistic." Yet it is precisely because of their different wiring that these individuals are responsible for some of the biggest insights and breakthroughs in science, business, and the arts, from the iPod to *ET*, from the theory of evolution by natural selection to $E = mc^2$. The world would be a worse place without each of those advances. Sure, we might have got there. But we wouldn't have got there nearly so quickly or directly without this A-list of neurodiverse talent.

Rather than being a drag on corporate life, Evans – and others – now see neurodiversity as a potential source of competitive advantage to those who build what he calls "whole brain teams". He now leads a Neurodiversity Council for I-COM, a global digital marketing and smart data organisation, and he has received deserved plaudits as one of the UK's most respected and senior marketers who also happens to openly promote neurodiversity.

It also turns out that neuroscience supports Evans' position. As we have seen earlier, people who are more elastic and less rigid in their thinking are more likely to have breakthrough insights. They are more innovative and take pleasure in finding new approaches to existing problems. Reporting the work of University of Georgia researcher Bonnie Crammond, Mlodinow shows how the stray thoughts of those with ADHD can sometimes prove relevant – relevant in exactly the way Evans suggests. Mlodinow says, "they can produce unusual but constructive connections and associations that wouldn't have been thought of by 'normal' people, making individuals with ADHD better at skills like idea generation and divergent thinking" (p. 66). Better – therefore – at insight. And how to be insightful.

INTERVIEW: BARONESS SUSAN GREENFIELD

Insightful interview 3 of 8

NAME	Baroness Susan Greenfield
ORGANISATION	Neuro-Bio Ltd
ROLE	CEO and Founder

Baroness Susan Greenfield has a long and distinguished career as a neuroscientist, having spent most of her 40 years in the field at the University of Oxford, including as Professor of Pharmacology. She holds honorary degrees from dozens of universities, and today runs Neuro-Bio, a biotech business spun out from research at Oxford that develops drugs to tackle neuro-degenerative conditions, including Alzheimer's disease.

For Greenfield, insight means seeing the connections that others haven't. This can often involve the application of learning and understanding from one field and applying it for the first time to another; seeing one thing in terms of another, combining old and old and making something radically new. It's like T.S. Elliot said of poetry, "One of the surest of tests is the way in which a poet borrows. Immature poets imitate; mature poets steal; bad poets deface what they take, and good poets make it into something better, or at least something different."[7] But what insight very definitely is not in Greenfield's mind is simply knowing the answer or giving a correct solution. That's analytical problem-solving, not insightful problem-solving, and the two are very different. The distinction is what historically separated divergent from convergent thinking.

Greenfield gives the example of Macfarlane Burnet, the Australian immunologist who first saw the connection between Darwinian evolution by natural selection in the wider world and the same principles at work in the human immune system. That insight – and application of learnings from one field of biology at a macro level to a completely different field at a micro, cellular level – revolutionised our understanding of the immune system, of virology, and immunology. It went on to shape public health policy, and as a result won Burnet numerous national and global awards and accolades.

Greenfield's 2014 book *Mind Change* sets out quite clearly where she believes neuroscience has helped us understand insight, particularly the 18th chapter, "Thinking Differently". Here she says, "the insight and the knowledge that characterises a gifted mind is more/than the regurgitation of facts . . . real intelligence requires a synthesis between facts, context and meaning that encompasses far more than efficient responding" (pp. 249–50). She goes on to say: "While collecting information is gathering dots, knowledge is joining them up . . . The more connections you can make across an ever wider and disparate range of knowledge . . . This is why the concept of context, beyond mere facts, is so important" (p. 250), and: "This ability to make connections where they didn't exist before, to connect the dots, could account for talents in a number of academic areas, including philosophy, mathematics, science and music" (p. 252). She concludes, "As I see it, the key issue is narrative. In a narrative there is a sequence, a chain of cause and effect in a non-random, strictly ordered sequence. Any narrative will, in some way, echo a life story. Stories arrange events into a context, a conceptual framework, and this order creates meaning" (p. 256).

In our discussion, Greenfield said that she believes neuroscience still has a long way to go before we can understand insight at a neurological level more than metaphorically. She is deeply opposed to the vogue in neuroscience that observes a particular area or set of areas "lighting up" in a brain scanner and researchers – who are necessarily ignorant of the whole – claiming to have identified the part(s) of the brain responsible for complex, cognitive functions. She dubs this "the tyranny of localisation". That said, the inherent plasticity of the brain – changing structures in response to environment and stimuli – is "an obvious correlate for joining up the dots, pruning and strengthening, and making firm associations". And our understanding is getting better and better, as the evidence presented earlier in this chapter from Kounios and Beeman show. This makes Greenfield optimistic that we will continually improve our understanding of the brain and brain processes, and she believes that scientific progress and "standing on the shoulders of giants still has a long way to take us with the brain".

Greenfield believes that there are very real dangers of excessive exposure to digital technology, especially for the growing brains and emerging minds of tweens and teens. The very act of becoming so absorbed in small, mobile phone screens removes perspective and reduces critical faculty. And perhaps most importantly, it stops us generating a proper breadth of view and opinion. What is fascinating is that physical limitations appear to have cognitive consequences. By narrowing attention to the small, insular world of the tiny screen, we become less able to see the forest from the trees more generally.

By contrast, Greenfield is convinced by an emerging field of psychology that shows how being somewhere big – open countryside; in the presence of rolling hills (or better yet mountains); in a desert or on the plains; out in the middle of a lake or the ocean; even in a cathedral (but not a church) – effectively slows down time. Being somewhere big allows us to process more incoming stimuli more quickly, hence the apparent time-bending benefits. On the other hand, being somewhere small and confined – which includes busy urban and office life, and which reaches its apogee when staring at a smartphone's screen – makes time appear to pass more quickly, allowing us to process fewer stimuli. "It appears as if there's a space-time metric in the brain," says Greenfield. "Large spaces make time slow down, and that's why so many of us deliberately seek them out. It's why they so often give us a sense of awe and calm."

The fact that we are able to process fewer stimuli in smaller, closed environments has two important consequences. First, we take in less information. And second, we handicap our subconscious mind by having less old stuff to combine with other old stuff and make it into something new. The busyness and relentless nature of modern, digitally mediated life appears to be counterproductive for those seeking to generate insights. Hence the benefits of being somewhere big, and hence also the benefits of timeout away from stimuli, to allow the subconscious mind to do its recombinatorial best.

Greenfield concludes: "I think from experience that insights are best developed when you divorce yourself from screens and screen technologies; they're pedestrian and distracting and you get too easily swayed, especially by the narrow and myopic echo chamber of opinion and dogma. To gain insight, don't go to Wikipedia or Google and only there. My best ideas come to me when I'm on holiday, sitting by a pool, where my mind can wander. You need a positive lack of distraction and space and time for connectivity to occur."

NOTES

1 John Kounios (2016). The Eureka Factor: Aha moments, creative insight, and the brain http://bit.ly/2H2YdGU

2 Image courtesy of Our World in Data, licensed under Create Commons BY license. Author: Max Roser. http://bit.ly/2N0HZ4I

3 With thanks to DeDoimedo www.dedoimedo.com/life/rice.html

4 A Most Remarkable Case. *American Phrenological Journal and Repository of Science, Literature, and General Intelligence*, 13 (4), p. 89, col. 3, April 1851.

5 It was a very great pleasure to get to know Marsh for a few years at the turn of the millennium around the time that he married a friend and long-term collaborator Kate Fox, the author of *Watching the English*. Apart from marvelling at how good he was at woodwork – redeploying his brain surgeon's hands to make beautiful furniture and buildings out of wood – I'll always remember the story Marsh told of a former colleague who was a true polymath with a great sense of humour. A brain surgeon in the second part of his career, his first had been as a rocket scientist. Marsh said he got bored with people saying to him, "Well, I guess it's not rocket science!" Ho, ho. So he decided on a whim to retrain as a brain surgeon so that he could retort – with genuinely unique knowledge – "No, and it's not brain surgery, either!" According to Marsh, his friend never missed an opportunity to trot out the line, often asking friends and family to set him up for the punchline. I still can't believe that Marsh – celebrated in the Storyville film, *The English Surgeon* on his pro bono work in the Ukraine and acclaimed for the candour of his two memoirs, *Do No Harm* and *Admissions* – didn't tell this story when he was on BBC Radio 4's *Desert Island Discs* in 2018. Perhaps he'd told (and heard) it often enough.

6 See for instance We All Lose by Overlooking Neurodiverse Talent. *Campaign*, 5 February 2018 http://bit.ly/2TsaDNo

7 T.S. Elliott (1920). *The Sacred Wood: Essays on Poetry and Criticism*, discussed in detail on the blog PLAGIARISMBAD in a post titled "Does talent borrow, genius steal?" http://bit.ly/2K4llji

4

HOW TO BE INSIGHTFUL

"Good ideas are not conjured out of thin air; they are built out of a collection of existing parts."

Steve Johnson, *Where Good Ideas Come From*

ON SHOE DOGS AND WAFFLE IRONS

Phil Knight, the founder of Nike, worked in close collaboration for many years with track and field coach Bill Bowerman. Bowerman is often credited as being the co-founder of Nike, although when he and Knight started working together on a handshake agreement, neither the Nike name nor brand existed. The company that went on to become one of the biggest names is running shoes and sports apparel started life in the early 1960s as Blue Ribbon Sports, importing the Onitsuka Tiger brand of running shoes from Japan and China. The Greek goddess of victory was not in their sights.

Slowly, gradually, the company started designing its own shoes, sourcing manufacture for many years in Japan, China, and elsewhere in the Far East. Bowerman wasn't necessarily an easy man – for social interaction or to work with. Come to that, neither was his co-founder, Phil Knight. Knight's autobiography, *Shoe Dog*, makes that very clear. But Knight and Bowerman were united by a love of running, and their companies provided a vehicle for their shared passion and Bowerman's obsession about creating the perfect, most lightweight running shoe possible. Hence – for example – his lateral, category-defining insight to use a waffle iron to create lightweight soles from plastic compressed and heated in the kitchen utensil. As Steve Johnson says, good ideas are not conjured out of thin air; they are built out of a collection of existing parts. This is a thought and a motif that we will come back to again and again.

With Nike, from our perspective, it's Bowerman's insights into the mindset and the motivations of runners in particular that drove the company from being A.N. Other importer and manufacturer of sneakers and sweatpants to where it is today. The Nike name, iconic swoosh, and values are universally recognised and pretty much universally loved – at least outside the Trump administration and his supporters and a few Russian bot farms. In 2018, the company turned over more than US$36bn, making it the world's biggest sports brand.

Perhaps Bowerman's most important insight was one of his most straightforward, fundamentally human, and least technical. For a man who'd try anything to shave another ounce off his latest shoe, the insight is simply this: **if you have a body, you are an athlete**. A self-evident statement, like many good insights. But also a universal human truth and a profound and deep understanding of athletic motivation for all which at once makes the company and its philosophy much more than just a shoe designer for elite track stars.

The company's declared purpose is "to bring inspiration and innovation to every athlete in the world". But by understanding that the simple act of being embodied makes one an athlete – no matter how trained, honed, or otherwise; no matter how many limbs; no matter how controllable those limbs – Nike created a platform to become the champion of all athletes in all sports at all levels, from "Couch to 5K" novices to Olympians. What is more remarkable – and this was enabled by the insight underpinning the purpose – is that "Nike's" first customers were world-class athletes. Bowerman's profound and deep understanding swept the rest of us along with it. From "if you have a body, you are an athlete", it's just a small hop, skip, and a jump to "Just Do It". Particularly if you're a triple-jumper. Insights, you see, have the power to shape and change culture. Even through something as ultimately trivial as commercial communication.

THE STEP PRISM OF INSIGHT

So here we are. In the course of the first three chapters, we've travelled 2,500 years from Plato to the third decade of the 21st century. We've considered what insight is (and what it is not). We've looked at the history of ideas and breakthrough thinking, as well as the etymology and language surrounding insight. From a clearly (and unashamedly) Western perspective, we've taken in the psychology and now the neuroscience of insight, moving from speculation and hunches to cast-iron proof. And all thanks to cumulative advances in both technology and understanding.

Scientific knowledge advances by each successive generation of labs seeing where we've got to so far, assessing what works and what doesn't, and using previous knowledge to inform new experiments and lines of investigation. As I trust I've shown so far, it's exactly the same with our knowledge and understanding of insight. What's even more satisfying is that it's true of our general conception of insight – what it is and how it comes into being. But it's also true of every individual's experience of looking for insights themselves. As the author of *Copy, Copy, Copy* Mark Earls (aka @herdmeister) has said, "Physicists don't have to discover gravity before starting experiments with gravity. Like Newton – and like Oasis with the Beatles – they stand on the shoulders of giants."[1]

Now is the moment when I get to formally introduce the model that's at the heart of this book and we start to play with it. And I have to say it is with some satisfaction that my model is itself the product of the model, in a delightfully meta way. Of curiosity, timeout, creativity, and testing.

So here it is.

The STEP Prism of Insight[TM, 2] is an unashamed act of borrowing (with full credit) and updating from those who came before, originally Graham Wallas and his *Art of Thought*, then James Webb Young and his *Technique for Producing Ideas*. It casts aside Wallas' arcane and archaic language, his obtuse and Latinate form of expression that did so much to keep what he stumbled upon as a dusty footnote in the history of cognitive psychology. It celebrates the clarity and simplicity of expression of Young – a vision that so captivated and inspired Bill Bernbach – though it renders unnecessary Young's new second step, keeping the model in four distinct

Figure 4.1 The STEP Prism of Insight™

phases, hence the four quadrants mentioned earlier. It takes encouragement from the findings of psychological experiments, and it welcomes
the confirmation of psychology via neuroscience, thanks to the physicist
Leonard Mlodinow.

In a cog-shaped nutshell – a designer's metaphor for cognition, the
whirring mechanisms inside the brain – the STEP Prism says this. If you
want to fulfil your uniquely human potential as a creature that advances and
evolves, you need insight. And to be insightful, you need to do four things –
consciously at first and probably always. For although the logic of Figure 1.1
is that unconscious competence is the desired end state, an unconsciously
competent driver can travel from London to Glasgow without remembering anything of the journey, and maybe that isn't nirvana after all.

So, this, top level, is how you do it.

1   **Sweat:** be curious. Absorb information, perspectives, and points of view from any and every source you can. Listen, read, turn up to events. Talk to people – people who know a lot about the area in which you're looking to solve a problem and innovate, but also those who know nothing about it. Take yourself outside your comfort zone and echo chamber. Seek out stimuli that help to reinforce your hunches, but also stimuli that contradict or are deeply opposed to it. Add some randomness and jitter into your data collection. And be curious forever. Not just for the current brief, today's quandary, this month's challenge. Ensure that the spirit of curiosity fills you always. Be like a shark, always needing to move forward in order to survive. Become crabby if you're confined or constrained and unable to flex your curiosity muscles. Be like a sponge with infinite capacity, taking in and absorbing new information and data at every opportunity, without becoming a slave to curiosity. There's no need to engender FOMO – fear of missing out – but if you want to give your subconscious mind the opportunity to do its brilliant, recombinatorial thing of mixing old things together to make something new, you have to fill the hopper and feed the beast. And don't worry about maxing out your data storage. The human brain is estimated to have a capacity of between 1 terabyte and 2.5 petabytes[3] (a terabyte is 1,000 gigabytes, and a petabyte is 1,000 terabytes).

2   **Timeout:** having absorbed stimulus, content, and information – however apparently irrelevant or off-brief – you need to step away from the challenge at hand and let your subconscious mind get to work. There are plenty of strategies and approaches you can take to make yourself stop thinking about the insight that you need to generate. Some of these are mental and work-related: go and work on another client or another project to distract yourself. Some of them are mental and diverting: read, do a puzzle, a sudoku, or a cryptic crossword. Once you get to a certain level as a cryptic crossword solver, you may well find that the strategies you use to find solutions to cryptic clues are the very processes that help unlock insights. Some involve other, non-verbal forms of creativity, from art to music, from knitting to dancing. It might involve going to a

gallery or museum. Some diversions are purely physical, including all sorts of exercise and individual and team sports. I find running and swimming – slowly – particularly good. Others – perhaps particularly those who lead large teams – find that football, cricket, and netball help to divert them. For others yet, it's drugs (legal or illegal), the gym, or riding a horse. It could be a spontaneous "duvet day", when a company allows – encourages – employees to call in and say, "I won't be coming in today". But timeout could be as simple as going for a walk at lunchtime or immersing yourself in someone else's world in a novel, a box set, the cinema, theatre, a musical or opera (well, I do live three miles from Glyndebourne). What matters is that you divert your conscious mind from the challenges you're seeking to address, from the insights you're trying to unlock. The great thing about physical things and exercise is that there's absolutely no chance of one of your sources of stimulus interrupting you with a ding or a beep of notification.

3 **Eureka:** during timeout – and timeout can last for five minutes to hours, days, weeks, months, or even years – your subconscious mind does its recombinatorial thing, trying mash-ups of the stimuli you've absorbed to create new solutions. To the problem at hand as well as to other challenges you didn't even realise you were trying to solve. And then – often without warning – you have conscious awareness of an answer to a problem. There's a lot of discussion in the psychological literature about whether a eureka moment is, in fact, a moment or perhaps a more gradual realisation that the period of timeout is paying dividends. I don't think it matters whether it's a millisecond or a growing sense of certainty. What matters is that you can recognise what's happening and get ready to capture your solution. I always say that Eureka for me is a "scalp-tightening" moment – I have a physical response which is similar to what I experience when my favourite guitarist from my favourite band hits the opening chord of my favourite song.[4] Genuine moments of insight often generate an emotional and a physical response, from increased heart rate to slight breathlessness. As well as excitement and anxiety, insight can be accompanied by confusion or irritation.[5] You know something's happened,

but you're not quite sure what. Emotional reactions occur, I believe, because of what's riding on an insight and the potential for the future. But you need to be able to recognise what *Aha-Erlebnis* is like for you because it can often be fleeting. This is why it's so important for you to realise you're having an insight and capture it as soon as you can – ideally immediately. From crayons in the shower to a pad by the bed, from a smartphone Dictaphone app to a virtual assistant. It doesn't matter how you capture your insights as they happen, but capture them you must. And express them as fully and completely as you can, at the time or just after they occur to you.

4   **Prove:** for many, it is tempting both during and after the act of creation to cosset and protect what you've made from the outside world. When we've created something we believe to be particularly beautiful and elegant – from woodwork to children, from a fine piece of prose to an insight – the temptation is to keep it safe from prying eyes until we've made it just perfect. Leaving analogies behind and focusing on insight, it's important to share your insights with others early – with colleagues, with clients, with collaborators. Yes, you'll want to work up your insight from the initial scrawls on Post-its made in the middle of the night before you get others to consider and pass judgement on what you've come up with, but don't leave it too long. Resist the temptation to polish and burnish and sandpaper your insight until it's too perfect. Early exposure from those who matter – particularly from those who stand to benefit from your insight – can help you determine early whether you're onto a winner or whether you need to abandon what seemed so strong and clear but actually doesn't move you on at all. What's more, others may see holes or gaps in your thinking that are easily and straightforwardly filled and turn your germ of an insight into a fully fledged insight. Think of exposing your insights to others as like sharing some initial riffs or the outline of a new song with other members of the band. They can help you work it up into something you might try out at an intimate gig. It won't be the finished article, but at both a jamming session and a low-stakes gig, musicians often try out new tunes that don't get taken any further. Or they do, but as the chorus to a totally

different song. What matters is early exposure as part of the process of the beginning of refinement.

Sweat is the *research* phase – Wallas' preparation
Timeout is the *thinking* phase – Wallas' incubation
Eureka is the *enlightenment* phase – Wallas' illumination
Prove is the *testing* phase – Wallas' verification

That's the model in summary. Simple as that. Rooted in Wallas – via James Webb Young. Supported by psychology and endorsed by neuroscience. Made more memorable than either, thanks to the cleverness and flexibility of English, that allows us to create the acronym STEP from Sweat – Timeout – Eureka – Prove – plus the Prism, as it's through this lens that we look at insight. What's more, the model is informed by more than 40 training sessions and nearly 500 delegates who've experienced the STEP Prism in the insight training courses I've been running since 2015. Oh you lucky people.

ON MADMEN AND WOMEN, REAL AND FICTITIOUS

Building campaigns – for products and companies, public health education and behaviour change – is the stuff, the output, of commercial communication. When agencies, consultancies, or practitioners receive a brief, they invest time and energy flexing the curiosity muscles, getting as well informed about the subject of the brief as they can, acutely. Ideally this is a well-established habit chronically, too, and the thinky bit is most often done by people who have the word planner of planning in their job titles.

With insights generated that articulate a profound and deep understanding of the brief and of target audiences' lives – often through a process not unlike the STEP Prism of Insight, though not necessarily with such conscious reflection or labelling – planners brief creatives to develop ads. If the insights are sufficiently powerful and well communicated, creatives will be sparked to produce on-brief work that answers the client's most pressing challenges. Account handlers – often nicknamed suits, especially by the creatives who don't often wear suits – will present creative executions to clients, and clients will be struck by the brilliance of the insights, buy the idea, put it into market, and meet the commercial, communications, or business objectives.

That's the theory at least.

LEARNING FROM THOSE YOU TRAIN

In very different rooms – of agencies, consultancies, councils, government departments, and industry associations – and with coffee and biscuits of wildly varying standards, our model has been presented, challenged, augmented, and validated by a wide variety of individuals and teams. Delegates of all levels of seniority – from MDs, CEOs, and board directors to interns and graduate trainees – have gotten to play with the model. Almost all have recognised its strength and usefulness. For many, it describes some or all of the stages that they intuitively use when they're looking to generate insights – particularly those who work with increasingly complex data sets (aka almost everyone). But what they've all found helpful has been putting some scaffolding around their thinking. By taking timeout from the everyday maelstrom of their working day and stopping to think about thinking, many have found that when they get back to their offices they have both a structure to do a part of their job they may have historically found challenging. And just as importantly, they have a set of tools and techniques in each of the four quadrants of the Prism that they can start applying straightaway.

What's been particularly gratifying – and what I believe you will find to be especially useful in the four chapters that follow immediately – is the broad array of tools, techniques, and approaches that delegates have shared with me over the past five years during our training sessions. Some of them have surprised me, some of them have come up once and only once, while others come up every time. That said, frequency doesn't make them any less or more valid. There are no right or wrong things to do in each of the four quadrants. What matters is what works for each individual. What matters is realising the potential that the model has to help unlock insight and how to be insightful, truly the superpower that drives innovation.

Getting good feedback on training is, of course, immensely satisfying. Trainers are privileged to be paid to have time in front of busy people who often don't have time to complete all the tasks demanded of them, let alone take timeout to attend training courses. So I believe it is incumbent on trainers to give delegates a good, memorable, useful time. Immediate positive feedback is a shot of adrenaline in the arm. But long-term feedback is – if anything – even more gratifying.

Often over the past few years, I'll train one team or cohort from a company or agency. And then, as delegates start to use the technique, and materials and frameworks from the training session are shared or referenced to those who haven't been on the course, a second course will be booked by the HR or training department. And I'll be walking through an open-plan office and one or more of my first cohort of delegates will wave or shout or come up to me in the office and tell me about new tools and techniques they've adopted. I'll often hear about specific new insights they've developed and expressed on behalf of their clients and how beneficial the framework has been in their development.

Training for insight teams and agencies or consultancies specialising in insight is common. There are courses aplenty in qual and quant, R and SPSS, coding and storytelling, data analysis and data visualisation. But training in what insight is and how to be insightful is more like hen's teeth. That's no doubt one reason why I'm remembered by delegates months after our training session.

Second, I trust that I give delegates a good time. There's something of the stand-up/improvisational comedian about being an effective trainer, flexing and adapting to meet individual and group needs. Some trainers I know – because I've been in their courses – have a fixed script and schedule they have to follow. I'm a bit more flexible than that, and I look to tailor content in real time.

And third, at the end of each STEP Prism of Insight course, I get all delegates to make a commitment – in front of their peers – that they will change. Having been introduced to the model and the different steps in the Prism and volunteered what they do each step of the way, I get delegates to complete a pledge card with which they commit to adopt the principles moving forward. They read these out to the assembled group.

And then, a few weeks later, I send wallet-sized pledge cards to each delegate so that they can remember and refresh their memories about what they've committed to. The commitment device: it's an old trick of behavioural psychology, and there are more details about the procedure in Chapter 9, together with a template you can start using with your team straightaway (see p. 202).

ON THE ALLURE OF TIMEOUT

Of all the steps in the Prism, Timeout is the most arresting and sometimes controversial. This is particularly true when there are members of the same organisation in the room, including the leader, when the role and power of Timeout in insight generation is discussed. Timeout can – clearly erroneously – be thought of as not working or, perhaps even worse, the antithesis of working. Bunking off. Playing hooky. Doing something other than work and still getting paid. More than once – in fact, more like a dozen times – I've sensed a disturbance in the force when I've introduced Timeout as an integral step in the model. Some leaders – often, it turns out, threatened, insecure leaders; uncertain of their leadership, uncertain of their team's followership – object to people not being chained to their desks 24/7/365, fulfilling every tick-box line item of their job description.

Timeout is instantly and universally popular with more junior members of a team, but not for the reasons leaders might fear. Having the freedom to step away from the task or challenge at hand when you want to is incredibly empowering. Permission to think about something else – and engage the superior skills of subconscious problem-solving – is a manifestation of trust and empowerment from leadership. What's more, as soon as the process and the science that support the approach are set out, leaders who want their teams to have the best opportunity to deliver in their own way soon come round to the concept of Timeout and of building Timeout into their team's way of working.

More than team dynamics, openly encouraging your team to take Timeout when they need to find a solution to a challenging problem is commonsense good business. Openly fostering and enabling an atmosphere and an environment in which insights and innovation can flourish is the cornerstone to success. Requiring people to work in old established ways just because that's served an organisation well in the past is irrelevant. Upstart start-ups and tech disruptors aren't hide-bound by archaic rules. Nor should those being disrupted by the upstarts. If Google's 10% policy – under which all employees are encouraged to work on a personal passion project outside their core team – were such a bad idea, parent company Alphabet would have killed it years ago. Yet it's the scheme that led to Gmail. If Netflix's "no working hours, no fixed working weeks, and as much holiday as you want" policy was harmful to productivity, the company's ethos and HR department would have been licked into "normal" shape by investors years ago. Objecting to Timeout as an integral part of insight generation is as forward thinking as questioning employees' commitment and productivity if they choose to work from home or – in Starbucks' memorable phrase – another Third Place.

Requiring individuals and teams to have breakthrough insights on demand is not only unreasonable. It not only runs against what we know about how the mind works and how insight works. It also makes insights *less* likely to appear. Undue pressure and stress to generate insights at will or on demand stifles the brain's recombinatorial creative genius. It closes down options and constrains free thinking. This makes it less likely that a problem will be solved in an innovative way and more likely that it will be solved in a predictable, habitual way that is likely to have been tried before and therefore likely to fail. Kounios and Beeman have done the experiments that prove that this happens, how, where, and why.

Organisations and organisational leadership should build daily, weekly, annual Timeout into their working practices. Timeout pays dividends by broadening horizons and making genuine, breakthrough insights more likely. It liberates insightful thinking in individuals and liberates an innovation culture in teams and organisations. Not seeing a colleague at their desk should be a cause of celebration, not a cause for concern. If they're walking round the block, have popped into a gallery, are attending a class for something that has nothing to do with their job . . . if they leave early or come in late, come in early or leave late . . . if they actively succeed in securing a life/work balance, managers should celebrate. Because the likelihood is, they're about to observe their teams generating the insights they need to solve the challenges they face collectively as an organisation.

WHEN INSIGHTS DON'T OR WON'T SHOW THEMSELVES

It's perfectly possible that the insight you think you've identified is indeed a banal platitude and doesn't advance the brief you're working on one iota. It's also possible that it's wrong or irrelevant. So too is the possibility that someone else – a competitor or rival – has used a version of this insight for years and you've just expressed it in a new way, but fundamentally there's no difference. It won't take long for colleagues, clients, and collaborators to point this out.

Imagine you are the brand manager of Bold, Procter & Gamble's home laundry brand. Working with your creative advertising agency, you're captivated by the insight that parents don't like being judged by how clean their kids' clothes are; kids should be allowed – encouraged – to explore the world and get dirty. Bold will take care of that. So you decide to champion a childhood lived out loud, outside, where mess and chaos is welcomed with open arms. Where muddy knees are a sign of success, not failure. It's a good thought, of course, because your number one rival, Unilever's Persil, has been saying "Dirt Is Good" for 15 years. Back to the drawing board, guys!

And that example is instructive. Because if your curiosity, timeout, ideation, and testing shows that what you thought was an insight isn't an insight – if it's just data or a casual observation and not a bona fide insight, or if it's someone else's insight that you've stolen and re-expressed without meaningful modification – then you need to go back one, two, or three stages in the insight generation process.

It could be that your subconscious mind has let through an insight that doesn't pass muster, so you need to give it some more Timeout – some more distraction from the task at hand to allow it to put more stimuli together and be left alone to do its thing. In this case, you'll be dialling back one or two steps and entering Timeout or Eureka. Try that and see if new thoughts emerge. But equally, it could be that your subconscious mind doesn't have enough stimulus and you need to increase the quantity and quality of content available for recombination. The marketplace or ecosystem in which you operate might have changed – through regulation, legislation, or competitive activity. Brexit might (finally) have been delivered (or put out of its miserable misery) and a new trading reality might have become a reality, providing new opportunities and threats you don't quite understand. In a case like this, you might get back into research mode, absorbing new content and stimulus for your subconscious mind to shuffle and recombine in novel and insightful ways when in Timeout.

But of course, if curiosity has become a way of life for the long-term future and not just for the brief you're working on now, this won't be an issue. If you're curious by nature or you successfully turn yourself into a curious character, you'll be absorbing new stimulus every day. On your drive to work you'll be listening to a podcast. On a flight to see a client, you'll watch a new favourite box set. When a colleague invites you to leave work early to go with them to a cooking or salsa or kick-boxing class – something you've never tried or even considered – you say yes. And if you're constantly curious and exposing yourself to new and different stimuli, it won't be long before your subconscious spits out a new solution to the challenge you're trying to unlock.

As James Webb Young puts it in the first step of his updated version of Wallas, *A Technique for Producing Ideas*: "First, the gathering of raw materials – both the materials for your immediate problem and the materials which come from a constant enrichment of your store of general knowledge." As canine welfare charities encourage us to reflect if we see a cute puppy in early December, "A dog is for life – not just for Christmas". In exactly the same way, curiosity is not just for today's brief. It's for tomorrow's, and next week's, and every brief you'll ever have to answer.

And so now we turn in detail to the hard work of Sweat, the first step in the STEP Prism of Insight.

INTERVIEW: THE ACTORS PETER FIRTH AND ALEXANDRA MCKIBBIN

Insightful interview 4 of 8

NAME	Peter Firth & Alexandra McKibbin
ORGANISATION	Actors
ROLE	From *Letter to Brezhnev* to *Spooks*

Peter Firth is best known for his portrayal of MI5 chief Harry Pearce in the long-running BBC TV series (and film) *Spooks*. Peter and his wife Alexandra McKibbin met on the set of the classic 1985 movie *Letter to Brezhnev*, where he played the character of Russian sailor Peter who swept the Liverpudlian factory worker off her feet and back to a pre-Perestroika Soviet Union. They became an item at the time, but drifted apart, had marriages and children. They are now an item once more, 35 years on, and are also now married. I spoke to them about what insight means to them and what they do as actors to get inside the heads of those whose characters they inhabit – when the director shouts "Action!" on the film and TV set, when the theatre curtain goes up. If insight is indeed a profound and deep understanding of people and things, the skill of the actor – particularly a well-known, recognisable actor – demands that they help us to suspend our disbelief that they are, in fact, someone else.

Peter's approach to getting inside the head of those he's portraying is intuitive, instinctual, and driven by human understanding. "Having learned a little about the character and the situation, I tend to make it up as I go along, in exactly the same way as we all do in real life – off the set, off the stage. You have to look in the script and the subtext and extract the meaning, emotion, and characteristics from what's written and what's implied."

Firth played Harry Pearce for 85 hour-long episodes, and he believes that in a long-running series a compact grows between script writers and actors and that what's intended from the writing becomes increasingly obvious. If a new writer comes onto the show and isn't so familiar with the character – or if they try to make them behave in new and unexpected ways – it's the responsibility of the actor to ensure the character behaves as she or he would. What's more, he believes that being a character is easier than being off-screen as there's no moral imperative to a drama-tised individual; there's no actual comeback if you behave capriciously, imperiously, appallingly. There's no sense of "I shouldn't do that."

Alexandra agrees, and goes on to say that the moment you become self-conscious in character is the moment that you become a bad actor because you immediately betray the fact that you're aware there is an actor and a character. While you're performing, you need to blend and sublimate identities. As soon as that doesn't happen, the audience picks up on it. To work, acting needs to be a totally unselfconscious act. Indeed, the mark of a good actor is to make even bad writing sound believable.

Belief in what's real and what's being portrayed is central to the actor's insight conundrum. "More than believe that you've become the charac-ter you're playing, you need to persuade the audience to suspend their disbelief in the whole artifice of drama. To do that, you have to provide a moment of magic to break what people believe and hold to be true and real. Break that, and you can win them over. In the case of Harry Pearce, I had the privilege of doing that for 13 years." Firth's elusive "magic" requires a finely tuned sense of vulnerability and showing the audience that you're just like them – even if you're playing the boss of MI5; that you're a human being, not a star or an actor. People flock to vulnerability. "Intuition is a talent, a gift", says Firth, "and experience helps too. It shortcuts things. If you've played a character 'like this' before, it's straightforward to channel that again. Just as in real life."

"There's absolutely *no* need to believe you actually *are* the person you're playing, as method actors would have you believe; that you're living their lives beyond the moments that you're playing them; between 'Action!' and 'Cut!', curtain up and curtain down. There's no need, quite simply, because you're acting. Get the audience to suspend their disbe-lief, suspend your own, suppress your own ego, and be unselfconscious. That's when you become believable."

Firth never went to drama school, started acting in his teens, and hasn't stopped since. McKibbin started as a dancer, which was all about technical performance, and she would always prepare for auditions phys-ically, with hair, make-up, and clothes. The character would come with her when she entered the audition room. Both of their routes into acting were unconventional, and both believe that their way of working – of getting the insights required to get inside the heads of those they portray – has less ego than classically trained actors.

McKibbin doesn't believe that playing characters as an actor makes you better able to navigate similar situations off-set, though Firth does say that being an actor gives you a fantastic, helicopter view of human social interaction; of what people are capable of. By getting insight into the human experience, actors do get to fine-tune their empathy muscles, and as we've already seen, while insight and empathy are not synonymous, they are most definitely connected.

Firth makes acting sound incredibly straightforward, after Noel Coward and many others. "There are two rules: 1. Learn your lines. 2. Don't fall over the furniture. The rest is magic." In my quest to understand and explain insight, I believe that his modest formula for acting success belies a profound and deep understanding on his and McKibbin's part of what it means to be human, which has allowed them throughout their careers to inhabit radically different characters.

NOTES

1 Mark Earls (2015). WARC Webinar: Copy, copy, copy http://bit.ly/33FjM9Z
2 My model is trademarked, but not because I want to stop other people using it or training others in this methodology of becoming more insightful. Quite the opposite. My whole purpose in building the model and sharing it in both training and this book is to get others to use this approach. It works for me, it works for those I've trained, and it can work for you, your colleagues, and your friends and family.

   I trademarked the STEP Prism of Insight for three reasons. First, when I developed it back in 2015, I was working with a lot of North American businesses, and I find that their eyes would twitch and ears prick up if they saw a™ or ® superscript after a product or service; they took it more seriously, so I played them at their game. It's a bit like when you persuade a publisher to edit, print, and distribute your thoughts. It shows you can concentrate long enough to string together a coherent streamofconsciousness and get others to buy into the ideas, too. Oh, and wrap some cardboard around lots of printed pages. As I found with *Narrative by Numbers*, suddenly people take you more seriously and are prepared to pay you to come and speak to them when before they'd be charging you.

The second reason I trademarked the model was that I wanted to find out what it was like to work with the UK Government's Intellectual Property Office, what the process of trademarking was like. I'm happy to report that, while formal and bureaucratic, the IPO's process was seamless, fair, and cost-effective. Actually, a confession: it's not the model that's trademarked. You can't trademark models, because models are abstract ideas. But you can trademark training courses, so that's what the ™ that appears after the STEP Prism of Insight™ refers to – the training course, which glories in the Trade Mark Number of UK00003118723 in Class 41, "Organising and conducting educational or recreational exhibitions/Organising and conducting of exhibitions relating to advertising and commerce".

And the third reason is my love off all things "meta" (see pp. 52–53): I was protecting a (training course of a) model whose purpose is to help others unlock the superpower that drives innovation; trademarking something that can help others surface genuine breakthrough ideas that themselves will need trademarking or copyrighting in due course.

3 Forrest Wickman (April 2012). Your Brain's Technical Specs. *Slate* http://bit.ly/31LY16z

4 Got a spare eight hours eight minutes, or fancy music for a full working day? My Spotify playlist "All Time 100 Favourite Songs" is here: 100 scalp-tighteners right there, from AC/DC to ZZ Top, via Half Man Half Biscuit and the Scissor Sisters https://spoti.fi/2TDZc5x

5 For students of insight, it might surprise you that I've not drawn the analogy – a powerful mental device – between insight and sex, and the eureka moment as an orgasm. For those who know me personally, this might come as both a surprise ("I thought he had a smutty sense of humour") and a disappointment ("He seems to have missed an open goal"). I resisted the temptation (a) because others have done it – like Anthony Tasgal in the *Inspiratorium*, getting rather carried away and typically full of puns when talking about developmental psychologist Alison Gopnik's seminal (ho, ho) paper on "Explanation as orgasm"; (b) because of the Bad Sex Awards (see http://bit.ly/2KIkUAY, though that report's not all that smart for the office), and I'll bet they're going to be extended to non-fiction any day soon; and, most importantly, (c) because I don't think the whole process of insight generation can be neatly fitted into a sex analogy. It's just too "pat" and convenient. Something that you start with curiosity and then put on one side before having a climactic moment? In my mind and experience, the analogy doesn't fit. It doesn't help. And it only titillates. Nothing wrong with titillation, but in this case I think it's an unhelpful distraction. And there's a fourth, even more important reason, too, but you'll have to wait for a footnote in Chapter 7 for that (see p. 170).

5

SWEAT – THE RESEARCH PHASE

"No one is dumb who is curious. The people who don't ask questions remain clueless throughout their lives."

Neil deGrasse Tyson

IT WAS ALL GREEK TO HIM

The Greek philosopher Socrates never wrote anything down – or at least nothing he wrote down survived antiquity. What we know about him comes principally from his pupil and disciple – his amanuensis – Plato. Most of Plato's work does survive from the fourth century BC, in the form of Socratic dialogues. In these dialogues, Socrates has conversations with others, looking to tease out answers to eternal questions. This reaches a crescendo in the theory of forms in *The Republic*, which we met in Chapter 2. You remember: purest green, purest courage, purest goodness.

In *The Apology* – a dramatisation of Socrates' defence at his trial for "corrupting the (minds of the) young" – Plato has Socrates say, "The only true wisdom is knowing you know nothing". Plato's Socrates can be irritating and gnomic. I know because I read most of the Socratic dialogues during my classics degree, tutored by a man more irritatingly Socratic than Socrates himself. Nevertheless, Socrates' "only true wisdom" line is a good dictum and maxim to live by when you start on the quest to

Figure 5.1 Sweat quadrant of the STEP Prism of Insight

generate an insight. It's a much better starting point than saying, "Yeah, I know all about that" and then falling flat on your face.

What's more, thinking you know the answer before you set out to test (never prove) your hypotheses is a futile exercise in functional fixedness. It's the very antithesis of Mlodinow's prescription of elastic thinking, and consciously thinking you know the answer closes down the options for your subconscious mind to suggest alterative recombinations. Premature certainty acts as a filter to reject innovative ideas, a break on creativity. It truly is an insight killer.

ON THE IMPORTANCE OF CURIOSITY

At the dawn of the internet era, I had a boss who despaired at how out of touch and ignorant he believed many of our brand manager clients were. He had a point, though he didn't always express it in the most empathetic manner. They seemed to him to have no cultural hinterland, no knowledge of film or literature, high-flown or popular, classic or modern. None of them appeared to read, either contemporary fiction or non-fiction. They were certainly the first generation to start dispensing with newspapers, at a time before morning and evening papers were freesheets. They didn't listen to the radio – particularly the heavyweight BBC Radio 4 or NPR – and they didn't watch the news. Any cultural reference my boss made – in an attempt to ignite their interest in an idea for a campaign we wanted to run for them – fell on deaf ears. The insights we brought them, often rooted in an appreciation of popular culture, often remained unsold because they didn't know their Arsenal from their Elbow.

This irritated my boss, and I shared his irritation (if not its intensity). It was unfortunate that good, insight-rich ideas were falling flat because elements of popular culture – today classified broadly as memes – were missing from our clients' worldview. So, we proposed a solution to this knowledge gap, a knowledge gap recognised by our clients' bosses, at board and marketing director level. The solution was to be a regular, interactive summary of popular culture, contemporary and historic. I think we even dubbed it "Instant Popular Culture". How we planned to deliver this multimedia, monthly summary is lost in the mists of the last millennium, in the land that CD-ROMs forgot.

Perhaps unsurprisingly, the idea was never bought. I suspect it might have been because the first dummy edition revealed to the bosses that they were nearly as ignorant as our direct clients, and they didn't like the cut of the emperor's new clothes any more than their charges did. This caused my boss further irritation, though that reaction, too, failed to improve things. He believed it was a generational thing, and he may have been right of that particular generation (Y, aka Millennials, born 1977–1995). With the benefit of hindsight, I'm pretty sure it's not an age thing, because Gen Z (aka iGen or the Centennials, born after 1996) appear to have plenty of that something that our clients seemed to be lacking. And that something is curiosity.

HOW TO BE INSIGHTFUL STEP ONE: SWEAT

If you want to increase the frequency and improve the quality of the insights you generate, the first step in the STEP Prism of Insight is to be and become more curious. If you want to give your subconscious mind the opportunity to combine more old stuff with other old stuff and come up with new stuff, you need to feed the beast. Stimuli cannot join together in surprising and innovative ways if they are not in the right place. And the right place is the melting pot of your memory, that repository of almost infinite capacity.

Your curiosity should be both focused *and* unfocused, dedicated to addressing the specific challenge that you need to unlock *and* curiosity for curiosity's sake. When your long-term memory lays down traces of facts, experiences, and opinions, it clusters them and makes connections between incoming data and data already on board. It makes these connections in obvious ways, according to the kind of rules we might set up in a database – same topic, same qualities, same sounds.

But it also makes associations between the new and the old that we don't necessarily consciously reflect on. Both thoughts might have the letter R in third position and rhyme with cough (but not bough, enough, or through). If you learn about one aspect of conflict resolution from a TED talker wearing a green dress and a recipe for lemon ice cream from a celebrity chef with a punky green haircut, the greenness of those memory traces – engrams in Karl Lashley's outdated but cute term – may form a connection between those two data points that you escape your own notice making.[1] Then, when it comes to recombination, there may be a genius, post hoc justification for why lemon ice cream is the perfect antidote to conflict, but you need to give you subconscious mind the time and freedom and the right conditions to do their recombining thing and link the two together.

Being curious specifically and generally, acutely and chronically definitely makes your life richer – as well as being an important first step on the road to being more insightful. You have a more immersive experience, and you start to observe or suspect there are relationships, even consciously, where you'd never imagined there could be any connection. It can deliver a permanently low-level feeling of déjà-vu,[2] the sensation that you've already lived through what's unfolding before your eyes, the place, the meeting, the whole experience. This can be unnerving, but I'd recommend that you get used to it. It's a small price to pay for better, richer, better-informed insights. By immersing yourself in potential stimulus, you're broadening your perspectives and horizons.

Experience is an important and invaluable by-product of curiosity and immersion. In his popular science bestseller *Outliers*, Malcolm Gladwell brings together a number of diverse sources to demonstrate that expertise in a domain typically requires in the region of 10,000 hours exposure or practice. True mastery requires the application of practice on top of a small innate advantage – when you were born in a school year, possessing perfect pitch, or having slightly-above-average kinetic intelligence. But if you want to bend it like Beckham, you also need to do what David did: go to the park every evening as a schoolboy and take freekick after freekick after freekick. From the same spot, curving the ball around an imaginary wall of defenders and in past the goalkeeper. Only then, deep into injury time, in the last gasp of a qualifier for the European Championships against Greece in 2001, can you score the perfect freekick.

One last point on curiosity. As you absorb information and data, as well as processing and allocating it for storage, you also analyze it, even without realising it. All the different formal and informal algorithms and heuristics you use to make sense of the world, detect regularities and outliers, come into play without conscious effort. Whether cognitive shortcuts are learned or innate, one of our fundamental drives and self-preservation mechanisms is to make sense of the world – logically and mathematically, grammatically and chromatographically – and look for examples that are out of the ordinary. Things that are as expected help to confirm the rules by which we live our lives: "There's a bird flying; birds fly." Things that are unexpected help to take us out of functional fixedness: "There's a man flying; it can surely only be Arthur Dent." Tales of the unexpected are of survival value. And they're also of value for the insight seeker. "X and Y together? That might just work . . ." As the astrophysicist Neil deGrasse Tyson – and the unexpected star of *Zoolander 2* – said, "No one is dumb who is curious."

To be reliably good at generating insights, it's not essential for you to understand the neuroscience underpinning our understanding of insight (or our insights into understanding, if you will). This isn't because it's unimportant. As a student and teacher of the art and science of being more insightful, I think that the neuroscience is both fascinating and incredibly important, particularly now it seems like it's been sorted out once and for all. But in terms of becoming a better practitioner of insight – of being more insightful – you don't really need to look under the hood. Or in this case, the cranium.

It's like being a good driver. You don't need to be able to describe the workings of the internal combustion engine to take passengers from A to B. Particularly in the era of hybrid and electric cars.

It's like being a competent user of a smartphone. Knowledge of semiconductor technology is irrelevant, as is the science of how haptics translate human gestures made with fingers into strings of ones and zeroes that lead to a like of a picture of a cute kitten on Instagram.

It's like being a restaurant critic. You're at no perceptible advantage if you appreciate the biochemistry of animal protein and plants and the conditions under which they bond for the optimal eating experience.

So it is with the neuroscience of insight.

It's now time for you to get into the nitty-gritty of making it happen. And because the process – and the component parts of the process – are the intuitive basis for insights that power innovations, you need to be able to identify and articulate what it is you do at each of the four quadrants of the STEP Prism. To start thinking about the Sweat phase – about how to be curious – you should read this short passage of guidance.

SWEAT

If you're going to solve a problem, if you want to develop breakthrough insights that will help unlock a challenge, you need to work at it. You need to immerse yourself – deeply – in the subject matter. You need to get your hands grubby and your nails dirty with the all the information and data that surround the topic. From social media analytics to expert interviews, you need to harness the most effective tools and techniques available to you, absorbing all stakeholders' points of view.

More than this, you need to pull on all relevant experience and information you and your team have on the issue or subject area, however lateral. Then share and disseminate it effectively. And as a dog is not just for Christmas, so curiosity is not just for a particular brief, this month's project, next year's innovation. Curiosity is a way of life, an attitude of mind that the most insightful individuals – the best problem-solvers – adopt for life.

To steer and shape your thoughts about curiosity, consider the following questions:

- How do you get as well informed as you can be on the brief you're trying to crack?
- How do you best summarise information so others can benefit from your research?
- How do you share information between team members most impactfully?
- What do you do to keep yourself informed?
- How do you satisfy and feed your curiosity?
- What are the best research resources you use?
- What are the best research tools out there, free or subscription? Websites, databases, apps?

You could do this alone; you could do it with or without a guide and someone to capture the ideas that you generate. My experience is that this process is best done in groups of at least four or five. We all have different experiences, and different points of view will help you to see and share the value of your own but also learn from others. If there are 15 or 20 of you upping your insight ante, tackle each quadrant of the STEP Prism in turn in smaller groups of four or five and then bring your thoughts and reflections back to the whole group. But however you approach the challenge – and as I say, solo is just fine – do so with an open mind and a willingness to be flexible and to learn.

The benefit for me of having run 42 of these workshops and counting is that I have regularly and repeatedly seen that many people – from many different businesses and diverse functions within businesses – often intuitively use the same tools, techniques, and approaches to satisfy their innate curiosity. In almost every session I find out something new. So, in teaching and training in insight, I get to learn new ways to become more insightful myself.[3] This is a Forth Rail Bridge of a project for me; by the time I've finished painting one end, I get to start all over again.

The benefit for you, dear reader, is that in this book I'm sharing with you all of the best ideas I've come across in many different training sessions

I've run. It's as if you've been riding side-saddle with me in all 42 sessions, and you're benefitting from a couple of months in the offices of my many and varied clients. Not all of these tools, techniques, and approaches will be relevant for you and the insight problems you look to solve in your organisation. What worked for a civil servant in the now-defunct Department for Exiting the European Union[4] may not be help a strategic planner in an advertising agency. If something in the lists of tools, techniques, and approaches given in this book doesn't feel right to you, discard it and ignore it. But if there's something that you know has worked for you in the past – or something that you can see might work for you in the future – add it to your checklist and build up your armoury of tools and techniques that can help you become more insightful. To make the process easier, there's a downloadable checklist at www.howtobeinsightful.com/sweat

Don't worry about curiosity overfilling or overstuffing your brain, overloading your subconscious mind with too much new stuff. However curious you are, you're never going to overfill your memory. Putting more stuff into the hopper will forge links between old, old stuff (information/facts/memories/representations in long-term memory). We've already considered the effectively infinite storage capacity of the human brain, and what we don't find useful for a very long time – what we're not triggered by unseen connections to retrieve from memory – will likely fade away.

THE BEST TOOLS, TECHNIQUES, AND APPROACHES TO FOSTER THE SPIRIT OF CURIOSITY

In no particular order of importance and hierarchy – because it doesn't matter *how* you absorb content, it matters *that* you absorb content – here are my (and my training delegates') top tips for satisfying your curiosity. Today and forever. For this week's brief, next week's, next month's, and your next job's. Chronically and acutely.

- Talk to people
- Read

- Travel
- Listen to podcasts
- Capture and analyze social media content
- Consume comedy
- Make friends with R&D
- Change the rules of meetings
- Minimise the use of email
- Watch a TED talk every week
- Go to events
- Read winning award submissions

Talk to people: Experts and ingénus alike can throw light on an issue. Make time to talk to people who are expert in a field (academics, sector analysts, investors, journalists) as well as those who know nothing about or are excluded from that field (your friends, partner, and family). In-depth, qualitative interviews with those in the know – and those in the dark – can be incredibly revealing. And don't just talk to people who like your organisation and will give you an easy time. Talk to critics and competitors and those who are openly hostile to you, your organisation, or your client.

Read: Read books, blogs, websites, journal articles, Wikipedia, analysts' reports. Set up Google Alerts and subscribe to industry- and sector-specific emails – provided you're prepared to unsubscribe from them as soon as they become a chore, when you've deleted five in a row without reading them. Join a book group. Read on the subject, around the subject, nowhere near the subject. Fiction, non-fiction, para-fiction, fan fiction. Content you like and that makes you happy, calm, and contented. But also content you don't like and that makes you unhappy, on edge, and nervous. Content produced by experts can shortcut learning for you, though don't suddenly think you're an expert too having read one article. You're bound to miss nuances and counter-arguments that have been casually set on one side.

If you're a bleeding heart liberal, see what the *Daily Mail* – one of the world's most read online newspapers, with 53 million unique monthly visitors – Fox News, and Breitbart have to say. You might be able to predict – through prejudice – their take on an issue. But you might also be surprised. And even if the position you find is 180 degrees from your own, actually taking the time to engage with content from the Dark Side might enable you to see how to disturb and undermine your opponents. David Hieatt, founder of purposeful jeans business Hiut Denim and creator of the Do Lectures, puts it this way in his book *Do: Purpose*,

> *If we read the same old books, we get to know more about the thing we know lots about already. We need subscribe to magazines that we wouldn't normally subscribe to; we need to go to places that we wouldn't normally go to, eat at places that may not be our kind of place.[5]*

For Simon Sinek, the crown prince of purpose, it's essential that we move ourselves outside of our comfort zones if we are to move forward. In his daily Notes to Inspire email from 23 August 2018, he said, "Curiosity is essential for progress. Only when we look to worlds beyond our own can we really know if there's room for improvement."

Travel: Experience different cultures as often as you can. In cosmopolitan capital cities and other major conurbations, this is also possible. If it's your own capital city and you're a native speaker, however, you'll miss out on the dislocating experience of speaking – or attempting to make yourself understood in – a foreign language. Different types of transport (perhaps the cities you know don't have vaporetti or trams), different food, different media, different social norms, different politics, different hand gestures, different climate, and different clothes and clothing conventions. Coping with very familiar tasks in unfamiliar terrain – buying a ticket for public transport, ordering a coffee, asking directions – demands that you think differently. Part of the benefit comes from coping. Part of it comes from having to deliberately and self-consciously slow yourself and your thinking down. This is particularly true if the alphabet is different from your own, especially if your native language uses Roman letters and the city's language does not. And part of it is the fact that everything is new.

Novelty attracts and commands and directs attention. New stuff is more memorable and less vulnerable to being filtered out because it's not familiar. A New Yorker who spends the weekend wandering the streets of Lisbon is likely to absorb many more novel experiences than if they hang out in the Upper East Side – and not just hill-climbing trams, *pastéis de nata*, and cherry brandy served from bars that are little more than ornately tiled holes in the wall, delightful as all those experiences are. And don't make the humble-brag mistake of telling friends and family, "All I saw was the back of a taxi, my hotel room, and the conference centre" when you do get to travel for work. Make it your intention and your duty to take in something of the city and the culture you're visiting, late at night or early morning. I always get up early and go for a run. Marketers have started to call this approach to business travel "bleisure". And if the portmanteau word of business + leisure makes you a little nauseous, it has the decency to have onomatopoeic undertones of vomiting.

Listen to podcasts: For every topic and every issue, there's at least one podcast. Often they come with production values, quality research, and informed commentary every bit as slick as professional talk radio. But often – as they're not regulated like radio – they can share thoughts in language that mainstream radio wouldn't touch. Five years working for the editors of *Viz*[6] (the "adult" comic) back in the 1990s taught me that swearing is both big and clever, done right. And on many podcasts, the conventional barriers and taboos about swearing are lowered. This means not only are the messages different – delivered in a self-serve, radio-like medium – the norms of acceptable expression are also changed. This can – and you'll have got here already – change your frame of reference and turn an apparently trivial titbit into very much more. For a completely non-definitive, entirely personal selection of podcasts, see Table 5.1.

Capture and analyze social media content: Before Twitter and Facebook, Instagram and Tik Tok, people had thoughts, took pictures, shared ideas, had discussions. They just didn't do so online, in real time, leaving a permanent trace – or at least permanent until such time as they choose to delete their posting history or change their data settings. Social media hasn't caused the polarised views that characterise modern political demagogy and debate, including vile expressions of hate and intolerance. It's simply surfaced it and made it obvious, particularly because the psychology of posting something anonymously lowers taboo thresholds and sees people saying things they might not have owned up to in the pub. I regularly consider the dark side of social media on the Small Data Forum

Table 5.1 A completely non-definitive selection of podcasts

Freakonomics Radio	Full of insights from the authors of the Freakonomics series of books. While University of Chicago economist Steven Levitt now spends more time on his golf handicap than Freakonomics, journalist and all-round Mr. Curiosity Levitt continues to apply the Freakonomics lens to increasingly diverse topics. Freakonomics' strapline is "the hidden side of everything", and every podcast is a lesson in insight spotting and insight hunting. It has 407 episodes in the tank at time of editing. Levitt also created an insight-rich game show podcast called *Tell Me Something I Don't Know* which, while still available, is not producing new episodes, sadly.
More or Less	A self-consciously wry BBC Radio 4 podcast on the use of data, numbers, and statistics in the media and public life. Developed by author Michael Blastland, a long-time collaborator of Sir David Spiegelhalter, the Winton Professor for the Public Understanding of Risk at Cambridge, the programme has been presented for the last dozen years by Tim Harford, the *Financial Times*' undercover economist. Much funnier and more inspiring than my description.
The Business of Story	Corporate and brand storyteller Park Howell has a little black book in the business storytelling world fatter than anyone else's. Now with more than 240 episodes, number 33 – "A Practical Guide to the Story Cycle and Transformational Business Languages" – is particularly listenable, in my opinion. I am the guest. http://bit.ly/2KZPZQL
Something Rhymes with Purple	Lexicographer and etymologist Susie Dent is joined by author and former politician Gyles Brandreth. Each week they share their love of words and uncover the origins of language. Nuggets ranging from nonsense to wisdom, but always useful.
Kermode & Mayo's Film Review	The creative arts are full of insights. Novels, TV miniseries, and films are convincing and compelling when they reveal a profound and deep understanding, when they are insightful. Film critic Mark Kermode and informed front man Simon Mayo have been broadcasting together for more than 20 years, podcasting for more than half that time. Their "Church of Wittertainment" is more insightful than the average pod.

Small Data Forum	I've already mentioned my role in co-founding and co-hosting this podcast, so recuse myself from commentary on quite how good I think it is. Founded a month before the EU Referendum, our 30+ monthly episodes to date have talked mostly about Brexit, Trump, Facebook, and Cambridge Analytica. This is also funnier than it sounds, particularly the Christmas specials.
James O'Brien's Mystery Hour	That rarest of creatures, a liberal talk radio host, O'Brien has one hour out of 15 each week on the UK's LBC Radio when he doesn't talk about the Small Data Forum's favourite topics. In Mystery Hour, he asks listeners for questions about anything (apart from driving), and for people who know – not people who can use Google – to call in with the answers.
Fortunately, with Fi and Jane	Two of BBC Radio's most authoritative and experienced broadcasters look behind the scenes of broadcasting and interview media personalities in a most entertaining and off-mic way.
No Such Thing as a Fish	John Lloyd created *The Blackadder*, *Spitting Image*, and many other British comedy staples. He also, with polymath author and actor Stephen Fry, created a company called Quite Interesting, which spawned the QI Club in Oxford and spoof game show *QI*. This podcast is a bit like James O'Brien's mystery hour in its scope, but carried out by the *QI* researchers (or "elves").
StarTalk Radio Show	It bills itself better than I could: "From the American Museum of Natural History in New York City, and beaming out across space and time, StarTalk is the podcast where science and pop culture collide, hosted by your personal astrophysicist, Neil DeGrasse Tyson."
The Curious Cases of Rutherford & Fry	Two science sleuths, Dr Adam Rutherford and Dr Hannah Fry, investigate everyday mysteries submitted by listeners. See what's happening with this list? There are lots of podcasts on this list that are all about curious people trying to find things out. It's a wonder there isn't a *Scooby Do* fan fiction podcast on here.
Serial	Investigative journalism, focusing in-depth on real-life cases of crime whose original conclusions and convictions turn out to be logical and understandable, but not necessarily right. Hosted by US NPR journalist Sarah Koenig.

(Continued)

Table 5.1 (Continued)

The Possibility Club	A mash-up of future-facing podcasts, in which host Richard Freeman talks to those at the coalface of change about what's around the corner in business, culture, education. I particularly like the 2018 episode on data storytelling: http://bit.ly/2qXebx0
The Allusionist	British godmother of podcasting, Helen Zaltzman, co-creator of the seminal *Answer Me This*, explores her passion for words and etymology around the world, particularly both sides of the Atlantic. *Answer Me This* – though now too knowing and self-referential – overlaps some section of a Venn diagram with *Freakonomics Radio*, *James O'Brien*, *No Such Thing as a Fish*, and *Rutherford & Fry*, though the self-selecting audience tends to be much younger.
Broad & Fry	Even if you don't like cricket (ah, oh no; you love it, ah, oh yeah!) the erudite and entertaining chat between odd couple Broad and Fry is a great mash-up listening of two world colliding. Giant England fast bowler Stuart Broad meets brainbox Stephen Fry. They talk about cricket as a sport, but also as a metaphor for life and beyond.
APG Podcast	The Account Planning Group brings together both experienced and novice planners in advertising to share knowledge and develop their skills. Planning is the insight function in advertising, and planners are required to extract insights from data to help build creative ideas.
The Savage Lovecast	Dan Savage is a Seattle-based agony uncle of the frankest, no-holds-barred sex advice show around. Not for the prudish, Savage's advice is guided by a set of core principles that manifest themselves with every answer. Authentic, raw, and often very listenable.
A Glass with . . .	"Jolly" Olly Smith is one of Europe's best-loved wine writers/presenters. His podcast involves him drinking a favourite bottle of his guests, from Sting to Sam Neil. Conviviality and *in vino veritas* makes for both very listenable and sometimes profoundly insightful listening.
The Griefcast	Actor and comedian Cariad Lloyd talks about death with other actors and comedians. A taboo subject treated with frankness and openness, with a standard set of questions drawing out very different answers and perspectives.

The Adam Buxton Podcast	Comedian, author, and documentary-maker Adam Buxton has "ramblechats" with actors, musicians, and writers. His butterfly mind and self-effacing manner often bring out profound and deep understanding from his guests.
Word of Mouth	Another wordy one, another one from the BBC, in which journalist Michael Rosen explores the world of words and the ways in which we use them. Often looks at (and pokes fun at) jargon. An oldie and a goodie.
The TED Interview	The man who bought and transformed TED from being a good idea to becoming the open access repository of the world's best ideas, Chris Anderson interviews the world's A-list. Bill Gates and Christine Amanpour ("How to seek truth in the era of fake news") are worth paying for. But – like all of the content on this list – they're completely free, downloadable, and can be taken with you to fill in a flight or commute or run.

podcast (www.smalldataforum.com). There, my co-hosts Neville Hobson and Thomas Stoeckle and I look at the uses and abuses of data big and small in politics, business, and public life.

More than just the bad stuff and the inappropriate and illegal analysis – think Cambridge Analytica[7] – social media also allows us to get a raw, unvarnished, unfiltered view of debates that used to take place less publicly. I've worked with communications consultancies that now have swapped out conventional market research for social media analytics entirely. There's so much conversation taking place online – about companies, brands, people, organisations, charities, issues, government departments, academics – that it's possible to get a good sense of public opinion for the price of a subscription to a social media analytics package. Mapping the conversation landscape about a product or an issue is easier than ever. It really is possible to detect the signal from the noise by looking at how people describe what your organisation provides compared with your competitors: the words they use, the sentiment attached to their comments, and how popular (or otherwise) those comments are. And in addition to trend spotting, social media analytics is also brilliant for finding outliers – rare, apparently random musings that might hold the key to a whole new programme of product evolution or radical innovation. Get listening, get analyzing, get thinking.

Remember: many people now use Twitter or Instagram as a search engine – even over Google – and Facebook as their primary news source. For others, LinkedIn is an invaluable business search engine. There are echo chamber issues to be wary of, particularly in Facebook, whose algorithms serve you content similar to the content you spend time engaging with and liking, and overreliance on social media as an information source is likely to introduce functional fixedness into your worldview. So, use social as just one of the sources you use to satisfy your curiosity. Tools and techniques will vary by market, but choose a couple from Brand-Watch, Google Analytics and Trends, HootSuite, Mintel, Pulsar, Factiva, Meltwater, and LexisNexis.

Consume comedy: Jokes in particular and comedy in general have a lot in common with insight, combining – as they often do – radically different and diverse stimuli and then serving up an expected twist or rupture of convention. Comedians and comic scriptwriters are particularly good at entertaining multiple possible outcomes and choosing the least obvious (or the most counter-intuitive, the one you least expected). Reading or watching satire is a good way of making your thinking more elastic to help with the insight generation process.

You can learn a lot by observing and then mimicking the trains of thought of satirists – from Juvenal to *Private Eye*, John Oliver to the unbowed *Canard Enchaîné*, Jonathan Swift to *Spitting Image*. Surrealists and Dadaists build on the work of satire and create impossible worlds, mostly artistically. Spending time with their work can free the mind to consider the merits what might have previously been impossible to entertain. Just imagine the insights you might have if you could think like Dutch modern art master M.C. Escher.

Make friends with R&D: If, as I contend, insight is the superpower that unlocks innovation, what better source of inspiration can you find in a company than the research and development department? Get a secondment to R&D if you work in the company. Shadow a research scientist for a week, just to see the tools and techniques they use to produce insight-driven innovations on demand. And if you work for an agency, ask your clients – most likely in marketing – if you can spend a few days embedded with R&D. It's in their job description to come up with new products and new ways of doing old things. This might be a small step, like adding fruit or chocolate to a favourite breakfast cereal. Or it might be a radical departure, like turning the essential protein found in cereal into a breakfast mini-drink. In the UK, R&D at leading cereal brand Weetabix did both.

Change the rules of meetings: Meet in unusual places – galleries, museums, libraries, car parks, parks; behave like a Cold War–era spy. Or follow the principles of the Xerox corporation, which only allows meetings for 30 minutes maximum, only at 12.30pm, and only standing up. Take a leaf out of the *West Wing* and hold walking meetings (we'll come back to walking under Timeout). Turn workshops into walkshops. Make it your objective to take no actions out of meetings. My best man and oldest friend, Pete, has done that for all his career, picking up this advice from a mentor in his early 20s. Despite several sets of underwhelming public exam results at school, he was a CEO by 36.

Minimise the use of email: Email is like a Dementor in *Harry Potter* – it literally sucks the life out of you. The apparent need to keep on top of email, to answer messages as soon as they arrive, the baleful politics of replying to all, whom to CC (and whom to BCC). Some office jobs today are little more than email firefighting. Minimise your use of email. Talk to people – in person, by phone, by Skype, by Whereby – rather than sending them an email. And if you work in the same office, walk across the floor and talk to them. Only open email three times a day – at the start of the day, around lunchtime, and about an hour before you leave. Only send an email when there's no other option. Make the most of different communications and collaboration, from Slack (my favourite) to Yammer, without becoming a slave to them as most of us have to email. Turn email notifications off. It takes ten times as long to get back into the flow of what you were doing before you were interrupted by a "Ping" and you felt the compulsion to reply to all.

Some enlightened businesses discourage the use of email. A few years ago, the ad agency Wieden + Kennedy – long-term partners of Nike – instituted a ban on its employees using email before 10am or after 4pm.

Email was completely verboten at night, on weekends, and on holiday – with the exception of genuine emergencies (there was a small but important list of these). The agency discovered its productivity, profitability, client satisfaction, and staff welfare and happiness all went up. And all because they made themselves less available 24/7, more able to focus on work, and more able to live a satisfactory life/work balance.

Watch a TED talk every week: TED is a great source of inspiration and stimulus for lateral thinking. You could – as I once did – commit to watching a TED a day. I found that turned an inspiring task into a mundane chore, so I dialled back to weekly. Subscribe to the TED daily email. You're bound to be served a new talk or a classic you've not seen at least once a week. Go to TED or to TEDx (independently organised "TED-like") events – there are thousands around the world each year. The great thing about TED talks – served serially from the TED server or in person at a TED or TEDx – is that if there's something you don't like you can zone out for 18 minutes and there'll be another one along on a completely different topic. Just be careful about TEDxes with force-fitted themes. TEDxes are independently organised, often by a close-knit clique led by a charismatic figure who can – in my experience – deliver their own agenda through the medium of the conference. If the theme interests you or is in some tangential way relevant, fine. If not, the event can be a waste of time.

Go to events: This is a more focused version of the encouragement to travel. Go to events and hear other people – often from very different organisations or walks of life – talk about what they do, how, and why. TEDxes can fill this niche. So, too, can networking events. And if speed-dating networking events – still popular – fill you with horror, there's a vogue for slow-motion networking, where delegates have more time to meet and tell their stories to determine whether there's any basis for collaboration. Putting two (or more) people together with all their knowledge and experience to produce something new is insight generation in human form. It's exactly what the Cambridge psychology department's morning coffee and afternoon tea rule routine aims to achieve.

Choose your events wisely. Some apparently low-key organisations run truly extraordinary and stimulating events. Before meeting the Brighton Chamber of Commerce, I had a stereotypical view of

Chambers of Commerce: male, stuck in the 1970s, moustachioed, full of attitudes and prejudices well beyond their sell-by date. My shorthand is "racist roofers". Not the Brighton Chamber, run by the inspiring Sarah Springford and her all-female team. Brighton's a different and vibrant place to do business, and Sarah's built the Chamber to reflect and serve the community incredibly well. My favourite event is the Chamber's annual Brighton Summit. Truly a hidden gem, I find it to be the most inspiring day of the year bar none. There'll be something similar near you. Sniff it out.

Read winning award submissions: Whatever industry or sector you work in, there are bound to be awards. Awards for innovation. Awards for creativity. Awards for new product or service development. And underpinning almost all successful award entries is an insight-rich awards submission. In commercial communication, the Cannes Lions, Effies, D&AD Golden Pencils, IPA Effectiveness Awards, and APG Creative Strategy Awards celebrate the best. Other industries have their own awards. In order to inspire other organisations and companies to enter these awards, many award-granting bodies provide open access to each year's successful entries. Absorb yourself in what they say, how they say it, and how they credit the role of insight in helping to create a new solution to a careworn challenge.

JUST ONE MORE THING . . .

For the past 30 years, *The Big Issue* magazine has "helped the homeless to help themselves", providing a product for homeless people to sell on the streets and generate income. Started in London, the magazine has spawned hundreds of welcome copycat projects around the world, providing thousands of homeless people with a springboard to get off the streets and back into mainstream society. In May 2019, the founder of *The Big Issue*, John Bird, launched a new magazine called *Chapter Catcher*, with the goal of doing the same for illiteracy that his first title did for homelessness. Each month, the title publishes an eclectic mix of chapters from a wide range of different authors – living and dead, fiction and non-fiction, serious and frivolous.

In an article marking the launch of the new magazine, *The Guardian* commented,

> *Editorially, the contents page looks as if it were compiled by an arbitrary drunk let loose in a municipal library. But such apparent randomness, Bird insists, is the whole point. We neither learn by reading what we already know, nor do we grow by reading what makes us comfortable.*[8]

The spirit and essence of *Chapter Catcher* is exactly the same as the drive for curiosity demanded by the STEP Prism of Insight. It's guided by the same, mash-up principles as *Cover* before it in the 1990s – a magazine that republished the best of the world's feature journalism each month – and *The Week*, which does the same for news. And although students of insight might not be the most immediate or obvious target market for this new title *Chapter Catcher*, I strongly recommend you check it out.

Chapter Catcher – like all the other tool and techniques, approaches and strategies identified in this chapter – fills the hopper of your memory, accessed without conscious awareness by your subconscious mind, with stuff. Like all the best quotes, "Talent borrows, genius steals" is attributed to more than one source, both Oscar Wilde and Picasso. As an observation of one of the qualities necessary to be creative, of course it should be something stolen. Picasso also said art is theft.

Artist Austin Kleon's 2012 book *Steal Like an Artist* is a manifesto for copying as the basis for originality. Not plagiarism, which is passing off others' work as your own, but self-conscious absorption of what's come before as stimulus for what you might produce. Exactly the principles espoused by Mark Earls in *Copy, Copy, Copy*. He shows how copying is our number one learning strategy, enabling us to outsource cognitive load from our brains to those of others. As the potter Grayson Perry said, "Originality is only for people with short memories." Don't ignore what others have done. Embrace it, copy it loosely, and allow mutations and other influences to creep in.

We leave the sweat phase with a summary of observations from Jim Carroll, the former chairman of London advertising hot-shop Bartle Bogle & Hegarty. In a 2016 blog on the architect Frank Lloyd Wright, he wrote,

I would suggest that the best and most successful creative professionals experience life in its infinite variety and infuse their work with their acquired knowledge and insight. A film or football match, a good read or bad play, a walk in the park, a dance in the dark, a word in the ear, a feast for the eyes. A life fully lived provides the material for creative thought. Random, extraneous, unrelated experiences inspire lateral leaps and imaginative connections. The personal stimulates the professional.[9]

So go ahead and fill your boots with everything that's come before. Stand on the shoulders of giants. And then . . . have a break.

INTERVIEW: ERIC BARTELS, INNER WHY

Insightful interview 5 of 8

NAME	Eric Bartels
ORGANISATION	Inner Why
ROLE	Founder and Managing Director

At time of writing, Simon Sinek's 2011 talk "How great leaders inspire action" from 2011's TEDxPugetSound was the third most-watched TED of all time, with more than 47 million views.[10] Also known as the "Start With Why" talk, Sinek sparked a movement – together with a very lucrative consultancy and speaking career, not to mention warehouses-full of book sales – with this humble talk and flipchart graphics. It's now a very rare business, charity, or third-sector organisation that hasn't at least considered its purpose. And the evidence is growing that brands and companies that put a clearly articulated purpose front and centre outperform those that are still groping in the dark towards their "Why?".

It was with this in mind that I spoke to philosopher, behavioural scientist, and entrepreneur, Eric Bartels – the brains and intellectual brawn behind Utrecht and New York–based business Inner Why. Bartels' purpose is all about purpose. He's developed a proprietary methodology to help businesses and brands find and express their true purpose, turn purpose into strategy and then – unlike so many consultancies – turn the resulting strategy into technical action plans. And as the company's name suggests, Bartels and his colleagues act as "idea midwives" (my phrase), helping executives to locate and articulate corporate purpose from within themselves.

Captivated by the success of Cupertino's favourite son, Bartels is currently writing his fourth book, *Be A Steve – And Build Your Own Apple*. He cites Jobs' contention that, in building the iMac, Apple never asked focus groups what type of computer they wanted; they built the computer they wanted for themselves, that was beautiful and elegant, and that made technology our slave, not our master. For Jobs, Apple's purpose involved domesticating technology, a phrase he used from the early days onwards.

Bartels' own research among high-performing executives suggests that it's the leaders who run businesses that operate from a clearly defined sense of purpose who thrive. Jobs' repeated experience – at least once he came back to Apple in the mid-1990s – and Tim Cook's ever since assuming leadership of the company on Jobs' death in 2011 runs counter to the orthodoxy that you need customer research to validate new product development. As Bartels points out, approaching 96% of all new product launches fail. "It's not because they don't research consumers or customers – they almost all do. Rather, it's because the businesses hadn't found or articulated why they were in business or why their new products should exist beyond making money."

For Bartels, the insights that are the key to an impactful, purpose-led value proposition exist within the individuals who make up the body corporate of a business. For Inner Why, companies are simply organisms made up of individuals. This is true of a centuries-old business every bit as much as a start-up. Of the CEO and those on the shop floor. And of the agencies who shape and articulate how the company communicates.

"Brand managers get stuck with the persona of what they think they should be," says Bartels, "of what they think their customers want to hear. Then they get paralyzed by the so-called rules that seem to compel them to research their products and target audiences to death. This leads to dysfunctional and inauthentic brand behaviour, to companies failing to express their purpose – their inner why. Our role is to be disruptive and change all that. To get companies and the individuals that comprise a corporate organism to look inside themselves for the language, the purpose which – often much to their surprise – they find was living inside them all along."

The rise and dominance of Big Data and the need for all decisions to be evidence-based is, Bartels believes, working against business' best interests. Many agencies and advisors arm leaders with data or at best casual observations, but certainly not insights. Business school teaches CEOs and CFOs to make bad decisions they can justify with logic, not the right decisions from within that intuition and instinct suggest are correct but cannot be proven unequivocally.

Bartels is clear that his approach is neither fashionable nor easy to accept. Many hyper-rational leaders he encounters struggle with his approach, and it's only those with a streak of rebelliousness who truly understand and embrace the journey within to find and articulate purpose. Entrepreneurs are much more open to his approach, and he cites his hero Steve Jobs' observation that if Henry Ford had listened to his customers rather than his purpose-led vision, "he'd have struggled to build a faster horse. Data-driven insights can only help give a business purpose if its meaning is assessed with empathy and without ego."

NOTES

1 Different languages have different ways of expressing themselves that others don't have at all. Ancient Greek, for example, has a whole mood – in addition to the indicative ("I eat") and the subjunctive ("I might eat") called the optative ("Would that I might eat"). The optative expresses the hypothetical desire that something might be the case. Ancient Greek also has a verb that no other language I know of has as a concept expressed in a single verb: *lanthánō*, "I escape my own notice doing . . ." + verb, such as "I escaped my own notice eating the left-over profiteroles out of the fridge". Escaping one's own notice doing something is – from the perspective of insight hunters – exactly what happens to memories as they're stored. It's outside both conscious perception and, *pace* Pinker, beyond human cognitive capacity. What's more, it's exactly what happens subconsciously, as the subconscious mind recombines old stuff with old stuff to make new stuff; insights.

2 The sensation and experience of "that terrible feeling of déjà-vu" has rarely been better expressed than in Monty Python's, It's the mind: A weekly magazine of things psychiatric www.dailymotion.com/video/x2tmmc2

3 Picasso said, "Talent borrows, genius steals". There is an itinerant, iconoclastic duo of marketing consultants, husband and wife team Faris and Rosie Yakob. Their business is named in honour of Picasso's quote. Their core belief is expressed in the line, "It's called Genius Steals because we believe ideas are new combinations and that nothing can come from nothing. But copying is lazy. We believe the best way to innovate is to look at the best of that which came before and combine those elements into new solutions." In the spirit of Faris, Rosie, and Pablo, I pay due homage and credit to the hard work of my training delegates and have distilled my thoughts and their experiences into the advice given in this and the next three chapters. More about Genius Steals at www.geniussteals.co

4 Small "p" political observation: I honestly don't think anything has ever worked in DEXU. It very existence makes the Department for Administrative Affairs in the long-running UK comedy series *Yes, Minister* and *Yes, Prime Minister* seem like the most necessary and vital government department, rather than the most useless ever to be dreamed up. Those I've met who were seconded – often against their will – to work in DEXU would make you favour a headless chicken as your lead strategist.

5 David Hieatt (2014). *Do: Purpose*. The Do Book Company, p. 68.

6 For details of the role a 30-foot blow-up of a cartoon strip from *Viz* had in helping me to develop an award-winning campaign for Tesco, see *Narrative by Numbers*, pp. 62–65, and especially p. 64, including its promise, "I'll talk much more about insight in my next book, *How To Be Insightful*)." Ah! The foresight.

7 For curiosity's sake on this topic – and to hear the full story from *Observer* journalist Carole Cadwalladr – I strongly recommend you watch the 2019 documentary *The Great Hack*. Netflix subscribers go here http://bit.ly/2NgXdCK

8 Oliver Balch (4 June 2019). Big Issue Founder Launches Magazine to Tackle Illiteracy. *The Guardian* http://bit.ly/2JVNfWF

9 Jim Carroll's blog (13 May 2016). Frank Lloyd Wright: When the personal inspires the professional http://bit.ly/2QbMbjR

10 On the very remotest off-chance you haven't watched this, have an 18-minute timeout right now over here forthwith http://bit.ly/36Srjnr. Actually, give it another spin if you haven't watched it for a few months. I'll bet you find yourself inspired.

6

TIMEOUT – THE THINKING PHASE

"Each person deserves a day in which no problems are confronted, no solutions searched for. Each of us needs to withdraw from the cares which will not withdraw from us."

Maya Angelou

AROUND-THE-HOUSE-CHESS

One of my father Kenneth's oldest friends and collaborators was a brilliant mathematician named David Champernowne.[1] Kenneth and David went to school together at the leading English public school, Winchester College, in the late 1920s. A few years after the Second World War, they were part of the team that founded and grew to quick prominence the Institute of Economics and Statistics at the University of Oxford.

But David's heart always lay at the more modest, considered, and thoughtful University of Cambridge.[2] Indeed, while Kenneth and David spent a decade together at the Institute, David would always rather have been in Cambridge. He even took a significant demotion to take up a role there in the late 1950s. David ended his career as a professor of mathematics in his favoured city and institution. But he started it there, too. On leaving Winchester, he was first an undergraduate and then a post-graduate researcher at King's College, where he took his PhD. It was while at Cambridge that David struck up a profound and lasting friendship

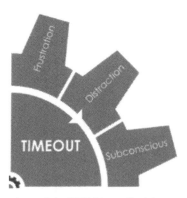

Figure 6.1 Timeout quadrant of the STEP Prism of Insight

with a man called Alan, with whom he collaborated closely over the next 20 years.

Alan. Alan Turing. Bletchley Park codebreaker of the Nazi's Enigma Machine, whose deciphered encryptions cut short the Second World War. One of the all-time most insightful Britons ever.[3]

My story about Alan – and David – relates to a game they invented and pioneered in the early 1930s, during their undergraduate studies. And it's a story that's never been told properly, until now. For that we have to thank David's son, Arthur, who retired in the early 2010s from a pioneering career in artificial intelligence in Silicon Valley. Arthur was a regular visitor to my family home in the early 1970s, bearded like a ruddy Greek god and riding bigger and more powerful motorbikes with every visit. He always told great stories of his tentative explorations in AI even then. He disappeared out of my life in 1975, only to reappear a few years ago. We struck up a conversation via email and he demonstrated that his storytelling prowess had not waned in the intervening 40 years. And here is what he told me, setting straight a story that has – until now – been lost in the fog of mythology.

Alan and David were peers in three different domains. They were great mathematicians. They were excellent, middle-distance runners.[4] But they were truly chess ninjas, able to hold flexible mental representations of complex games and boards in their heads, playing five, six, seven moves ahead.

Photo 6.1 Statue of Alan Turing in Sackville Park, Manchester
Source: author's own picture

Being smart and curious, Alan and David wondered how best they could combine their passions. It was mathematics that brought them to each other's attention, but it was chess and running that glued them together as friends. And so was born the much-misunderstood and often misreported game of "around-the-house-chess" or "run-around-the-house-chess". And it's thanks to Arthur that we now know the truth.

The game did not – contrary to rumours and inventions on bulletin boards – involve one or both players making a move and then running around the house in which either man lived. Even in the 1930s, the grounds of Cambridge student accommodation weren't big enough to give Alan and David the space and so the time they needed to experience sufficient time away from the game to benefit from that period of Timeout; to help unlock what Leonard Mlodinow calls "frozen thinking".

The original and most authentic version of the game went like this.

- Alan and David would take a folding card table with a green baize top – plus two collapsible chairs – to the Cambridge University running track.
- Dressed in shorts, singlets, and the 1930s equivalent of running spikes, they'd sit opposite each other and set out the pieces.
- Whoever was white – in this example, let's say it's Alan – would set off round the 440-yard track. This was the **house**, around which they would run.
- On his return from running round the "house", Alan would sit down and immediately make his move.
- At this point, black – David in our example – would set off, retaining a mental representation of the board and Alan's move in his head. The faster he ran – and Alan and David were both excellent runners, and so could complete 440 yards in under a minute – the faster he would breathe. The quicker his pulse. The more he would sweat. And – potentially – the more inspirational, outlandish, and insightful the move he would make.
- On his return from his lap "around the house", David would sit down, make his move, and send Alan on his way for a lap and to consider his next move.
- So this would continue, one running, making his move, sending the other off for 50–60 seconds of timeout and consideration of his next move.

What Alan and David created with their game was an extraordinary and extreme experiment in insightful thinking, over a shortened time frame. Their chronic curiosity for chess over the previous 15 years had delivered to each man an ability to look at the unique challenges of each configuration of chess pieces with the eyes of informed experts. They'd put in their 10,000 hours.

By mashing chess together and middle-distance running, they'd blended their favourite hobbies in a uniquely creative way, for sure. But they'd also introduced the critical Timeout phase, required to allow the subconscious mind to work its wonders between moves. They subverted the norms of chess playing – from school gymnasiums to Washington Square Park, from Istanbul cafés to the International Space Station[5] – of seeking inspiration for the next move while sitting, almost always in silence, facing one's opponent across the eight-by-eight checkerboard.

Being chess ninjas and excellent runners, Alan and David were able to stay some of the effort required to run and still keep an accurate mental representation of the board at play in their minds as they ran. When we're used to doing something – anything – it becomes increasingly automatic and demands less of our conscious attention. This is true of mental just as much as physical exertions. I well remember when I started running, I genuinely thought I was going to collapse in a heap from utter exhaustion when I'd only put one foot in front of the other for but 60 seconds. Things are rather different – if not much quicker – now I'm used to running.

But the harder and faster Alan and David ran, the more attentional resources were demanded by the sheer physical exertion of running, the more consciously focused on running they would become: heart beating faster, breathing more deeply, blood and oxygen coursing more quickly round their bodies. As the mind – conscious and subconscious – is material, physical, corporeal; as it is as a metaphysical instantiation of the brain – fed and oxygenated by the blood, 140, 150, 160 times a minute while running – these periods of Timeout could have quite extraordinary effects on the moves that Alan and David played.

Their rules required the runner to make his move as soon as he sat down at the card table beside the university running track. The other would then get up, run as fast they judged right, considering where they should move next. After a particularly effortful, fast run, the internal homoeostatic state of the players would be more extreme and more different from normal chess competition as it's possible to make it. And reportedly, according to Arthur, it was at these moments that each player could make a move – a eureka decision on where to move next and why – that apparently defied logic, beggared belief, and utterly confused his opponent. As they set off on their lap, they took in the new information – the new stimulus – pondered it more or less consciously, pushing themselves as fast as they thought right given the state of the game. But they were also looking to test or prove their own and their opponent's insights as to where the game stood and where it was headed.

Sometimes, a move after a sprint was madness. Suicidal or ill-thought-through moves were more likely after an arm-pumping, chest-rasping lap. But so, too, were genius, insight-rich moves that anticipated how the game could turn out five, seven, or ten moves ahead. Such was the insight petri dish of experimentation of around-the-house-chess, told here in all its brilliant glory for the first time. Thanks for sharing it, Arthur.

David and Alan went on to take – in Churchill's memorable phrase – their "corkscrew thinkers' brains" to Bletchley Park, where they were they were joined by my father, Kenneth. Kenneth died in 1988, never breaking the Official Secrets Act, never letting any of his family know what he did during the war, apart from his coded mutterings of being "a protected mind". It took another Oxford collaborator, Asa Briggs, to "out" him as a "BPite", as someone who had worked at Bletchley Park.[6] In one of his last books, 2011's *Secret Days*, Briggs wrote,

> *I did know, however, that one non-collegiate institution in Oxford, the Institute of Statistics, where at least one ex-BPite, Kenneth Knowles, worked, reproduced, in part at least, the open, experimental and superficially rankless flavour of BP [Bletchley Park]. Certainly there were mathematicians working there of the kind that BP always took to heart.[7]*

In 1948, Turing and Champernowne created the world's first computer game, Turochamp.[8] The program was able to play chess at a low level – well below the level that either man could play himself, even if he'd been running hard around the house. The code for Turochamp is now lost, and it was too complex to be coded into the primitive computers of the time. It is a coda to Alan and David's story, told right for the first time. And to me, this truly is a tale of insight, of old + old = new, and the potential of the brain's recombinatorial brilliance. It's a tale that takes its rightful place in a book about insight and how to be insightful, and in terms of our model, what it tells us about Timeout is particularly instructive – if, to some, a little bit extreme.

ON THE IMPORTANCE OF DISTRACTION

The artist and author Austin Kleon says in his most recent book *Keep Going* that to be creative, everyone needs to visit or create their own "bliss station". Interviewed by US author Dan Pink on one of his regular "Pinkcasts",[9] Kleon cites the storytelling mythologist Joseph Campbell, he of the Hero's Journey storytelling framework fame. In his classic book *The Power of Myth*, Campbell defines a bliss station as something we all need to have; a special time or place in which we disconnect from the world so that we can connect with ourselves.

For Campbell, a bliss station can be a physical place at home, in the office, or in a third space. Alternatively, it can be a time of day that you dedicate to unplugging from the noisy world around you. And if you're travelling, Kleon gives two tips: put your smartphone in airplane mode and put in some earplugs. No calls, no texts, no notifications. Set the timer on your phone for 15 minutes, sit back, and relax, uninterrupted. That makes an enclave in which you can do your really intense, creative work. And by being cut off from dings and pings and notifications, you can properly connect with what Kleon calls JOMO: Joy of Missing Out. The very antithesis – and so much more productive – than that tyranny of the social media age, FOMO: Fear of Missing Out.

Now it is true that not many people run. Only one in ten of the population do so regularly. Many people say it's too hard, they can't do it, it makes them hurt for days afterwards. They claim they get no pleasure from it and it's a unique combination of dreaded anticipation before, pain during, and no compensatory rush of endorphins afterwards. I was like that until I started on Couch to 5K in 2011. But just as with writing, so with running. As the very wise novelist, writing coach, and book whisperer Beth Miller says, "If you're going to write, write." With running, it's the same. "If you're going to run, run." There's no substitute for it. You many not write much that others deem to be good, let alone readable, or even literature. You may not run in a style or a pace that elite or even good club runners would consider to be anything more than a lolloping jog. But running you will be.

But for some people, running is too vigorous and too distracting an activity to undertake with the acute or chronic aim of distracting your conscious mind from the task at hand and allowing your subconscious to do its recombinatorial best. For me and many other strategists, innovators, and inventors I've spoken to, that is precisely the point of running. It's so absorbing, so all consuming, that the act of raising your heart rate, increasing your rate and volume of oxygen ingestion, and sweating hard . . . these are precisely the diversions needed to make us focus on the very moment – in the now. It's the closest we can get to a meditative state (because meditation isn't our thing or we've not invested time in it).[10]

I've found you can enhance the benefits of running and make it more like meditation – a running meditation, if you will – if you count to ten, odd numbers on in-breaths, evens on out-breaths. Constantly monitor the connection between your counting and whether odds and evens fall on in- or out-breaths, and if the order switches, start again. For me, that makes running the most perfect form of diversion, of Timeout from the insights I know I need to generate. It's the perfect antidote to conscious thinking and gives your subconscious free reign. It also has the added benefit of being the best form of exercise there is, always available, requiring minimal equipment (with the addition of a judicious headtorch, hat, and gloves in winter), and it's free. Stop me if I'm getting too evangelical.

WALKING BEFORE WE CAN RUN

But as I say, for some people – for most people, for nine out of ten of us – running isn't their thing, either for exercise and fitness, or distraction and timeout. For others, walking is the thing. The Roman philosopher and tragedian Seneca said, "It does good to take walks out of doors, that our spirits may be raised by the open air and fresh breeze". Early Christian theologian Saint Augustine of Hippo put it even more snappily when he wrote, *solvitur ambulando*; "a solution comes [literally "it is solved"] by walking". Augustine's maxim is usually taken to be a little bit metaphorical, suggesting that problems are solved thanks to the application of practical experiments. But from the perspective of taking Timeout as a means of allowing the subconscious to get recombinatorial, I think we can take it more literally, too.

The writer Ferris Jabr wrote an excellent, extended essay titled "Why walking helps us think" in *The New Yorker* in 2014, bringing together many strands from different sources, cultures, and genres of writer and philosopher whose work has been helped by walking. It's well worth the detour and features some of the arguments advanced here, covering the psychology and neuroscience of walking's impact on cognition. He concludes, "Likewise, writing forces the brain to review its own landscape, plot a course through that mental terrain, and transcribe the resulting trail of thoughts by guiding the hands."[11]

Turing and Champernowne, remember, were combining the act of more and more extreme exercise with imminent problem-solving, which chess piece might they move next to where. They were stepping away from the problem to be solved, running full pelt, attempting to hold a mental representation of the chessboard in their heads, then sitting down and making their move. The distance between problem-setting (opponent makes a move) and problem-solving (making one's next move, with the medium-term goal of winning the game) are removed but not far removed.

In the STEP Prism of Insight, there are no prescriptions about how long it might take for Timeout to have its effect, but Timeout in our model is about distracting yourself long enough for your subconscious mind to do what it does best. And it's because 90% of us don't run that I believe many people don't associate the Timeout given by running with problem-solving. They mistake the direct stimulus (running) with the direct response (solution, insight generation), whereas the direct stimulus is more running that distracts the conscious mind as a form of

Timeout. The common misconception is an understandable one, but for me it's too linear and logical an explanation for the ethereal qualities that Timeout can bring.

Daniel Kahneman is probably the best-known cognitive psychologist alive (at least at the time of writing).[12] Much of the experimental work he undertook – to elucidate and explain the shortcuts or heuristics that lead us to make predictable errors of judgment under uncertainty – was done in partnership with his long-term research partner, Amos Tversky.[13] Indeed, Kahneman would only accept the Nobel Prize for Economics if the committee gave it jointly to them both, even though Tversky was by that time no longer alive. Neither Kahneman nor Tversky were runners, though they did approve of St Augustine's approach to problem-solving and insight generation done on the move. Walking, but not too briskly. Just enough to change the scene and get thinking in a different modality and environment. We'll come back to the role and value of walking and the potential of "walkshops" shortly.

A MORE INNOCENT APPROACH

Artist Austin Kleon and his wife go for a walk every morning, come rain or shine (more likely shine, as they live in Austin, Texas), before they start their day. Walking, Kleon believes, is good for physical, spiritual, and mental health. He quotes the Swedish film director Ingmar Bergman, who advised his daughter: "The demons hate it when you get out of bed. Demons hate fresh air."[14]

Innocent Drinks today has a strong presence across Europe, but it started life in 1998 as a side hustle of three management consultants. They'd been friends at university and spotted an opportunity to build a business out of selling better, fresher, and smoother smoothies than anyone else. Between 2010 and 2013, they progressively sold more and more of the business to Coca Cola – its stake today is now 90% – and in 2018 the brand recorded annual sales of more than £350m.

Innocent's tone of voice and capacity for powerful, emotional storytelling have always been trademarks of the brand, from packaging to advertising. This has not changed since the sale to Coke. In their decidedly non-corporate-speak book *Innocent: Our Story and Some Things We've Learned* (2009), the founders say,

> We had our big idea on holiday. You might have yours in the park while feeding the ducks, or in bed, or out walking in the country. Pretty much any place where your mind can be liberated. Your brain is hemmed in at a desk, thinking about desky things. Don't expect it to be creative when you're there.

Pesky, desky things like spreadsheets, timesheets, and organisational charts. Not insightful things like how to reinvent the soft drinks category.

Timeout is such an important – and at the same time such a counter-intuitive – aspect of insightful thinking that many people when first hearing that it's such an integral part of the STEP Prism of Insight look quizzical. "Surely taking Timeout and time away from what we're required to do is bunking off or playing hooky?" their puzzled faces – and mouths – often say. But just consider what Leonard Mlodinow, the physicist who helped us to unravel the neuroscience of insight back in Chapter 3, says:

> The result of our addiction to constant activity is a dearth of idle time and, hence, a dearth of time in which the brain is in its default mode. And though some may consider "doing nothing" unproductive, a lack of downtime is bad for our well-being, because idle time allows our default network to make sense of what we've recently experienced or learned. It allows our integrative processes to reconcile diverse ideas without censorship from the executive brain. It allows us to mull over our desires and shuffle through our unattained goals.[15]

Timeout allows us – if you'll allow me, Leonard – to be insightful. More often, more reliably, and with more impact. As the madmen's madman David Ogilvy wrote in his career retrospective *Ogilvy on Advertising*, more than 30 years after he set up shop on Madison Avenue, New York,

> Big ideas come from the unconscious . . . But your unconscious has to be well-informed, or your idea will be irrelevant. Stuff your conscious with information, then unhook your rational thought process. You can help this process by going for a long walk, or taking a hot bath, or drinking half a pint of claret . . . if the telephone line from your unconscious is open, a big idea wells up within you.[16]

Half a pint of claret, indeed. The perfect volume in which to drink fine Bordeaux. Certainly the route to a long, fuzzy period of Timeout.

HOW TO BE INSIGHTFUL STEP TWO: TIMEOUT

So, I contend that if you want to make insights a more frequent and likely part of your life, you need to distract your conscious mind from the challenge that you're wrestling with. Insight problems are not – repeat not – like analytical problems. They don't respect the time you put in to solve them and, when you've thought about them long enough, give up their secrets, hold up their hands, and say, "It's a fair cop, guv, and no mistake. You've got me."

By contrast, insight problems demand that the conscious mind takes Timeout to allow the subconscious mind to play with the stimuli we absorb – both acutely to consider the challenge at hand, but also chronically out of a spirit of curiosity – and to piece them together in new configurations. Many of these new permutations will be nonsensical and irrelevant and will never be let through the gate to consciousness. But some will. And what we need to allow and enable the subconscious to do its stuff is not so much time as timeout. Robert Poynton celebrates the power of the pause in his Do Books Company book, *Do: Pause*, as the key to making us "vibrant, irregular, and delightful".[17] Our story of Alan and David showed how they took pausing to a physical extreme, but that doesn't work for everyone. But what does work for everyone is taking time away from the task at hand and doing or thinking about something else. It's channelling your inner Arthur Dent from Chapter 1, not thinking about flying, tripping over, and soaring above the trees. Or getting into the mindset of Ray Bradbury's antihero in his dystopian novel *Fahrenheit 451*, Guy Montag, described as "thinking little at all about nothing in particular".

So, let's get back into the training room – or the learning suite, if you work in an agency that likes to give its rooms fancier names.[18] Now you've had a think and a talk about curiosity, let's move around the STEP Prism cog and onto Timeout. To get you (and your colleagues) thinking and talking about what you intuitively, instinctively do to take Timeout and divert your conscious mind(s) from the insight challenge at hand, read the following short passage.

TIMEOUT

Conventional wisdom suggests that to crack a problem, you have to work and work and work away at it until the problem yields to the force of your intellect, respecting the time you've put in. Conventional wisdom is wrong. That's how you solve analytical problems, not insight problems.

Presenteeism and management demands that we make progress – at times even to innovate on demand – reveal that many leaders believe insight problems are like iron; you just need enough heat and pressure to make them bend. More often than not when you're trying to innovate and establish a profound and deep understanding of something, this leads to frustration.

To allow ideas to connect in your subconscious mind, you need to stop trying to address your challenge, distract yourself from the task at hand, and do something else entirely. Whether for minutes, hours, days, or more, insight problems thrive on Timeout.

The questions you should consider about Timeout include:

- What's your favourite diversionary tactic that you use to distract your mind?
- What works for you outside of work, in your personal life?
- What's the best de-stressor you've got, that allows you to disconnect from the day-to-day?
- What's the difference between a distraction and a displacement activity or full-on procrastination?[19]
- How do you distract your mind?
- What form of exercise works best for you?
- How can you square indulging in Timeout without feeling like you're bunking off?

Again, you can download a checklist of the best tools, techniques, and approaches for timeout at www.howtobeinsightful.com/timeout.

THE BEST TOOLS, TECHNIQUES, AND APPROACHES TO GIVE YOURSELF TIMEOUT

As in each of the four key practice chapters, these are listed in no particular order. It doesn't matter how you take Timeout, it matters *that* you take Timeout. Make sure that you actively build Timeout into your working life so that you train your mind to know that it's going to get an opportunity to do some recombinatorics in its own time. The best strategies include:

- Work on something else
- Change your perspective
- Go somewhere big
- Get moving
- Get spiritual
- Make and have a cup of tea or coffee
- Get some sleep
- Don't go to work
- Do something creative
- Get into the limelight
- Turn a workshop into a walkshop
- Do boring tasks
- Play games

Work on something else: The joy of agency life – the joy of having clients – is that when you're faced with a challenge from one client that just won't yield, you can put it to one side and get on with working on another client's challenge. This is true of any service business, from marketing to web design, from law to financial advice. But it's also true when you work inside a business. Say you work for an insurance company, in the insight team. You have all kinds of different internal clients who ask you to help them understand different aspects of customer behaviour, for example – finance, sales, marketing, ecommerce, legal, regulatory affairs. If the chief financial officer has asked you to help make sense of the fourth-quarter surge in sales and there's no obvious cause you can identify in the data, get stuck into the report you're writing for the head of customer care on complaints. As you distract yourself in a different domain – a strategic document instead of a presentation – you'll often find that the solution to the CFO's question springs fully formed into your head, triggered by something you're writing – a word, a number, a topic. Just be sure that you're ready to capture the insight when it comes to you. We'll go into more detail of the hows of that in the next chapter.

Change your perspective: Physically remove yourself from your workstation, taking a leaf out of the Innocent founders' playbook. Staring into the screen where you answer your emails and fill out your timesheets is unlikely to help you crack the insight challenge you face. Stand up, walk around, sit somewhere else. Thanks to mobile technology, WiFi, and very portable yet powerful laptops, modern offices often have hot desking set-ups, meaning you don't sit in the same place every day. From the perspective of being more insightful, this is a good thing. But even if you do have an allocated desk or team area, many companies also have meeting rooms and break-out spaces, libraries, pods, or areas where you relocate temporarily. Take advantage of these when you are attempting to secure a profound or deep understanding of someone or something. If it's not come to you in your usual workspace, it may well come to you if you move somewhere else.

When I taught undergraduate psychology seminars, I used to arrive in the teaching room 15 minutes early. I didn't want to go over my notes "just one more time"; I was always well prepared in terms of the subject matter. What I wanted to do was rearrange the furniture. Sometimes, I'd set the room out like an "anonymous" meeting, a circle of chairs. Sometimes, we'd have a horseshoe of desks; at other seminars a square or a rectangle. If I was feeling impish, the desks might form chevrons or follow no coherent pattern at all. And on very rare occasions, I'd even set the room out classroom style. My reason for doing this was to change the environment of learning. By changing office topography, we burst out of functional fixedness and so can grasp a different perspective and point of view. And though my students at first thought I was a bit weird – that was actual feedback I received – they usually came to love the novelty of having somewhere different to sit each week. Judging by their fresh insights as the terms passed, they also became freer, more elastic thinkers.

I have always found it difficult to work in the same place for more than three days in a row. Ask any of my former colleagues about the "ants in my pants" that arrive after three days. My dear late mother, Bay, often used to quote that Italian maxim of hospitality: *"Dopo tre giorni, gli ospiti puzzano comme pesce"* – "After three days, guests stink like fish". Even today, more than 30 years into working life, if client, training, or consultancy demands don't require me to work somewhere different on day four, I'll make myself do that. Changing your perspective, outlook, and point of view can be as energising and impactful on creativity and productivity as a good night's sleep.

Go somewhere big: The evidence from environmental psychology that Baroness Susan Greenfield shared with us in the interview suggests that insightful thinking benefits when the person attempting to unlock a thorny insight problem is somewhere big. In the open green countryside, not the closed, narrow, concrete cityscape; in dales and valleys and mountains, not just hills; in the rolling ocean with no land in sight over rowing on the river; in a desert or the wilderness; in a cathedral, not a church; walking around the office or running around the block, not just staring into the screen of a laptop or a smartphone, however big Samsung and HTC may make their phablets these days. The bigness of these environments does two critical things. It broadens our perspective, our worldview; what the Germans gloriously call *Weltanschauung*. And – this is what blew me away in the research Susan shared with me – it effectively slows down time and allows us to process more stimuli more quickly, something that being somewhere small (like staring into a smartphone) hinders. It enables us to take in more stimuli and for our subconscious mind to make more connections, most of which will be futile, but more of which may just be on to something.

Get moving: The first album I owned as a child was *Wombling Songs* by The Wombles, those fictional, long-nosed animals believed to live on Wimbledon Common in South West London, whose purpose in life was clearing up litter. One of the defining tracks on this (admittedly novelty) album was sung by the Wombles' keep-fit fanatic, Tomsk, who was athletic but rather dim. The track was titled "Exercise Is Good for You (Laziness Is Not)".[20]

One of the best ways of changing your perspective, inside and out, is to do exercise. Alan and David's approach may be too extreme for most of us, and I've already extolled the very real virtues of running – even very slow running. You may be more Kahneman than Turing, in which case a walk around the block, into and round a park, may be all that you need to get the pulse beating a little faster, your breath a little deeper, the oxygen into the brain a little faster. That may be the only catalyst you need to divert your conscious mind sufficiently to get it joining more dots. At a conference recently, I met a remote-working, software sales support guy who has a treadmill set up under his stand-up desk. He said that by keeping his pace to 3.1 mph or less, he could do his job just as well as sitting down, but with many more physical and metaphysical benefits. The 3.1 mph figure is important. At that pace, he doesn't get out of breath and sound like a heavy breather on the phone.

Many find swimming and total immersion of every external cell of your body to be beneficial, and I believe that's for two good reasons. The first is that water temperature is very rarely the same as body temperature and it's usually colder – particularly for wild swimmers in rivers, lakes, and seas. This brings down your body temperature and diverts blood supply to warm you up (or at least stop you from becoming hypothermic). A bit of blood redirected to the skin and muscles and the periphery of the body means marginally less in the resource-hungry brain. This doesn't lead to brain shut down, but it means that non-essential services – including worrying about how we're going to satisfy client or colleague demands – get second billing. The total sensation of coldness can dominate conscious thoughts, too. "God it's cold this morning. Can I really face another lap?" That also bumps conscious concerns down the priority list, again upping subconscious activity.

The second reason why swimming is such a powerful catalyst for insight is that it makes diversion by smartphone and other nagging, electronic devices practically impossible. Exercise generally cuts you off from the close-up, closed-in world of mobile devices, objects that are so valued and prized by their owners that they wouldn't think of taking them in the water with them as they plough up and down the lanes. We don't have enough hands to be able to do front crawl *and* check our Instagram feed. And despite waterproof claims of manufacturers, almost nobody would risk killing or drowning their phone for the sake of the dopamine rush of another three likes, favourites, or retweets. So in that way, swimming liberates us by removing the potential for distraction.

This is very different from taking a walk around the block. I live about a mile from the station which connects me to many of my clients in London, just too far – for me – to think it's worth walking rather than cycling. The walk takes 15 minutes, but it's five on the bike. And if I'm required to be with clients first thing, I often ride past commuters scurrying to the station, too. Very often, they're already glued to their phones, captured in their always-on, on-demand worlds at the very moment they could be benefitting from the simple act of walking.

Over the years, my insight training delegates have offered every sport, exercise class, individual and communal, as their brilliant way of taking Timeout. Before, during, and after work. Football, rugby, cricket. Running, power-walking, skiing. Gym work and weightlifting, ballet and soul barre, Pilates and yoga. Yoga comes up often, and not just because of its physical benefits. There are also a lot of advocates for hot, power, and Bikram schools of yoga, and I believe there are similar benefits that come from these forms of the practice that result from raising the body temperature that swimming brings by lowering it. Similar benefits are often singled out by aficionados of saunas, steam rooms, and hammams.

Get spiritual: For those who delve deeper into yoga, there's the opportunity to discover the eight limbs of yoga – the ashtanga – and the set of eight yoga sutras established by the semi-mythical sage, Patanjali. Those that Western yoga bunnies experience most often are the asana (the postures) and pranayama (the control of breathing), and maybe – with more committed and learned teachers – dharana (concentration) and dhyana (meditation). But there's also niyama (observances), yama (abstinences), pratyahara (withdrawal of the senses), and samadhi (absorption). Master all those (in a lifetime) and you'll have a powerful toolkit to help you become an insight yogi or yogini.

And if the physicality of yoga isn't right for you, explore one of the many and growing schools of meditation, ancient and Eastern, or modern and Western. Tai chi, mainstream religion, spirituality. For millennia, these approaches have brought benefits to their practitioners. If they work for you in taking you away from the challenges you face – and so in that way enable you to crack them – I'd say embrace them wholeheartedly. I may be a godless rationalist, but if it works for you, carpe diem.

Make and have a cup of tea or coffee: Get up from your workstation, stroll to the kitchen, pop on the kettle or coffee machine, and make yourself – and maybe others – a hot drink. Doing something simple, physical, repetitive – something programmed into a mental schema – is like a mini-meditation in and of itself. There's a lot of mythology around the power of caffeine to make us sharper, quicker, better able to spot connections between apparently unrelated phenomena. From the three years I spent in a human psychopharmacology lab, getting students drunk and a doctorate into the bargain, I often took part in my fellow researchers' caffeine experiments. I learned that I, personally, received almost imperceptible benefits from even high doses of caffeine. And I also learned that caffeine – like nicotine – generally doesn't make you sharper and perform better than you otherwise would. Rather, when you're in withdrawal, you perform worse than your normal baseline. It takes a cup of caffeinated beverage to lift you back to baseline.

The writer Dan Pink in his book *When* shares the secret of the Nappuccino. About seven hours after waking up, our daily biorhythms really want us to have a quick snooze, to recharge us for the second half of the day. Those in Latin countries have long acceded to this demand of biology with the institutionalisation and enduring appeal of the siesta. Pink throws caffeine into the mix. He recommends that after lunch, you make a double espresso, go into a quiet space with a bed or a couch to lie down on, drink the coffee, set a timer for 25 minutes, put on an eye mask and pop in some earplugs, lie down, and (at least try to) go to sleep. Whether you drop off or not, lie there and let your mind calm down.

The 25-minute timer is chosen for two reasons. If you do go to sleep, you'll be roused before you go into a deep sleep, which can take time to slough. And when the timer goes off, the caffeine will just be kicking in, entering the bloodstream, and taking you out of withdrawal. Try it. You'll be amazed at the impact and how you enter the second half of the working day as if you're having a second morning. This truly is the caffeinated version of Austin Kleon's travelling bliss station.

Get some sleep: Why do we sleep?[21] While that's not the topic of this book, sleep is a very important way for the brain – the subconscious, indeed non-conscious mind – to make sense of the new stimuli you've taken on board since the last time you slept. The brain shuffles and organises, retrieves and stores, categorises and looks for connections – connections that may not be obvious in periods of conscious introspection. When we turn to the third step of the STEP Prism in the next chapter, we'll see how often insights come to us in dreams or when waking up. We'll also see how important it is to have some way of capturing these permanently, by the bed. But know for now that sleep is really critical to the process of insight generation, both taking timeout from the act of conscious insight spotting and giving the brain the mental space it needs to join the dots. So many insightful, creative people – from McCartney to Poincaré – wake up inspired with fresh insight. My mathematician sister Kate told me that one of her heroes, the Indian mathematician Ramanujan, even claimed that his theorems were written on his tongue during the night by the goddess Namagiri; a beautiful, metaphorical explanation for the insight-generating powers of sleep.

Don't go to work: At its simplest, not going to work can mean working from home. Gone are the days when bosses freaked out at the prospect of their employees working from home rather than in the office. "Surely they'll slob about in pyjamas, eating toast, and watching daytime TV all day!" Well no, actually. The vast majority of those who work from home are more productive, achieve more in less time, are less stressed (by the commute, office politics, and everyone else getting to and from work), and happier. If an employer chooses to allow their team to work just one day in five from home, if they operate a hot desking policy, their offices can be 20% cheaper and smaller.

Not going to work can also mean having a duvet day, embracing the spirit epitomised by Maya Angelou and her encouraging each person to "have a day in which no problems are confronted". If you're really up against it – there's a pitch or new business tender next week – but you just can't crack the creative idea that's going to underpin your sales pitch, call the office and tell them you won't be coming in this morning. Go instead to a gallery and wander around, in part out of curiosity, in part to change your perspective, in part to take yourself out of the maelstrom of preparing for the pitch. More junior members of teams can find this suggestion intimidating and likely to land themselves in trouble; more senior members of teams and departmental or company leaders fear that if everyone started doing this, no one would ever get anything done. Often when I suggest this approach in training sessions, leaders fear I'm about to foster a palace revolution. But quite the opposite is true. Organisations that offer the opportunity to have duvet days – allowing their team members to decide, when they wake up, that they won't be coming in today after all – have fewer bogus "sickies" and more motivated and more productive teams.

Not going to work can mean spending purposeful, mindful time away from social media and connected digital devices, either regularly every day, every week, or slotted into your life as works best for you. In *Do: Pause*, Robert Poynton has a lot to say about how and why pauses of all sorts need to be bespoke and tailored for the individual, not just blindly copied and adopted. That makes them very much less likely to be sticky and enduring.

The actor Joseph Gordon-Levitt made a compelling case for the relationship between attention and creativity – and ultimately happiness – in a 2019 TED talk.[22] In his presentation, Gordon-Levitt blended personal experience with psychology and neuroscience to show how craving attention via social media makes us less creative. Social media has a profound and real "unintended consequence for anyone on the planet with an urge for creativity". By narrowing our attentional capacity, the very act of seeking attention blocks our ability to take in diverse stimuli and in this way blocks creative breakthrough. In the context of the model at the heart of this book, social media gets in the way of curiosity and makes it less likely that we will give our subconscious minds sufficient freedom to recombine old stuff into new. It's not so much that technology is the enemy of creativity but more that the attention-driven business model of the social media industry is a eureka blocker.

Not going to work also means taking holidays. If I ran the world, I would fine employees who failed to take their annual holiday entitlement. For every day's vacation not taken, I wouldn't roll it over to next year or pay them extra in lieu. I'd subtract the number of days' salary not taken in the year from the last month's pay packet. And holidays mean holidays. Not constantly checking in on emails, behaving to clients and colleagues as if you're working despite your "out of office" autoreply. No one ever says on their deathbed, "I wish I'd answered a few more emails when I was on holiday." We need time away to recharge. But we also need time away to allow our brain the space to do non-worky things. And it's amazing how often brilliant insights that help to create new businesses come to us while shark watching, windsurfing, sunbathing, or quad-biking over the Namibian dunes. Just be ready to capture them.

On the spectrum of not working, we go from working from home and the duvet day to the planned holiday and on now to the sabbatical. More and more progressive employers offer sabbaticals after a certain amount of service – typically a month after five years' service. If you like your job and plan to stay, seize these opportunities with both hands. Negotiate a sabbatical into your contract up front. You'll be amazed at the benefits on your ability to spot insightful connections if you've just spent four weeks kayaking down the Amazon, your perspective jolted.

Do something creative: Draw, paint, play music, knit, sew, crochet, cook, sculpt, throw pots, unleash your inner Banksy. Develop a hobby and a passion outside of work that has nothing to do with what you do day to day. Music is particularly good, but you don't have to be the Rolling Stones, Tyler the Creator, or David Devant & His Spirit Wife to benefit. Listening to and getting absorbed in music – on a commute, while walking or running, at gigs or in clubs – helps take you out of yourself in an almost shamanistic way. Music takes you out of a verbal, problem-solution frame of thinking, diverting you from the challenges you face. If we know little about the actual mental representation of words, we know even less about how we encode and communicate music. But what we do know is that musical phrases and lyrics – not to mention the sheer joy of being in the melee of a mosh pit for three hours – can trigger associations and help your mind to join up old stuff to make new.

Get into the limelight: Go dancing. Go to an improvisational comedy class. Join an amateur dramatics group. Perform. In the modern knowledge economy, many more of us have roles that involve performance and the presentation of information in environments or circumstances that we can find intimidating. If you're used to performing in public in something you enjoy, you're more likely to make a more insightful, persuasive, and moving presentation of quarterly sales figures or make a better case for why we need to hire a new head of internal communications.

Turn a workshop into a walkshop: In *When*, Dan Pink's prescription for the perfect workplace break involves walking, away from your desk, with someone you like, walking together, not talking about work, and – if it's not too hot, cold, or wet – ideally done outside. Fans of the early 2000s' series *The West Wing* – liberal porn at the time of the hawkish George Dubya Bush administration – will be very familiar with the walking meeting. Given the very real benefits of both movement and not sitting in meetings in the same place you always have meetings, why not turn your next offsite workshop into a walkshop, ideally somewhere out in nature and somewhere really big?

Related to walkshops, in researching the benefits of movement to insight problem-solving, I was delighted to discover the school of management known as MBWA: management by wandering around, a haphazard approach of randomly sampling and assessing employees' performance by wandering in an unplanned and unstructured way, serendipitously.[23] And the British classical composer Benjamin Britten had a habit of composing music all morning, then going for a walk after lunch, considering his morning's work, then coming back and refashioning it. In his writings, Britten made several references to his "composing walks". He used to say, "I work whilst I'm walking."[24]

Do boring tasks: Make yourself deliberately bored, or do really boring, mundane, automatic things that don't require concentration. Things like ironing, mowing the lawn, or doing the washing up. I love all three of those tasks. In part because they allow me to make order out of chaos. In part because – as a consultant and a completer-finisher – I don't often get the opportunity to completely finish any one piece of work. And in part because they free my mind to do its recombinatorial best.

Play games: The best games are absorbing and take you out of yourself. We've considered chess at length with Alan and David. For some it's

FIFA or Call of Duty, for others it's Sudoku that diverts and distracts and dislocates their minds. The mental gymnastics required to solve cryptic crosswords is the very stuff of insightful thinking, done consciously, shuffling and recombining existing stimuli in creative ways to make something new. So, too, is playing with LEGO; the enduring appeal of LEGO is recombinatorics made plastic. LEGO Serious Play is a set of tools that use mini-bricks to help teams solve problems, enhance innovation, and communicate better. But if you don't want to invest in a set of expensive workshops, buy the game Creationary for the office and introduce it into your process for generating ideas.

This set of tools and techniques for Timeout doesn't pretend to be exhaustive or comprehensive. But it shows you how very many methods and approaches there are within easy reach – of both individuals and the organisations where they work – that empower and enable them to distract their conscious minds from the task at hand. The benefits of Timeout are not just designed to avoid burnout. In the STEP Prism of Insight, Timeout is an essential part of the process of being more insightful. Of joining old stuff together with more old stuff to make new stuff.

What's more, all of these tools and techniques have the opportunity to turn work into something which it still isn't for too many people. It has the opportunity of actually making it fun – but fun with a purpose. And by letting the cogs whir in the background, that purpose is more, better, more creative ideas.

Perhaps Timeout is a palace revolution after all.

INTERVIEW: PROFESSOR ANGELA GALLOP, STRATHCLYDE UNIVERSITY

Insightful interview 6 of 8

NAME	Professor Angela Gallop
ORGANISATION	University of Strathclyde, Glasgow
ROLE	Professor of Practice, Strategic Director for Forensic Science

Angela Gallop, CBE, is the forensic scientist of her generation, the forensic scientist's forensic scientist. After hitting her head on the glass ceiling of the Home Office in the 1980s, she founded and ran three hugely successful private forensic science businesses – Forensic Access, Forensic Alliance, and most recently Axiom International. She is Professor of Practice and Strategic Director for Forensic Science at Glasgow's University of Strathclyde. In 2019, Hodder & Stoughton published her book *When the Dogs Don't Bark*, sharing details of how she and the teams she led solved many of the UK's most complex and intractable criminal cases, including the murders of Rachel Nickell, Damilola Taylor, and Stephen Lawrence. In full disclosure, she is also my sister.

Forensic science is a profession defined by insight problems. Inconclusive, incomplete data sets. Stimuli that appear to lead somewhere but then go cold. Evidence that practitioners accumulate both acutely for the case at hand, but also chronically so you can recognise patterns and understand the significance of outliers. Cases are often solved when the recombinatorial engine of the subconscious mind draws together apparently unconnected data in new and surprising ways. The solutions can be counter-intuitive because those who perpetrate crimes often attempt to interfere with or cover up evidence, and getting to insight can mean ignoring or going against logic. As Gallop says frequently, it's often more important to look for evidence "when the dogs don't bark". Hence the title of her book. "Always ask," she urges, "why the dogs aren't barking. Particularly when experience tells you they should be." As she says in her book, "One of the fundamental principles of forensic investigation is that absence of evidence can't be assumed to be evidence of absence" (p. 66).

For Gallop, insight is "that wonderful moment when you've carved through everything you've been thinking about and you see a direct line of where you want to go – a straight line to where you need to be – and that is the point at which you mustn't become distracted". As we saw in Chapter 3 on the neuroscience of insight, just before an insight comes, our visual cortex dims and narrows our focus of attention. Gallop's rejection of outside stimulus and her overwhelming desire to focus on the tip-of-the-tongue insight as it emerges – away from all distractions – echoes the neurological reality of insight.

There are a number of necessary (if not sufficient) conditions that Gallop believes are central to insight generation. These include:

1   **Experience** – learning from failures (false positives and true negatives) and from previous successes (true positives). Taking in stimulus (aka our Sweat). Sometimes, however, experience can be a hindrance. It can make you close down possibilities too soon, make you too confident. It's important to keep an open mind for as long as possible.

2   Making sure there's the **time and the space for insights to germinate**, and not being too choked up with other stuff (Timeout). When working in teams, make space for others, too. For Gallop, insights can appear "like a fish in a river, flitting and flickering in the corner of your eye, so make sure you're alert to the possibilities". Remembering things matters. Remembering where – and in what context – you saw them is just as important, if not more so.

3   **Not letting others distract you** when you're getting close to the moment of insight (our Eureka). "You can't always – often – ever – tell when insight's going to come. It might be when you're taking the rubbish out, so you need to be prepared to capture insights whenever they arise."

4   **Sharing your insights with others** quickly when the time is right (what we might call Prove).

Gallop cut her teeth on a case of the notorious English serial killer Peter Sutcliffe, the so-called Yorkshire Ripper. From the very beginning of her career, she's been aware that the time-pressured world of forensic science means that not having an insight that could catch a killer might lead that killer to strike again. That's why she advocates both effective delegation and the ability to carve out time to allow the mind to develop and articulate insights.

The Big Data revolution has had a paradoxical impact on forensic science, narrowing the different types of data sources used to assess crimes. When Gallop was training and for the first 20 years of her career, forensic scientists looked for a wider variety of physical evidence, albeit often at a microscopic level, dubbed "the five Ds: drugs, Doc Martens, digits, DNA, and documents". Evidence of blood splashes and bodily fluids on clothes, carpets, and skirting boards. Cells under fingernails revealing evidence of a struggle. Hairs and fibres at a microscopic level uncovering who'd been where with whom. Broken glass. Footprints from distinctive trainers or wellington boots showing people weren't where they said they claimed to be – or rather were where the wrongdoing was taking place.

But progressively over the last 20 years, the categories of evidence used by forensic scientists looking for insights to solve crimes have boiled down to (i) the hardy perennial of fingerprints, (ii) DNA, and (iii) digital data. The widespread availability and tumbling cost of DNA profiling have been driven by its accuracy; the probability of the DNA profiles of two unrelated individuals matching is less than one in a billion, on average. The lure and rise to dominance of digital data in forensics is because of the traces we now leave on laptops, mobiles, and CCTV footage. In many ways, the digital revolution has spawned quicker, faster, better evidence. But just as in other fields that have rushed headlong into digital – most notably marketing, finance, and IT – the mere presence of data does not guarantee either evidence or genuine insight that can unlock the challenges the forensic scientists face.

In 1910, the French criminologist and pioneer of forensic science Edmond Locard said, "Every contact leaves a trace." In the case of Stephen Lawrence, for years those investigating his murder could find no evidence of blood on his clothes. He was stabbed twice, through six layers of clothing. Eventually, Gallop and her team did find the blood they knew had to be there, but it had been repeatedly overlooked. Often, there can be as much art as science in finding the evidence – in understanding how the evidence could be where it should be. To learn the specifics of that (and many other cases besides) you should get hold of a copy of Gallop's book.

"It's like CSI," she says. "Only much, *much* more interesting."

NOTES

1 As this obituary (http://bit.ly/2m36F16) from *The Guardian* relates, Champernowne was such a good mathematician that he had a paper published while he was still an undergraduate student on "Champernowne's constant", the number 0.1234567891011. . . . Further evidence of his originality as a mathematician

comes from this story my father often told. When a visiting professor from Japan suggested that mathematics should be recast in base six – because that was the number of petals on a lotus flower – Champernowne reflected, "She's quite right, you know. It would make everything much easier."

2   I have to recuse myself, here. I was an undergraduate at Trinity College, Cambridge, the college where David ended his career as a fellow and emeritus professor of mathematics. And while it would be a gross oversimplification to say, "Oxford people are like this while Cambridge people are like that", I'm convinced there is a difference. Oxbridge, as the combined output is often called, has run the UK for generations – politics, media, and business. But for me, the fundamental difference between Oxford and Cambridge is well evidenced by the arrogant, self-serving mess that Messrs Cameron, Gove, Johnson, Rees-Mogg, and Cummings have made of the UK over Brexit – the first by accidental misjudgement, the rest by Machiavellian opportunism.

3   It is a matter of enduring national shame that Alan Turing was hounded to his death by the government of the country he helped to save from Hitler. After being arrested in a police sting and a set-up for cottaging – seeking sex with another man in a public lavatory, at a time when homosexuality was illegal – and prosecuted for gross public indecency, Turing chose the barbaric option of chemical castration over jail. But changed by the treatment, Turing soon took his own life by cyanide poisoning at the idiotically young age of 43. The unequivocal apology issued by the then British prime minister, Gordon Brown, in September 2009 on behalf of the UK government and his imminent appearance on the new British £50 note are scant compensation, even if they do represent baby steps in the right direction. In a rare statesmanlike act in an otherwise pretty shambolic premiership, Brown described Turing's treatment as both "horrifying" and "utterly unfair". "We're sorry," said Brown. "You deserved so much better."

4   Turing trialled for the British Olympic team in the marathon in 1948, with his time of 2 hours 46 minutes just 11 minutes slower than British runner Thomas Richards, who won silver at the London games. Turing is said to have – on occasion – run from Bletchley to the War Office in London for meetings, an 80-mile round trip.

5   Chess is played in unusual places. According to the repository of all things chess, chess.com, the five craziest are 5. In a boxing ring, 4. Underwater, 3. Atop the Eiffel Tower, 2. In space, and 1. On a roller coaster. There are some amusing photos here http://bit.ly/2AI3Tmc

6   It is odd and an unsolved family mystery that Kenneth never told our family of his time at Bletchley, particularly after his treatment at the hands of the US embassy in 1953 when he had been recruited to open an institute of economics and statistics at Berkeley. Like so many in Oxford in the early 1930s, Kenneth had been an active communist; had he not started a family shortly after graduation, he would undoubtedly have gone to Spain to fight Franco – and most

likely been killed. In 1953, the paranoid McCarthyite US government attempted to coerce Kenneth to publicly recant his 1930s' communism with two days of high-pressure interrogation in the cellars of the US embassy at 1 Grosvenor Square. Despite the promise of a hike in salary of more than 400% – from £2,000 to US$25,000 a year – Kenneth refused to write articles in either *The Economist* or *The Economic Journal* disowning his earlier "communist misdemeanours", and so stayed at Oxford. Indeed, he never even went to the US, despite his second son – my half-brother Jeremy – becoming professor of chemistry (and later dean) at Harvard in 1974 as part of the so-called brain drain. The best explanation of Kenneth's silence about Bletchley is the loyalty he felt to his own country, contrasted with the lack of loyalty and duty he felt to presidents Truman and Eisenhower. For he never tired of telling the story of his two days in the Grosvenor Square cellars.

Champernowne's obituary, referred to in footnote i, above, does mention his friendship with Turing, but it omits their time together at Bletchley, most likely because Champernowne – like my father – never mentioned it to his friends and family either.

7 Lord Briggs of Lewes (2011). *Secret Days: Codebreaking in Bletchley Park: A Memoir of Hut Six and the Enigma Machine*. Frontline Books, p. 211.

8 "The History of Computer Chess: Turochamp", https://www.chess.com/blog/Ginger_GM/the-history-of-computer-chess-part-2-turochamp and see also https://en.wikipedia.org/wiki/Turochamp

9 Dan Pink's Pinkcasts are pithy slugs of micro-content, a two- or three-minute monthly video, and well worth a subscription. See www.danpink.com/pinkcast/ These Pinkcasts also inspired my own series of (60- to 90-second) micropodcasts on insight, which I started while writing this book – http://insightagents.co.uk/podcasts/ – of which there are now more than 70.

10 In Zen Buddhism, the word *satori* means awakening, comprehension, or understanding. It describes *kenshō*, the experience of "seeing into one's true nature, one's inner essence", a very useful metaphor for generating insight.

11 Ferris Jabr (2014). Why Walking Helps Us Think. *The New Yorker* http://bit.ly/2AL6XOg

12 Kahneman's 2011 popular science bestseller *Thinking, Fast and Slow* has firmly established System 1 and System 2 thinking as Things – Things One and Things Two, in Dr Seuss' terminology. And the book has helped to establish the orthodoxy that we make our decisions emotionally and we justify them rationally. But the book – by Kahneman's own admission, for instance when interviewed by the comedian-polymath David Baddiel at Westminster Central Hall, London, in 2014 – is not brilliantly written. It provides proof point after proof point to make its arguments, and some of the language is elliptical and at times less penetrable than a popular science book should be. But those are minor quibbles. What matters is that the central message is so compellingly clear.

13 *Moneyball* author Michael Lewis has written a stimulating and touching account of the lives of Kahneman and his long-term collaborator Tversky in his book *The Undoing Project*.

14 Austin Kleon (2019). *Keep Going: 10 Ways to Stay Creative in Good Times and Bad*, Workman Publishing, p. 175.

15 Leonard Mlodinow (2018). *Elastic: Flexible Thinking in a Constantly Changing World*. Allen Lane, p. 125.

16 David Ogilvy (1985). *Ogilvy on Advertising*, Vintage, p. 16.

17 Robert Poynton (2019). *Do: Pause*. Do Books Co http://bit.ly/2VpTp4o – Poynton has also summarised succinctly the thesis of his book in a powerfully argued piece in *The Guardian* http://bit.ly/2LSc6dl

18 In the 1990s, the London office of PR agency Burson Marsteller dedicated a room to creative thinking and insight, which it called Room 42. It was named in homage to Douglas Adams's *Hitchhiker's Guide to the Galaxy* in which 42 was the "Answer to the Ultimate Question of Life, the Universe, and Everything", calculated by a supercomputer named Deep Thought over a period of seven-and-a-half million years. The advertising agency Mother names its rooms – often no more than curtained-off spaces in a former biscuit factory – after the mothers of its founding employees. BBC Broadcasting House names its rooms after its most successful ever celebrities, leading to hilarious misunderstandings of colleagues calling other colleagues who are late for meetings and saying, "Where are you? We've been in Lord Reith for hours!"

19 One of my favourite TED talks is Tim Urban's 2016 exposition "Inside the mind of a master procrastinator" http://bit.ly/33cEltz – very well worth putting off what you were doing, including reading this book, for 14 minutes.

20 For the Womble-curious, you can hear this fine track here www.youtube.com/watch?v=vE1jvGwhSC0

21 For an excellent, contemporary round-up of all the latest evidence about the role and purpose of sleep, see Matthew Walker's excellent *Why We Sleep: The New Science of Sleep and Dreams*.

22 Joseph Gordon-Levitt (April 2019). How craving attention makes you less creative, TED2019 http://bit.ly/2ZyILMU

23 MBWA: Management by Wandering Around. *Business Dictionary* http://bit.ly/2AM18QD

24 The Echoes Benjamin Britten's Composing Walks. *The Guardian*, 30 January 13 http://bit.ly/2rwSioJ

7

EUREKA – THE ENLIGHTENMENT PHASE

"Mr Bond, they have a saying in Chicago: 'Once is happenstance. Twice is coincidence. The third time it's enemy action.'"
Ian Fleming, Auric Goldfinger in *Goldfinger*

ONE PLUS ONE EQUALS MORE

Most famous for the 80/20 rule, Italian philosopher and polymath Vilfredo Pareto once said, "An idea is nothing more or less than a combination of old elements." Inspired by Pareto, US advertising pioneer James Webb Young – whom we got to know in Chapter 2 – observed, "The capacity to bring old elements into new combinations depends largely on the ability to see relationships." And the ability to spot, appreciate, and express relationships – adding old stuff to old stuff to make something new – is what the third step of our model is all about. Eureka!

Steve Jobs is rightly regarded as one of the most successful businesspeople of all time. Despite a haphazard, non-linear trajectory – including being sacked in 1985 by the company he had co-founded nine years earlier – the foundations he put in place after his second coming in 1997 propelled Apple to become the world's most valuable business. In August 2018, its market capitalisation passed $1tn, the first company to achieve such scale and success.[1]

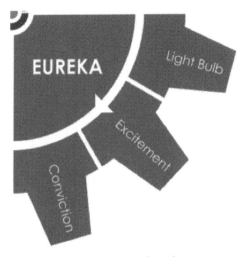

Figure 7.1 Eureka quadrant of the STEP Prism of Insight

Apple owes its corporate success to its beautiful, functionally superior, effortlessly user-friendly products, their screens and their cases, their haptics and even their packaging. For much of that, Jobs and Apple have British industrial engineer Jony Ive to thank. Ive was chief design officer at Apple for 27 years until 2019, not a Jobs' hire originally, but they developed a formidable partnership. What set Jobs apart from many other leaders of hugely successful corporations was his capacity for insight. This is true of Jobs himself, of the individuals he recruited and nurtured, and of the teams they built together. In his book *I, Steve* (2011), p. 69, George Beahm quotes Jobs as having said, "Creativity is just connecting things . . . [creative people] are able to connect experiences they've had and synthesize new things."

British advertising guru Dave Trott – the master of the one-line paragraph and the most exquisite copywriter – says in the introduction to his book *One Plus One Equals Three* (2015), p. 2: "The more varied the input, the more unexpected the combinations, the more creative the ideas. As Steve Jobs said: the broader our understanding of human experience, the more dots we will have to connect, the more creative our ideas will be." And as the journalist and author Matt Ridley says in his 2010 TED talk, leaps of innovation happen when "ideas have sex".[2] To allow the amazing, recombinatorial engine of your subconscious mind to do its thing, you need to create an environment in which your ideas can meet, dance, mate, and procreate. At the same global TED event in Oxford, our friend Steve Johnson from Chapter 4 observed that the coffee house was the "foundry of the enlightenment" (my phrase, not his). This is interesting for two reasons. First, the one everyone notices: it provided a safe, inviting place for people to take their ideas, share them, blend them, and come up with new and better things. And second, innovation flowered at the time that when a depressant (alcohol, historically drunk because water wasn't safe and alcohol kills bugs) was replaced by a stimulant (caffeine, and boiling water also kills bugs to make it safe to drink but not intoxicating).

ON THE IMPORTANCE OF ENLIGHTENMENT

The STEP Prism of Insight requires those looking to solve insight problems to combine extreme hard work and curiosity (Sweat) with distracted indolence and a complete lack of focus (Timeout). Like data storytelling, which yokes together number-dense analytics with millennia-old story structure, the journey towards insight is about fusing apparently contradictory, fire-and-ice disciplines. The curiosity demanded by the Sweat phase is not just curiosity for stimulus that might help crack the problem at hand; it demands curiosity and inquisitiveness be a permanent state of mind and way of being, an endless thirst for knowledge both chronically and acutely. Mercifully, with effectively limitless storage capacity, users of the human brain don't need to worry about running out of memory.[3]

And then, having absorbed whatever there is to be absorbed and then some, gone down rabbit holes, followed leads and links with capricious whim – having gorged on input like an all-conquering king at a medieval banquet – you must step away from the insight problem you're trying to crack. Famine follows feast, focus is replaced by blur and fuzziness, and pinprick spotlights give way to floodlights. Taking Timeout, time spent away from the problem, is designed and required to enable the subconscious mind to pick up the many and varied jigsaw pieces you've taken on board, put them together in a dazzling array of new combinations, and see if any of them fit in novel and interesting ways. In time, some of these new combinations will slip through the gate between the subconscious and conscious mind, often triggered by tinges or echoes of one of the original stimuli. And one of them may be the answer to your problem. The challenge now is to recognise and capture them as they emerge.

On first exposure, Timeout often feels like a luxury that the busy-ness of business just cannot afford. And when I start talking about duvet days and sabbaticals, those in charge of teams, departments, and companies often start to panic, afraid that my model prescription for the superpower of innovation is actually just an excuse for doing nothing. But quite the opposite is true. For in order to divert your mind sufficiently from the insight problem at hand, Timeout itself needs to be demanding and all-encompassing so that – whatever the activity of choice of distraction – the conscious mind doesn't sneak the opportunity to have another go at a solution. And very often, particularly during the working day, Timeout will involve working on another client's business, doing a different type of work, serving a different internal team.

- Struggling with the abstract for your conference paper or impact case study? Do some low-level, exploratory analysis of that data set you've always ignored because you thought it was irrelevant.
- Can't develop the strapline for a new campaign designed to increase the uptake of reusable coffee cups? Fill out your expenses claim, bringing to mind a vivid memory of each purchase. Some of those purchases will almost certainly have been for coffee . . .
- Stuck in a rut with developing a more effective way to synthesize data from timesheets? Wander around the exhibition of wartime propaganda posters at the museum.

Building Timeout into a model of insight problem-solving isn't done lightly or on a whim, just to be perverse. I did it because the psychological and neuroscientific evidence shows quite clearly that for the brain to have the scope to do its recombinatorial thing, it needs conscious anti-focus. And

Timeout doesn't mean shut down. It means working on analytical problems, attending to other new stimuli, and getting on with other aspects of your life and role. It means preparing yourself for enlightenment.

The challenge with enlightenment is that you can't know when or where it's going to strike. For logical, clock-watching managers who yearn for their charges to deliver all aspects of their work on demand like conveyor-belt factory workers, this can appear to be frustrating. But genuine, breakthrough insights are comparatively rare, at least until you hone and perfect your insight generation skills. Even insight ninjas spend comparatively little of their working, productive, or creative time actually experiencing the epiphany of insight. How could they otherwise? Genuine insights – profound and deep understanding of people or issues – take Sweat. Indeed, even once you do become more insightful, you should be wary if you feel as if you're having insights all the time. That may well be because there is an insufficiently tight, metaphorical sphincter between your conscious and subconscious, and 20-insight-a-day folk will doubtless find they're surfacing too many, ill-thought-through false positives.

I considered false positives at length in *Narrative by Numbers*.[4] Indeed, "Avoid false positives" is the third golden rule of data storytelling in my previous book, where we met the perennial Harvard Law student, Tyler Vigen. Tyler became diverted from the law and obsessed with spurious correlations.[5] One of the very real challenges of our Big Data world – with vast quantities and very many different types of data available to integrate and build into models that might explain a phenomenon – is what statisticians call GIGO. Garbage In, Garbage Out.

This is particularly true of time series data: Thing One happens over time, Thing Two happens more, while Thing Three happens less. "Therefore", we conclude, "Thing One promotes Thing Two and suppresses Thing Three". Or, "The co-occurrence of Things One and Two suppresses Thing Three". Or even – and most dangerously of all – "There is a causal relationship between Things One, Two, and Three, and the extent to which they co-occur". We humans like – and always look for – cause and effect. And insights that join different data sets together very often include cause and effect inferences. Well, insight hunters beware, and always make sure you've considered what might be a hidden, third cause.

THE PHYSICS AND METAPHYSICS OF INSIGHT

So, because you can't know when insight's going to strike, you might as well get on with something else until it does. And because you're doing something else – including something else that distracts your attention from the insight problem at hand – it's really important that you come to be able to recognise what having an insight is like for you, that you capture it as quickly as you possibly can and articulate it as fully as possible. Insights are often physical and emotional experiences as well as cognitive, and it matters that you learn what it's like for you.[6] You need to know what's happening to you so that you can label it and act upon it. And because insights can be fleeting and ethereal and feel like oh-so-nearly, tip-of-the-tongue phenomena, you need all your wits about you to write or draw or play them.

Labelling mental experiences which have clear physical manifestations is important. I well remember during the London 2012 Olympics, the BBC TV commentator John Inverdale repeatedly asking successful Team GB athletes the same, rather dumb question: "But weren't you nervous?" Time and again, they would answer in the same way. "Well no, I was excited!" they would say, followed by some variation on this sort of line: "After all the preparation, planning, and envisaging possible scenarios, I knew what was coming. As a result, I was prepared and calm and ready for the final, and incredibly excited to be here." Excitement and anxiety, you see, are physiologically identical; it's the mental label we attach to them that separates out the experience we have.

The same is true of experiencing insights. People often talk of excitement and mild breathlessness around the time they have a breakthrough insight, just as their mind is combining multiple old stimuli to make something new. Having an insight prepares you to recognise what it's like to have an insight, so that the next time you have one you'll know what's happening and you won't just dismiss it as déjà-vu or trapped wind. And one of the defining characteristics of experiencing an insight is the feeling of intense relief that you've nailed it down.

Sometimes a eureka moment truly is a moment – a blinding flash when everything becomes clear. When the insight reveals itself and springs fully formed – fully grown and in a suit of armour. Just like the birth of Athena, when the blacksmith god Hephaestus split open Zeus' skull with a wedge and out she came. Ok, probably not quite that dramatically (or messily), but there are indeed moments when insights present themselves as eureka moments. Just like the moment of religious epiphany experienced by John Belushi's character, "Joliet" Jake Blues, in the 1980 movie *The Blues Brothers*, when he realises the way to raise funds to save the nunnery where he was raised as an orphan is to "get the band back together". "Jesus H. Christ!" he exclaims. "I have seen the light."

At other times, insight comes more gradually, over a period of days, weeks, months – maybe even years. As you take on more stimuli and find more and more confirmation that your hunch might actually be a fully fledged insight, you can get a growing sense of certainty as your subconscious puts the relevant pieces of the jigsaw into a new configuration. But even if a particular insight is a dawning realisation – or if the way that you experience insights is more gradual than instantaneous – what we know about the psychology and now neuroscience of insight tells us that it is a characteristic of the phenomenon that when the pieces do fit together, eureka truly does happen in a flash. Kounios and Beeman have shown that, just before we experience Bühler's *Aha-Erlebnis*, general visual processing dims. Visual acuity (or sharpness) at the periphery of our field of vision is also dialled down, and we focus only on the insight – like a single character in the middle of the stage, picked out with a spotlight not a floodlight, preparing to give a soliloquy.

Whether you experience today's insights or insights generally all-at-once or gradually, followed by a sudden flash, you need to be prepared to do two things and do them fast.

1   To recognise that you are indeed having an insight. To recognise what that feels like – physically, emotionally, physiologically. What is the moment of giving birth to an insight like for you; what are the necessary and sufficient conditions in your mind-body nexus?
2   To capture the insight there and then, as it presents itself to you. That's why you need a pen and paper by the bed, a voice recorder

app on the home screen of your phone, and waterproof crayons in the shower. We'll come back to this very soon.

Three strands of evidence have convinced me that moments of insight – eureka moments – generate more than just a mental, brain-centred manifestation.

1   **Introspection**. When I have a breakthrough insight – like the insight that the way Tesco should talk about the quality of its products was to get their producers to become their storytellers (see *Narrative by Numbers*, pp. 62–66) – I get quite profound physical symptoms. Symptoms of conviction that I'm onto something, that the planets have aligned (that brilliant word for Scrabble, syzygy). I feel excitement, a slight breathlessness, and an overwhelming desire to stand up and share my breakthrough with others. In Chapter 4, I described the overall experience as "scalp tightening", the feeling I also get when my favourite musician plays the opening chords of my favourite song at a gig. Others have their own physical symptoms. What is important is that you can recognise, name, and identify your symptoms. That's another step on the road to being more insightful.

2   **Other people's experience**, including many of those I've interviewed for this book. An "*n*" (or sample) of one may have been good enough for Victorian psychologists, but when I started out on my journey to becoming more insightful half-a-dozen years ago, I wanted corroborating evidence. You'll find some in the interviews with the actors Peter Firth and Alexandra McKibbin (pp. 89–91), as well as in the summary of my conversation with the artistic director of the Royal College of Music, Stephen Johns (pp. 50–52).

3   **What psychology and neuroscience reveal**, as detailed in Chapters 3 and 4, and most particularly in the work of Kounios and Beeman's labs, which has made clear exactly what happens inside the brain at the instant a eureka moment happens.

My experience + other people's experience + what the science says. As management gurus are fond of saying, "One's a dot, two's a line, three is a trend." Or as Ian Fleming put into the mouth of his villain Auric Goldfinger: "Once is happenstance. Twice is coincidence. The third time it's enemy action." Quite so. Eureka moments do indeed have both metaphysical and physical consequences, helping to nail mind/body dualism once and for all.

HOW TO BE INSIGHTFUL STEP THREE: EUREKA

If you've got this far – and I truly hope you have, because this is where the rubber of the process underpinning the model really starts to hit the road – you'll be familiar with what happens next, in this third of four practice chapters. For those who want to have more insights; for those who yearn to generate profound and deep understanding of people, issues, and topics; for those who crave to make the process of insight generation less random and more certain . . . for all of you, my insight-seeking friends, we come to the moment of insight.

You've been curious during the Sweat phase. You've stepped away from the insight problem you're trying to solve, taking Timeout to give your subconscious mind the time and space it needs to juxtapose the stimuli you've absorbed, both acutely and chronically. And – all at once – your subconscious has put a candidate insight forward. Like a DVD or download of a movie sent to a member of the Academy of Motion Pictures, Arts, and Sciences around the turn of the year, it comes with a label attached marked "For your consideration". And before you can judge whether it's an Oscar-worthy insight, you need to recognise it for what it is (a candidate insight), capture it, and articulate it clearly.

First off, have a read of this short piece of stimulus in the following box. If you're doing this exercise in a group, use this as the basis for your discussion.

EUREKA

When you have an idea – when you combine existing information to create something new – the appearance of this new insight is often unexpected. To capitalise on the hard work you put in during the Sweat

---

phase and to reap the benefits of the Timeout phase, you need to be able to recognise when you're having a genuine insight.

And you need to be able to distinguish an insight, innovation, or new idea from a casual observation that just pops into your head. Once you master these abilities, you'll invest your energies in exploding and expanding something worthwhile. And not chasing rainbows. Knowing when to leap out of the bath and when to add a little more hot water is critical.

Next, you can use these questions to frame your thoughts and discussions about enlightenment:

- How do you know when you're having a eureka moment?
- What feelings do you experience when you have an idea?
- What emotions do you feel when you crack an insight problem?
- Do you have a physical as well as an emotional reaction?
- Why are you so convinced that your insight solves the challenge?
- Can you distinguish genuine eureka moments from false positives? What criteria can you use to separate them out?
- What is the connection between the strength of conviction you feel of an insight you think you've found and how powerful that insight is?

The checklist for eureka tools, techniques, and approaches is available for downloading at www.howtobeinsightful/eureka.com.

THE BEST TOOLS AND TECHNIQUES TO ACHIEVE ENLIGHTENMENT

As usual, the tools and techniques aren't listed in any particular order; they're not ranked in order of importance, with the exception of the first, which I would urge everyone to get under their belts before they do anything else, if they've not mastered it already. Otherwise, I'm sharing them as strategies that work for me and for many of those I've spoken to about insight. Pick and choose as if from a dim sum menu or sushi restaurant conveyor belt. Find the ones that work for you and share them with others. And if you find something new, adopt that and discard what you did before. Be ruthless in your pursuit of insights and don't be held back by tradition, precedent, or what colleagues or bosses think is the right way to do things.

Here's a selection of the optimal approaches for Eureka:

- Learn and articulate what insight feels like for *you*
- Invest in stationery fit for a strategist
- Locate recording devices wherever you might need them
- Keep an ideas journal
- Accept that what's apparently obvious may well be insightful
- Be as complete as you possibly can be
- Flick through your ideas journal(s)
- Distil your ideas
- Master the mindmap or spidergram
- Do other things that join dots and combine ideas
- Go to events
- Learn not to get too attached to your ideas

Learn and articulate what insight feels like for *you*: I put great store in everyone taking the time to learn and get to know what happens in and to their body at the moment of insight. Unless you've stopped to think about it, consciously, you're unlikely to know intuitively how your body reacts. Although we're a uniquely cognitive species, we're not – by and large – terribly metacognitive. As discussed in the text (and extended footnote) in Chapter 2, taking the time to stop and think about how we think is one of the very real benefits of the STEP Prism of Insight, the model, the training course, and now the book. By giving everyone the time to reflect on how they think, we can move up the competency ladder, at least as far as conscious competence.

Now that you know more about insight and insight problems and how we solve them (as distinct from analytical problems), monitor yourself over the coming weeks and months. Note down – perhaps in an

ideas journal (see later) – what happens to you physically and emotionally when you have a breakthrough insight. Learn what that feels like, think about what it feels like, and label it. Once you've started to think about it and subsequent insights come, write about the experience – again perhaps in your ideas journal – and label different elements and aspects of the experience. Do you blush? Do your palms go clammy? Do you feel slightly breathless? Are you with me in the scalp-tightening club? Do you laugh, perhaps not as uncontrollably as Jürgen Klopp or Joaquin Phoenix's *Joker*, but still? Once you've mapped your unique cluster of eureka symptoms, you'll know better what's happening next time it does and at each subsequent eureka moment.

One of the defining qualities of a genuine, breakthrough insight is the strength of conviction that the person who has created the insight feels for it. It drives them to capture it and share it and try to explain it as completely as they can. It's often the case that, to begin with, we can't articulate precisely what the insight is and what it means – the critical "So what? Now what?" of insightful problem-solving. But if your subconscious has done a decent job and combined old stuff with other old stuff and produced a profound and deep understanding that is genuinely new and insightful, that brings with it a powerfully strong sense of conviction that it answers a problem in an innovative way. And that can be infectious. Just sanity check it quickly to make sure it isn't a statement of the bleeding obvious, an idea or insight that others have already had, or an obvious mistake. We'll come to techniques to help with this process in the next chapter on the Prove stage of the model.

Invest in stationery fit for a strategist: The simple, analogue tools of the trade for an insight hunter include big paper – a block of A3 paper, a flipchart of A2 or A1, or a continuous roll for a kids' easel (just a few pounds, dollars, or euros from any IKEA); a planner's pen with four colours (Bic makes my favourite, with clickably interchangeable red/blue/black/green Biros in one chunky barrel); Blu Tack, White Tack, or frankly Any Colour Tack to enable you to attach your big paper productions on walls or windows, and then move them around; and Post-it notes of different sizes, shapes, and colours – you'll soon find your favourites. Oh, and an ideas journal.

Locate recording devices wherever you might need them: I'm not – necessarily – suggesting you need to invest significant resources in high-tech recording or memorial devices, all over your home and your office. But because you need to be ready for insights to appear at any time of the day or night – during the working week, at the weekend, or when you're on holiday or sabbatical – channel your inner girl guide or boy scout and Be Prepared. A pad and pen by the bed is particularly important. Many's the idea I've had at 4.46am and, rather than switch on the light (or fire up the Notes app on my phone and likely wake my wife), I've scribbled my moment of inspiration on that pad in the dark. The act of memorialising what's come to you while it's fresh is important – be that in a dream like Kekulé and his autophagic snake, when nodding off, or when lying awake. Insights don't hang around for long or respect your bleary-eyed intentions, however good they may be. Thinking "that's good, I'll write it down tomorrow morning" will almost certainly consign it to the dustbin of history.

If your smartphone doesn't come pre-loaded with a notes app, find one and download it – including Evernote, if that multi-platform ecosystem works for you. Very often on a train, a bus, or a plane, on a run or a walk, ideas will pop into your head. And a pad and paper aren't so handy in any of those environments.

We've considered at length how often ideas present themselves when we're in water – the bath or the shower, the power of total immersion, cooling (or heating) the body, changing your resting homoeostatic state. If you're a frequent aquatic insight monger – and you'll know what sort you are once you've learned and articulated what insight feels like for you – why not invest in a set of waterproof, non-permanent pens or crayons?[7] Then, when insights come to you in the middle of the shower, you can write your *bons mots* straightaway without having to get out, towel yourself dry, and go and look for your phone or the pad by your bed . . . by which time, the insight will have expired as quickly as it came in to being. Just make sure you also invest in sponges, scrubby pads, and cleaning sprays or creams that remove your watery scribblings quickly and easily.

"Hey, Siri (Google, Alexa, Cortana) – take a note" and then dictating a response to your virtual assistant can also work well. As can "Hey,

Siri – send a text (or email) to [my mobile number/my email address]". Much better to capture the inspiration that's come to you and have people look at you slightly strangely than to lose what might be a cracking insight. As voice becomes more and more prevalent, those bemused and quizzical looks from those around us will become less common.

Keep an ideas journal: Because insight is a capricious, unpredictable sprite that doesn't always reveal itself fully articulated, you need to be prepared to capture nuggets and snippets that might be insights or might be the building blocks of insight. And you need to be prepared to do this whenever they occur to you. Start an ideas journal or scrapbook, in which you write down ideas or quotes or facts or campaigns or sketches or snatches of music or charts or or or.... It doesn't matter what you write down in your ideas journal. It doesn't matter what order the ideas area written down. There doesn't need to be any logic to it. Think of it as a place where you can set down useful stimuli for the insight problems you're working on today as well as those you might not even be briefed on for another three years.

For some people, a physical book is the perfect artefact for an ideas journal. For others, it's a folder and set of files on their computer desktop, where they can keep jottings, virtual Post-it notes, photos, links, presentations, sound and video files – all kinds of stimuli. For others yet, an application like Evernote – which allows the magpie in you to stash away the ideas silver that you steal, and do so across devices – or writers' favourite, Scrivener, work better than a book or folder.

What matters is that you choose and decide upon a means of capturing ideas or building blocks of ideas. Whether it's a book, Microsoft Word, Evernote, or Scrivener doesn't matter. You just need to find the means of recording that makes it easy for you to capture what you need to capture. Today's software is intuitive and comes without manuals or tutorials. But Evernote and Scrivener have their idiosyncrasies, so if you choose to go for either of them – or other applications – invest time in mastering at least the basic functionality. The last thing you want, in the fleeting world of insights, is for form to interfere with function. If the medium holds up recording of the message, abandon the shiny new tool and go back to something simpler and easier to use like pen and paper.

Some find that a simple book doesn't feel special enough, so they invest more in a book than a simple, spiral-bound, reporter's notebook. Depending on your budget, you might choose a Black & Red, a Moleskine, or even a Smythson. A special book – cheap, expensive, or deluxe – is what counts. Somewhere that only admits entry to insights, proto-insights, or nuggets of stimulus that might one day for the building blocks of insights; a physical manifestation of the stimulus you encounter.

Accept that what's apparently obvious may well be insightful: Those charged with mining for insights often say that they nearly reject insights that feel like they're too obvious. The genius of an insight that truly resonates – one that really does deliver a profound and deep understanding of an issue – is that it can often feel like a statement of the bleeding obvious, as we've already considered. Easy to understand, easy to explain but – in Pope's memorable phrase from Chapter 1 – "What oft was thought, but ne'er so well express'd". Tolerate the apparently obvious until such time as you've found that's what it is. Because it may well be an insight, and you don't want to dismiss one of those rare beasts too early.

Be as complete as you possibly can be: However and wherever you're seeking to capture the thoughts and insights that occur to you, try to capture them as completely as they've occurred to you. The more you can get down in the moment just after enlightenment, the more likely it is you'll capture what matters and the easier it will be for you either to reject them as wrong or else expand on them, embellish them, and explain them to the others you need to convince.

Flick through your ideas journal(s): There's no point in your keeping an ideas journal, physical or digital, if you don't go back to it and flick through it and remind yourself of the interesting stimulus you've captured. You may not remember why you were interested in or captivated by the stimulus as the very act of capturing may have subcontracted some part of the memory to the act of so doing. But if you flick through your ideas journals from time to time, you may trigger fresh associations between this and that recorded stimulus and cascade a new process of insight generation, giving your subconscious mind the opportunity to build new links. Over time, you may build up a small library of ideas journals. You may choose to have some that are about specific areas of your life (personal, clients, your own business) or put everything in one place.

Equally, if you go digital and use folders, Evernote, Scrivener, or the next clever app that's developed, your archive may quickly become sizeable. Electronic archives have the advantage of allowing you to add tags which are searchable, so if particular stimuli are about specific people, topics, or companies, you can access them all at the same time if you've gone to the trouble of tagging them as you record them. And even if you're logging your entries manually in books, systems of colour-coding and tagging with client/topic names can make future access and retrieval more straightforward when you flick back through them.

However you magpie potentially relevant stuff, to make it genuinely useful eureka fodder, be sure to go back to it. Not just acutely, but also chronically, over time. Dip into your ideas journal randomly when you're looking for inspiration. Use a random number generator – www.random.org is as good as any and rather more mathematically correct and pure than many. Set the upper limit as the number of pages in your journal(s). Then click "Generate" and go to that page. Capriciously obeying the virtual dice, you'll be summoning the spirit of Luke Reinhart's *Dice Man* and going with the will of the Cosmos (man). Who knows what you'll find and what your random access of management information will throw up? It's unlikely to be nothing, and it might just be something that leads you to an insight. If you've built up a library of journals over the years, you'll first need to decide – at random – which volume to access.

Distil your ideas: Once you've begun a practice of capturing snippets and nuggets in a journal, take the time to revisit them with purpose. Particularly more fully fledged ideas that join together multiple stimuli into what may be approaching a full-blown insight, or what may be a profound and deep understanding that you just haven't noticed yet. Reassemble your thoughts, taking a bit from over here and a bit from over there, on a new sheet of paper (Word file or PowerPoint slide). Use different language and synonyms to express the same ideas or constellations of ideas in new ways. The very act of rewriting them (or typing – or playing, if they're musical notes and phrases) may forge or reveal links and relationships you hadn't spotted before and in that way make manifest the insight you've been looking for.

Master the mindmap or spidergram: I remember well my primary (elementary) school art teacher encouraging freedom of expression in artistic experimentation by "taking your pencil for a walk". She wanted us, her young charges, to be unconstrained by the boundaries and restrictions we brought with us to the art room. The spirit of this approach I took with me when I started to plan answers to essays in secondary school and throughout all stages of university, up to and including writing academic papers for peer-reviewed journals.[8] And it's something I've held onto ever since, in more than 30 years of work.

When you're looking to develop a profound and deep understanding of a subject area – when you've filled the hopper of your curiosity and taken Timeout from consciously trying to crack the insight problem – get some big paper and whatever else you need from your strategist's stationery kit and start to map out your understanding of the issue free from the constraints of lined paper or a page of Microsoft Word.

Put down the most important elements of concepts, perhaps in capitals letters on Post-it notes. Move them around, until they make a constellation around the central concept or "exam" question. Join them with lines and arrows, of association or causation, and annotate them. On one level, you're imposing order and structure on the component parts of your potential insight in much the same way as the human mind does. In so far, of course, as we understand it.

The spidergram or mindmap is an incredibly powerful tool to help you shuffle and reorder elements of the topic you're considering and attempting to understand in greater depth. The freeform, rule-free, unbound nature of this form of expression encourages more conscious association-making than other, more linear forms of idea alignment like Word or PowerPoint or even its travel-sickness-inducing cousin, Prezi. And while mindmapping or spidergramming the issue or topic you're trying to unlock won't guarantee you'll liberate a hidden insight while you're doing it, it will get you to look at the component parts in new and interesting ways, from new perspectives, points of view, and vantage points. And that can be incredibly helpful on the journey towards insight.

As I was writing and refining this chapter, I went to my favourite annual stimulus event – a tremendous exercise in curiosity or Sweat. The event in question is the annual Brighton Summit, run by the Brighton Chamber of Commerce in Sussex, Southern England.[9] Perhaps improbably, this regional trade event attracts national (and international) quality speakers, and in the last three years these have included the writer Misha Glenny (*McMafia*), the economist Guy Standing who coined the term "the precariat", and the campaigner Gina Miller. The success of the event is down to the Chamber's impressive and quietly magnetic director, Sarah Springford, and her team.

At the 2019 event, I attended a workshop run by the Brighton Comedy Course. Founder Louise Stevenson showed us how to use the spidergram as the stepping-stone to building stand-up comedy material. First, write a down a list of topics or issues that you want to rant or rail against. Then choose the one that irritates you most. Summarise that in a couple of words in the middle of the page. Draw satellite arms out from the focus of your ire and list out reasons why the topic irritates you. Some will naturally join – with complete or perhaps dotted lines – to others. Unexpected stimuli will start to connect together when you commit them to paper, even in scribbles. Then, use the completed spidergram as your guide for writing comedy material.

The same is true for insights, and I strongly recommend using Louise's twist on the spidergram when you're getting towards an insight – perhaps if you have an inkling but no eureka – as a means of helping to articulate it. It's like writing out an elevator pitch using data and statistics and then reading it out. You can find and understand things you didn't realise before you articulated a proposition, and this is an invaluable technique for those looking to crack insight problems.

Do other things that join dots and combine ideas: Cryptic crosswords are great diversionary tactics for Timeout. But they're also a brilliant way of training your subconscious mind to be more recombinatorial, which is an integral part of the art of insight. The same can be said for taking part in an improvisational comedy class, writing jokes, and even just watching or listening to comedy. All of these enable you to see ideas and elements come together which are ultimately subverted by twists and unexpected punchlines, the core of humour. Suggest radically different genres of writing each month if you belong to a book club. Even doing jigsaw puzzles can help. So, too, can DJing and mixing radically different genres that happen to share a common rhythm or beat. Likewise culinary mash-ups, fusion cooking from different cultures.

Every one of these experiments might produce results that are cacophonous or disgusting – just like the candidate insights your sub-conscious may or may not let through to your conscious mind. But by playing like this and doing other things that join the dots – this all gets you thinking in a recombinatorial fashion, and insight hunters can't have too much of that.

Go to events: I have a novelist friend, Brigid Coady, who introduced me to the work of *Story* author Robert McKee and then convinced me to go to his three-day Story training course. On the third day, McKee spends 11 hours going through *Casablanca*, beat by scene by sequence by act. Without doubt the finest training course either of us has been on, and brilliant, Sweat-type stimulus and input. Except that Brigid doesn't use McKee's Story course to satisfy her curiosity. At least not any more.

At time of writing, she's been on the same course three times. The same material delivered by the same no-nonsense, slightly cantankerous, genius story doctor. Brigid goes on McKee's course not for the benefit of Sweat or indeed Timeout. She goes on it for Eureka reasons. Being in his presence, talking about story and story structure, helps her to unblock wherever she might be in her novel-writing journey and to have the insights she needs to make her characters work and interact and inhabit a more real world. She uses his course in particular to give her subconscious mind a framework with which she can make sense of the stimuli she's already absorbed, created, and written about. And she's not alone.

That's why I'd encourage anyone to use events not just as input, but also as metacognitive happenings that can help you get closer to eureka, whether they're industry conferences, talks, or training sessions. I use the Brighton Summit in this, among other ways.

Learn not to get too attached to your ideas: Although insights are really special and can truly be the superpower that unlocks innovation, non-insights aren't all that helpful. And the difference in the expression of a genuine, breakthrough insight and something that is either a statement of the bleeding obvious – or an idea so old and unoriginal that literally everyone else has already had it and dismissed it before it occurred to you – is very small. As the character David St Hubbins says in Rob Reiner's 1984 rockumentary *This Is Spinal Tap*: "It's such a fine line between stupid and clever". And if your insight turns out to be a non-insight – even if the truth is pointed out to you in the nicest possible way – be prepared to drop it like a hot potato, move on, and look for new insights.

We leave the ideation phase for now with a nod to how Nike founder Phil Knight felt when he absolutely categorically realised that he was going to create his business and why, at the end of a particularly gruelling run. In the preface to his book *Shoe Dog* (2016), p. 4, he says,

> *I was suddenly smiling. Almost laughing. Drenched in sweat, moving as gracefully and effortlessly as I ever had, I saw my Crazy Idea shining up ahead, and it didn't look all that crazy. It didn't even look like an idea. It looked like a place. It looked like a person, or some life force that existed long before I did, separate from me but also part of me. Waiting for me but also hiding from me.*

INTERVIEW: RICARD SAPIRO, AGÊNCIA DE BRANDING, SÃO PAULO

Insightful interview 7 of 8

NAME	Ricardo Sapiro
ORGANISATION	Touch – Agência de Branding
ROLE	Proprietário

Ricardo Sapiro has dedicated his career to brand marketing. Training with Johnson & Johnson before moving on to Wyeth Whitehall, both roles in Brazil, he made his reputation during a 15-year tenure at Unilever. With local, regional, and global brand marketing roles, he ran the business in Brazil and across Latin America, as well as spending four years in London running Sunsilk. In 2010, Ricardo set up Touch Branding, a São Paolo–based agency dedicated to developing and articulating brand positioning. Insights – what he likes to call human truths – are his currency.

"It's not fashionable to say this, but . . ." is one of Sapiro's favourite ways to start a sentence. He goes on, "Insights about products don't come from an in-depth knowledge of a product or a category. They don't come from analysis of how consumers use your products, about shopper behaviour. Insights – genuine, transformative insights – come from understanding people as people, not as shoppers or consumers. Marketing people need to be able to put themselves into the shoes – into the lives – of those who buy their products."

For Sapiro, insights emerge when we shine a light on the hidden tensions of human existence, tensions which brands can adopt to build relevant and empathetic propositions. They're not developed by 20 people playing games in a room for two days with unlimited Post-its, familiar as that approach is to anyone who's worked in marketing since 1985. Rather, they're created by small, intimate, informed teams made up of people who are characterised by keen curiosity and – a signature Sapiro word – repertoire, characteristics that modern business fails to value at its peril.

"Many leaders don't see the point of mining for insights. Leadership often thinks that insight and growth are opposing forces, and there's profound prejudice against harnessing insight and business as parallel routes to the same end: to growth. That's the most significant barrier we need to overcome to help leaders root product propositions in human truths. Once you allow that, it's amazing to see how using insights can energise and transform a business."

Unusually for a consultant, Sapiro has seen at first hand the positive business benefits of embracing genuine insights: he was a pivotal part of the team that developed "Dirt Is Good" for Unilever's laundry category in the mid-2000s, a process led by Unilever's current global head of marketing, Aline Santos. Inside Unilever, he helped to usher insight-led leadership from a peripheral "nice to have" to a central principle of purpose-led marketing, working in the company that bought the world Dove's Campaign for Real Beauty and the corporate brand's Sustainable Living Plan.

As to the critical distinction between instinct (a gut reaction) and insight, for Sapiro the magic comes from repertoire. Those who cultivate a rich repertoire borne of curiosity become much better at judging whether ideas are genuine insights – higher human truths – or not. Without an open-minded, always-hungry repertoire, unperceptive folk can think they're having insights every few seconds, when in fact they're just making casual and often banal observations.

Repertoire is less about experience and more about an open, positive attitude of mind. "Too many experienced people are incredibly narrow-minded," says Sapiro. "Ten thousand hours can get in the way. In fact, experience can lead you to dismiss too quickly those very ideas which could be developed into insights. And if you become immersed in product or category or business specifics, you close yourself down to the potential that looking up enables. Repertoire is about breadth over depth."

Not all brands are lucky enough to have human-truth-grade insights as the foundation of their storytelling. In beauty, only Dove has the insight that most women don't think they're beautiful (whence the Campaign for Real Beauty); in laundry, only Persil/Skip/OMO has "Dirt Is Good" (enabling the brand to engage parents and families in the very real, learning benefits of outdoor play); in running shoes and athletic gear, only Nike has Just Do It (allowing the brand to celebrate the athlete in all of us). In terms of communication, these brands are very definitely not all about face cream, washing powder, and sneakers. Insights come first, products second.

"Dirt Is Good" illustrates well Sapiro's compulsion for repertoire. He recalls that some of those in the team charged with creating a new platform found the proposition very difficult to grasp. Specifically, those who struggled were people without children, but also men – including fathers – who were not actively involved in the day-to-day job of bringing up young kids.

For decades, the category had been focused on consumer washing habits, foam, enzymes, and whiter-than-whiteness. The entire medium of soap opera was developed in the 1920s as an advertising vehicle for Procter & Gamble, after all. But the disruptive manifesto cry that "Dirt Is Good" has nothing to do with category norms or direct product benefits. It is an emotive appeal for parents to encourage an over-protected, indoors-only, video-game-sated generation to get out into the fields and woods and roll about in the grass and make dens. Of course parents can depend on modern-day laundry products to get their clothes clean again. But they can put their energy into focusing on enabling their kids to learn and grow through outdoor play rather than worry about what muddy trousers might say about them. Not only that, but "Dirt Is Good" also allowed Unilever to overtake P&G in global sales for the first time in decades. The idea made sense to consumers, and they voted with their wallets.

Sapiro is ambivalent at best about the modern marketing world's obsession with data, often at the expense of insight. But his prescription of curiosity, repertoire, and universal human truths – wrapped up in his signature Latin American passion, emotion, and empathy – have served him well in a career on both sides of the client/agency divide. It's the stuff of the STEP Prism of Insight, from Sweat to Prove.

NOTES

1 Since Tim Cook replaced Steve Jobs as Apple CEO in 2011, Apple's share price has quadrupled (see this report in *The Guardian* http://bit.ly/32amS4h). But it was Jobs' oversight and development of the iMac, iPhone, and iPad – not to mention iTunes (which became Apple Music) and Apple TV – that set the company up for long-term success. The first $1bn company was US Steel in 1901. The benefits of scale, inflation, and globalisation are reflected in the fact that US Steel took 117 years to become the world's first billion dollar business, while it only took Apple 42 years to amass market capitalisation 1,000 times as big.

2 Matt Ridley (July 2010). When ideas have sex, TEDGlobal2010 http://bit.ly/3432lk8

3 When I was a baby coder back in the early 1980s – with my Sinclair ZX81 and then Spectrum attached to a tiny old black-and-white TV – running out of memory was a constant cause of anxiety. I remember once trying to write a machine code version of the arcade classic Pacman in just one kilobyte of memory on the ZX81, but there wasn't enough space to build a maze and have ghosts follow the chomping-mouthed hero without drifting through the walls of the maze. Then, for my 15th birthday, I was given a 16K RAM pack to push onto the back of my computer. At last! My memory (or computer's memory) had increased 16-fold. Coding Pacman after that was a walk in the park, though my code became flabby and repetitive. And I became carless, jogging the ZX81 too hard in coders' frustration before I'd saved the definitive version of the game onto cassette

tape. The RAM pack fell off, and the code was lost. *You tell kids that these days and they won't believe you.* And fortunately, this is not a concern for the user of the human brain, with its effectively limitless capacity.

4 See *Narrative by Numbers* Chapter 3, and pages 55–58 in particular.

5 For 30,000 spurious correlations using publicly available data sets, see www.spuriouscorrelations.com and www.tylervigen.com

6 Some writers, commentators, and thinkers in this area use a sexual analogy for the moment of insight, equating the eureka experience with orgasm. I think this is an understandable but ultimately lazy and mistaken analogy. I appreciate that orgasm is a profoundly personal and individual experience which some find very easy and others find next to impossible; that the circumstances, antecedents, and environments which some require for orgasm would lead to a complete lack of desire in others. But the real reason I think that the analogy sucks is that, once an individual and their partner(s) discover what they need to attain sexual nirvana – which can indeed be a moment of insight – the stimuli required to produce the response are predictable, even if there's a repertoire of stimuli that can achieve the same end. That makes sex much more like an analytical than an insight problem.

7 There are lots of different suppliers of waterproof crayons, but I like those from Kidly – see http://bit.ly/2Jd6ysu. Usually these are products aimed at children and not strategists, planners, and others with solving insight problems, which says something telling to me about both problem-solving and the freer rein we give to children for expression of their more elastic thinking. Something we tend to squash once people have "grown up".

8 For example: S.K.Z. Knowles & T. Duka (2004). Does Alcohol Affect Memory for Emotional and Non-Emotional Experiences in Different Ways? *Behavioural Pharmacology*, 15 (2), 111–121 http://bit.ly/31cox8G. I followed a similar – though more involved – process for my doctoral thesis, The effects of alcohol on memory for emotionally significant events https://ethos.bl.uk/OrderDetails.do?uin=uk.bl.ethos.407733

9 See www.brightonsummit.com

8

PROVE – THE TESTING PHASE

"To doubt everything and to believe everything are two equally conve-nient solutions; each saves us from thinking . . . It is by logic that we prove, but by intuition that we discover."

Henri Poincaré, *The Foundations of Science: Science and Hypothesis*

THE PROOF IS IN THE PUDDING

Proof is in the air – fluttering in the Zeitgeist – but it's not always getting a decent press.

In 2016, the *Oxford English Dictionary* declared its "word" of the year to be "post-truth". Not to be outdone, rival dictionary publisher Collins announced 2017's winner to be "fake news", closely followed by "echo chamber". Notwithstanding that dictionaries on either side of Hadrian's Wall seem to be mistaking phrases for words, evidence, facts, and proof are having a bit of a rough ride in the era of Trump and Brexit. During the EU referendum campaign in the UK in 2016, pro-Leave supporter Michael Gove famously scoffed in a TV interview, "We've had enough of experts – with their acronyms". And while I have sympathy for his distaste for jargon-rich acronyms, the scourge of clear communication, I'm definitely not with Govey for his scathing attack on expertise. As I argued in *Narrative by Numbers* (pp. 22–23 and Chapter 4), I believe that

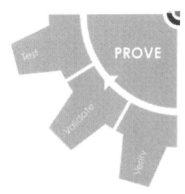

Figure 8.1 Prove quadrant of the STEP Prism of Insight

the data that surrounds every organisation and individual today provides an opportunity for more powerful and persuasive storytelling than ever before – provided that data is used in the right way. That means sparingly, as the rational support to an emotional story, and in that all-too-rare dialect of Human.

Proof matters because, when laid out clearly and simply, fairly and accurately, it is evidence that can help our rational System 2 thinking to justify and confirm the decisions that our emotional System 1 thinking has accepted. Equally, it can help System 2 reject hunches or ideas that System 1 galloped towards because they seemed like a good idea at first, second, and thirty-fourth glance. When we take on more and more stimuli, chronically and acutely, and we give our subconscious mind free reign to arrange it and make connections between it, we are hypothesis testing. In the model of null hypothesis significance testing laid out by Karl Popper, we hold that null hypothesis – that there's been no change in the world – until and unless we find evidence to the contrary. Hypotheses are there to be disproved by counterfactual data. For Popper, falsifiability was the cornerstone of scientific knowledge, and any hypothesis that is incapable of being falsified just isn't science.

With insight problems – so different in genesis and in solution from analytical problems – once the magic has occurred and a plausible, exciting insight has manifested itself in your conscious mind, you need to test it and share it early to see whether it is genuinely as insightful as we feel it to be. And that is a process of hypothesis testing – looking for nay-saying evidence just as much as we look for supportive evidence. Indeed, counterfactuals should demand more of our attention and effort than my-side evidence. This is because hypothesis testing is very different from hypothesis proving, which is a fancy-pants way of saying "cooking the books". As the mathematician Poincaré said, "It is by logic that we prove, but by intuition that we discover", and verification of intuition is what the fourth step of the STEP Prism of Insight is all about.

If we have the breakthrough insight that all swans are white – not all that powerful an insight in these days of global knowledge, the internet, and international travel, I'll grant you, but bear with me . . . If that is our insight, and we go to places where we know white swans live – game reserves, rivers, lakes, countries – we will find more and more proof that our hunch is right. Some member of the awkward squad might say, "Yeah, but have you been to New Zealand? They've got loads of black swans." The challenge threatens to make our insight crumble, and we often feel protective of our insights because of the power we know they have to drive us forward and help us to innovate.

But rather than turn your back on evidence that threatens to make your insight unravel, I say embrace it. Go looking for evidence that exposes the flimsiness of your insight, however strong or right or breakthrough it might feel to you. Expose your insights early, before you've invested too much time and energy in chasing a false prophet. Think how foolish you'd feel, having pioneered your unique new milking stool, with its three days of sanding and eight layers of varnish, if one of your competitors or critics shouts from the back of the launch press conference, "Nice stool, but it's only got two legs. It's going to fall over. This is useless!"

When an insight occurs or appears to you, you need to capture and articulate it quickly and accurately, elegantly expressing its component parts and the key data points that you've successfully recombined to make something you believe to be genuinely new. We've already touched on a wide variety of tools and techniques that can help you do just that in Chapter 7, from an ideas journal to a pen and paper by the bed, Ever-note to waterproof crayons for the shower or bath. When you're dry or fully awake, do some more work on refining and expressing your insight, marshalling your supportive evidence, and setting out your case. As we've seen, spidergramming and mindmapping – analogue or digital[1] – can help here. So, too, can writing out your insight a few times, editing it, and making it more succinct but still complete. And then – once you're happy that your expression of it does it justice – you need to share it with others quickly, before you invest too much time in it and you become too invested in it because it's taken you so long. It came to you in an instant, so you don't need to spend six months writing it up.

ON THE POWER OF CO-CREATION

I don't like cricket, uh, oh no. I love it, uh, oh yeah. On Sunday afternoons and evenings between April and September each year, I play low-quality cricket with a group of 40- and 50-something friends in Sussex in the South of England. We go by the name of the Gentlemen of Lewes. Now cricket is a fascinating game, a game of mental robustness just as much as technique, for batsmen, bowlers, and fielders under a steepling catch in the outfield.

A common view of cricket is that it's not a team game at all. Yes, there are two teams of 11 players who have a common goal of representing the city, county, or country, but cricket teams are really groups of 11 individuals all out to do what they do best. In past-our-prime, middle-aged cricket, this sometimes appears to be particularly true. A promising school or club career put on ice when work or family took priority can be rekindled in later life, but before a good eye or excellent hand-eye coordination has completely disappeared. Someone who may have been slightly better than average aged 15–25 can appear to be a titan of the game from 40 onwards. Often, a figure like this – let's call him Craig – can take on superhuman status in a team, and a team game can then appear to depend unduly on just a handful of players, the rest being just ornamental padding.

The same can be true of the professional game. Australia's disgraced former captain, Steve Smith, returned from a 12-month ban – for allowing his charges to sandpaper the ball while fielding and bowling – to score an eye-watering 774 runs in just seven innings in the 2019 Ashes battle with England; England just couldn't get him out. India's skipper Virat Kohli is known to do the same – dominate and apparently win series single-handedly. The same is true of bowlers in cricket, as well as the best pitchers and batters in baseball. Individual trials masquerading as team sports.

But while the Craigs and Steves of this world may appear to be individuals just pretending to be part of the team, in fact the reverse is true. With no other players to bat with, with no fielders to catch or stump or run out opposition batsmen, there is no platform for a stand-out player of cricket, baseball, or any other team game. While there may be significant overlaps in the psychology of batting in these sports with the psychology of golf – and particularly the phenomenon of the yips, when nerves trump ability; when excitement morphs into anxiety – cricket and baseball are very much team sports. And in just the same way, so is testing the veracity, integrity, and insightfulness of insights.

In agency life – particularly in medium-sized and larger agencies –often several other people do the same job as you do, at a similar level, with similar years and types of experience, just working on different accounts. In medium and large businesses, the same is true. Members of a peer group – of accountants, account managers, insight directors, whatever – can often see other members of the same group as competitors. For the higher you go in most organisations, the fewer, senior roles there are. Promotion to even more senior roles is secured by a combination of opportunity and expansion in the business, time served, and capability. In increasing numbers of roles in a wide variety of sectors and disciplines, the ability to have, express, and make use of insightful problem-solving is a critical aspect of capability. And where it's not, it certainly should be, because as the subtitle of this book says, insight truly is the superpower that drives innovation. From innovation comes growth and from growth comes success.

By their very nature, peers are a perfect audience to judge whether your insight is original, persuasive, and powerful; whether it is – in fact – an insight at all, whether a competitor has been saying this for years, or whether it's just a statement of the bleeding obvious. But because they are also competitors for the next rung on the ladder, peers can be perceived to be competitors determined to knock back your ideas at the earliest possible moment. As the judge sings – screams – in the song *The Trial* in Pink Floyd's 1982 concept album *The Wall*. Or worse yet, they might dismiss your insight, tell you you're barking up the wrong tree, then steal it, repurpose it, and present it to your joint boss as all their hard work. If they earn a promotion off the back of it, you'd feel foolish for sharing it with them and believing their quick dismissal of it, and your boss won't believe you if you bleat.

Corporate dynamics notwithstanding, I'd encourage anyone who has an insight to share it with their peers as soon as they're confident they're onto something insightful and as soon as they've articulated it clearly enough to allow others to judge it – and no later. They, potentially, are among the best judges of whether you have an insight and likely to pressure-test your idea more honestly and quickly than others. In addition, asking for quick-and-dirty feedback from peers shows a vulnerability and openness that tends to be reciprocated, not seized upon as weakness and an opportunity to get one over on you. What's more, this approach will help your peers help you build on and co-create your insight to make it more powerful yet – or else consign it more quickly to the scrapheap. And you'll also find them coming to you to road-test their ideas, insights, and innovations more often. Before you know it, you'll have set up an informal skunkworks, and joint ventures will be springing up all over. You'll be replicating the spirit and the impact of the MRC Cognition and Brain Sciences Unit at Cambridge we met earlier, with their morning coffee and afternoon tea clubs.

Peers are good sounding boards, but so too are colleagues who know relatively little about what you do. When running data storytelling training, an early exercise I get delegates to complete is writing an elevator/barbecue/cocktail party pitch, weaving in relevant data and statistics they've brought with them to the workshop. After barely 15 minutes' writing, I get everyone to read out their pitches to the rest of the room, both asking for peer review – "Did that data-driven story work for you or not?" – and providing real-time feedback from my role as a professional data storyteller. I then encourage delegates to find a buddy in their business – not necessarily in a peer role – with whom they can share the opening to a pitch or presentation, asking for a critique, and offering the same ad hoc service in return on an open door basis. This can be the difference between winning a pitch and coming that irritating – and perennial – "close second".

Peers and colleagues can be joined by clients and commercial partners. If you're developing a project or a campaign together and you think you've had an insight that can unlock the challenge you're facing together and on their behalf, again share it early. There's also a great benefit to road-testing insights with friends from completely different careers – teachers vetting insights from criminal barristers, designers assessing IT insights, blacksmiths evaluating insights from advertising executives. Adland used to encourage planners and creatives to use their grandmother as the ultimate naïve expert, though that is usually and quite rightly today deemed to be both sexist and ageist. "Simple enough that even my children can understand it" has some merit in it too (though that's ageist in the other direction). But the principle is clear.

Sharing insights late enough (so that they're properly developed) but early enough (so that you haven't overinvested in them and can still willingly give them up and start again) is the first step on the road to co-creation. I'm not encouraging you to give your ideas away to colleagues, peers, competitors, or clients – nor to grandparents, parents, or children. But I am urging you to harness the power of the hive mind of your friends, family, and colleagues to help you (i) see if you have an insight, (ii) pick holes in it if there are holes to be picked from which your overinvolvement in the stimulus has blindsided you, (iii) reject it if rejected it should be, but also (iv) build on your insight to develop it into something much more powerful. The vulnerability and honesty you exhibit – like a dog baring its neck to another; like a cat purring; like a human smiling – I warrant you'll be repaid many times over for sharing your insight early.

HOW TO BE INSIGHTFUL STEP FOUR: PROVE

Now we've reached the fourth and final step in the STEP Prism of Insight, you know clearly what's coming next. When you're developing real insights in the field, you'll have filled the hopper of your brain with stimuli, taken Timeout from the specific challenge at hand to allow your subconscious mind to take over, and experienced that scalp-tightening moment of insight. Now is the time to find out whether your insight is truly an insight. At this point, consider this short piece of stimulus to start thinking and talking about step four.

PROVE

When you've put in the hard yards, walked away from the inputs, and had a moment of insight, it's time to road-test your innovative idea. Ideas feel special – like creations; like our children – and we're often tempted to cosset and protect them. **Do precisely the opposite***.*

Expose them before your harshest critics, your strongest competitors in your organisation, and your broader circle. Encourage them to pull your ideas apart, to test them to the breaking point. If you're going to verify that you've got more than just a hunch – if you're going to validate your insight – it needs to go 15 rounds before you use it to inform a new strategy, campaign, or product.

To help stimulate the spirit of co-creation, consider these questions:

- How certain are you that this is a new idea and not a rehash of something old? Genius steals, but it needs to recombine too.
- How does your insight stand up to criticism and questioning?
- Is your insight really shining a new light on the challenge you're trying to address?
- How do those your peers in your organisation react to your idea? How about people you know who are at a different level or in a different role? What about clients? Commercial partners? And friends or family who know very little about what you do?
- Is your insight a statement of the obvious, a spurious correlation, or a false positive? Are you sure it's not just data or a re-presentation of data using a clever dashboard or data visualisation tool?

- What's distinctive and genuinely new about your insight? In what way has it recombined old stimulus with old stimulus to making something new?
- Does your insight provide the inspiration needed by your team?

You can download a checklist for co-creation at www.howtobeinsightful.com/prove

THE BEST TOOLS AND TECHNIQUES AROUND TO PRESSURE-TEST YOUR INSIGHT

As in the three previous chapters on Sweat, Timeout, and Eureka, for Prove the tools and techniques aren't listened in a particularly logical order. They're what I – and those I've spoken to – have found to be useful and helpful in determining whether we have insights, how our articulation of it should change, or whether we need to get curious (or take Timeout) anew.

- Google it
- Look yourself – and your insight – in the mirror
- Go shorter and shorter
- Call a tissue meeting
- Be like Einstein and "shave with" Occam's razor
- Hold a vox pop with naïve experts
- Represent your insight in a different medium
- Submit your insights to structured questioning
- Hold a balloon debate
- Enter the dragons' den
- Take the "last £100" test
- Offer your insight-testing capabilities to others
- Put yourself in the stocks

Google it: Before you take your insight very far into the world outside your creative imagination, search online with key terms to see if someone else has already had the same idea, is running the same campaign for a competitor product, or has launched a product, service, or app that does exactly what your apparently blinding flash of insight proposes. It's remarkable how often good ideas have already been had. After all, you're unlikely to be the only one who's taken on board the stimuli you've taken on board, or the only one whose subconscious mind has recombined these stimuli into something similarly new. If you can find evidence of the same (or at least a very similar) insight underpinning a campaign or a product, ask yourself – and others – if there's enough difference in your articulation of your insight to develop it in new and interesting ways.

It's also remarkable, in a world fast approaching eight billion living souls, how often good ideas *haven't* been had already. It's easy, when insightful thinking is part of your job description, to come to a brief, work on it with a blend of curiosity and Timeout, and reject insights too early. It's easy to dismiss insights because they feel too familiar or too right, such that someone must have had them before. It's easy – from Dr Google to peers, colleagues, and clients – to have your hunch confirmed that your insight is someone else's or isn't an insight at all. But the same, simple process of enquiry can quickly help you see that your insight really is differentiated. There's no shame to having had someone else's idea, just remarkably little commercial or competitive advantage.

Look yourself – and your insight – in the mirror: The emotional excitement – often with physical consequences – of having an insight can be overwhelming and cloud your judgement. When you've had what you believe to be an insight and have started to articulate it well enough to share with others who matter, present it to yourself behind closed doors. You really do want to make sure that your insight is something genuinely new and not just a clever reframing of an old stimulus that hasn't been successfully combined with other old stuff to make something new. And so far as you can – so far as you have conscious recollection of the origin of your stimulus – credit your sources of inspiration: "the tailfin of a 1958 Chevy Impala", "the opening riff of Prince's *Purple Rain*", "the chapter in Dan Pink's book *When* about time management". As Austin Kleon says in *Steal Like an Artist*, "The reason you want to copy your heroes is so that you might somehow get a glimpse into their minds . . . and that's what you really want – to internalise their way of looking at the world."[2] When

@herdmeister Mark Earls encourages us to do smarter marketing with the rallying cry "Copy, Copy, Copy" by using other people's ideas, he's keen to squash the stigma around self-conscious absorption and assimilation of others people's work because he knows "old + old = new". He's particularly keen to encourage the application of an idea from one sphere into another.

Go shorter and shorter: When you've written a version and an explanation of your insight, write a shorter one. Go from one page to one paragraph, from one paragraph to a single sentence, from a single sentence to a phrase, from a phrase to a word, from a word to a facial expression. Mark Twain, Oscar Wilde, and Winston Churchill would all have written you a shorter letter; they just didn't have the time. Make sure you make the time to write a shorter version of your insight – but don't take too long. Write it using none of the key words you used in the version you thought you were happy with. Translate it – yourself, if you speak another language; with Google Translate if you don't – into another language that you know a friend or colleague speaks. Road-test it with them.

Call a tissue meeting: Many creative advertising and design agencies like to share their creative ideas with their clients as part of the process of creation – or, more accurately, co-creation. These interactions are called tissue meetings because concepts are shared just loosely sketched out, often on cheap tissue paper.[3] They allow creatives to share their thinking without it appearing to be too set or definitive, as they would be if they were printed and shared on expensive Foamex boards. This allows agencies to incorporate client feedback into the creative process and course correct in real time if they've taken a wrong turning or failed to accommodate some key stimulus or data.

Tissue meetings with clients and colleagues when developing insights can be tremendously helpful. They can help flush out whether an insight is an insight, whether it's new or a rehash of something that's been tried or articulated before. And they can help to identify whether further work will turn a promising proto-insight into an insight or kill it off early.

When organisations are looking to find the most powerful and persuasive language to talk about themselves, they need to look inside themselves. Some companies – with no disrespect; they'd be the first to say the same thing – do really technical, arcane, and abstruse things, crucial as they are in the infrastructure of business-to-business supply. In my experience, the best way to extract distinctive phrasing, stories, and a clearly articulated purpose demands a sense of fun. It involves playing games – games like Enemy, Mission, and Product Truth (see pp. 209–213). Essentially, individuals from roles right across the spectrum of the organisation and all levels of hierarchy need to do the same thing again and again to tell their own stories. Like Eric Bartels, the founder of Netherlands-based consultancy Inner Why whom we met at the end of Chapter 5, I believe that the clearest expression of why organisations do what they do lives inside those who own, run, and work at the organisations.

Getting it out can be messy and complex – not least because most people aren't used to talking simply and straightforwardly about the enterprise they work in. They're hampered by the Curse of Knowledge: often they know so much about the organisation – what it does, how, and why – that they can find it challenging to put themselves in the minds of others who don't know what they know. But with some gentle coaxing, sugar-coated with not a little fun, the words and stories and core purpose come tumbling out. In order to capture and corral these tales, the role of an experienced consultant here is more like that of a midwife or a doula. Difficult birth pangs, unfamiliar pain, but ultimately resulting in the delivery of something beautiful and life affirming. Through experience, I know how to help those who will give birth to the words and story and purpose to just that.

Be like Einstein and "shave with" Occam's razor: Einstein said, "It can scarcely be denied that the supreme goal of all theory is to make the irreducible basic elements as simple and as few as possible without having to surrender the adequate representation of a single datum of experience."[4] This has been simplified to "Everything should be made as simple as possible, but not simpler". Einstein was channelling his inner William of Occam, a 14th-century philosopher-monk, whose "razor" states that "the simplest explanation is usually the correct one, all things being equal".

Apply Occam's razor to your insight. Shave away all unnecessary elements until you're left with an irreducible core. Does it still make sense? Have you embellished and embroidered it unnecessarily? Would it be even more convincing and compelling if you simplified it? Simplifiers – and I distinguish simplifiers from those who dumb down to the simplistic – are heaven to work with. They make the complex comprehensible and accelerate the path to progress and innovation. The more you can resolve complexity in your insight, the more likely you are to both land on something truly powerful – and, by the same token, show your insight to be rather less than you thought it was. The "Go shorter and shorter" technique is classic Occam razoring.

Hold a vox pop with naïve experts: Take your insight on the road, onto the pavements, into part of your life that has nothing to do with the organisation in which you work. If you're a teabag technologist, talk to members of your five-a-side team. Take a smartphone with you, and record a series of vox pop interviews with a random selection of people who know little or nothing about the challenge you're seeking to understand with insight. Present your insight to them – simply, succinctly, clearly – and see how they react. Do they understand it? Does it make them have their own moments of *Aha-Erlebnis*? Or do they look more confused than when you started talking to them, cartoon bluebirds circling round their temples?

Represent your insight in a different medium: Most insights are expressed as statements. But can you express your insight in a different medium? Does it lend itself to a mood board, that stock-in-trade of market researchers, with images and words ripped out from magazines and assembled as a collage on a flipchart or big piece of cardboard? Could you make a short film, scripted and dramatic or documentary cut-and-shut from content online, that would express the idea you're trying to convey? In Plasticine or LEGO? Crossing into different and multiple sensory modalities – verbal, visual, auditory – can help your insight mean more to more people. Equally, if your insight isn't insightful, you can soon tell if that's the case when you start to represent your insight in different media. And don't waste too much time and energy creating a transmedia representation of your insight. Summon the spirit of the tissue meeting to make something rough and ready but well-enough put together such that it facilitates (and doesn't actively hamper) understanding.

Submit your insights to structured questioning: If insight generation is an important part of your role – and for many people, being insightful is becoming increasingly important – develop a set of common, critical questions in the form of a discussion guide to pressure-test your insight. Have a colleague or friend not directly involved in the project ask the questions of you, the holder and creator of the insight. Record your session on a voice memo or video app. Listen back to how you answer the questions, with what degree of confidence and competence. Do you believe yourself? Seeing yourself defend and explain the indefensibly inexplicable can be a chastening process.

Hold a balloon debate: If more than one of your team – or more than one team – has been set the same insight problem, set a deadline by when you need to share first thoughts. When that deadline has passed, bring together all those involved – in sourcing and analyzing stimulus, in articulating the insights arising from the process of idea generation. Then hold a balloon debate, with competing visions or answers to the insight problem pitched against one another – five or ten minutes maximum per person or team, with a 60-second elevator pitch in summary at the end. Hold a vote at the end of the debate and chose the most insightful idea. Most likely, your insights will – in Matt Ridley's memorable phrase – have sex, and you'll end up combining the best of all candidate ideas. Try not to turn out a camel by committee instead of a horse, and don't allow your decision to merge insights to add complexity. Keep Occam's razor close at all times. In balloon debates, those representing ideas whose time is up are required to jump from a metaphorical, overloaded balloon basket.

Enter the dragons' den: As a variation on the balloon debate, pitch your idea to a set of putative "dragon" investors. Ensure your dragons are not involved with/don't have any personal stake in the insights being pitched in the den. Once the insights have been pitched, see which one or ones attract the most investment. The energy attracted by the winning pitches should give you a good indication of which have most potential, which represent the most profound and deep understanding of the topic, issue, or challenge.

Take the "last £100" test: Imagine that you'd had a run of really bad luck in business and business investments; perhaps you've played too much dragons' den, and all of your recent investments have been duds. Imagine that you have just £100 left. Would you invest that last £100 behind your idea, bringing your insight to life? Does it open up potential in ways you just hadn't appreciated? Again, those that offer potential are likely to be the most insightful.

Offer your insight-testing capabilities to others: Mutuality – you scratch my back, I scratch yours – is a fundamentally human characteristic. Let it be known among your colleagues and peers that you're up for helping them evaluate their ideas, insights, and potential innovations. In the spirit of "Google 10% time", where you make 10% of your time available to projects that are completely outside your day-to-day responsibilities, offer your time to others in your organisation to interrogate their insights on the basis that they do the same for you.

Put yourself in the stocks: Ritual humiliation isn't de rigueur (or even legal) in most workplaces today. But when it comes to showing useful vulnerability that enables your insightful ideas to be tested to the limit, create and participate in forums in which you invite others to test your ideas to the limit. Screw your courage to the sticking point, Lady Macbeth style, and invite mockery, ridicule, and metaphorical rotten tomatoes be hurled at your ideas. This is really just more extreme structured questioning, a balloon debate or dragons' den pitch on steroids. But far from making you the company whipping boy or girl, this act of ultimate vulnerability will also let you know pretty soon how robust your insight really is.

All of these tools, techniques, and approaches start from the perspective that, convinced as you are that you've had a genuine, breakthrough insight, you could be wrong. By putting yourself and your ideas in the firing line and showing that you're open to rejection, you're giving your potential insights the chance to fail – but also the chance to succeed. By contriving any number of different ways in which others can question and pull your insights apart, you're again showing a vulnerability and openness that is attractive and will encourage collaboration.

This collaboration will be for the particular challenge at hand, but will also most likely be for other projects or tasks, too. Many people believe and say they're "just too busy" to help pressure ideas in this way. But if they do and can see quite how helpful this cooperation can be – and how it can lead to co-creation and cut down development time – they're more than likely to seek out the same services from you. And as we know, adding an old stimulus (in this case the approach of one department) to another old stimulus (the approach of another) can very often lead to something new. Something powerful. Something insightful. An insight.

INTERVIEW: DR PETER COLLETT, UNIVERSITY OF OXFORD

Insightful interview 8 of 8

NAME	Dr Peter Collett
ORGANISATION	Oxford University
ROLE	Body language guru

For more than 20 years, Peter Collett was an Oxford don in the university's Department of Experimental Psychology. There his research gave academic rigour and a profound and deep understanding to the perennially popular topic of body language. His expertise on what our tics and tells reveal about our state of mind found a natural home on TV, from the BBC to Channel 4, where Collett was one of the first *Big Brother* psychologists. Today, he regularly tells viewers on Sky TV what world leaders really think and mean in his occasional *Uncovered* series. He has written widely on body language and is perhaps best known for his 2003 publication *The Book of Tells: How to Read People's Mind from Their Actions*.

For someone who's made a career out of piecing together tell-tale clues and tiny giveaways of what's really going on inside other people's heads, Peter Collett has a clear sense of what insight is and how the best insights are developed. He says it's "the ability to gain an understanding of the essential elements of either a problem or circumstances or someone else's state of mind – though it's not a conscious thing, by the way". Collett has a number of conditions that he believes need to be satisfied to make insight generation more likely. These include:

- **Reflection** – making time to be still, to allow the mind to do mind-y things. Modern life doesn't give us the luxury of time to let the mind get on with what it's so good at. And we waste too much time on worrying and fretting about how we're going to solve an insight problem when we really should be mulling, cogitating, and rolling the problem around in our minds.
- **Timeout** from a problem is really important. "Sleep is the best form of Timeout, and paradoxically, that's the time when the brain is really busy, shuffling and reshuffling what it's taken on board and trying to make sense of it, to categorise it, to find connections."
- **Scribbling and doodling**, taking your pen or pencil for a walk, creating shapes and connections between ideas, idly free-associating on an issue when you've done your research and seeing if a new configuration makes sense gets you to insight.
- **Writing** and expressing your thoughts, even if they're only just beginning to come into focus. "The act of writing can be intensely creative. Characters and contingencies can emerge when you set your ideas out in words." A combination of doodling and writing is how Darwin developed his tree of life (see Photo 8.1), and these tools and techniques for Collett can be both "the product and the progenitor of insight".

Darwin says in *On the Origin of Species*:

> "The affinities of all the beings of the same class have sometimes been represented by a great tree. . . . As buds give rise by growth to fresh buds, and these, if vigorous, branch out and overtop on all sides many a feebler branch, so by generation I believe it has been with the great Tree of Life, which fills with its dead and broken branches the crust of the earth, and covers the surface with its ever branching and beautiful ramifications."[5]

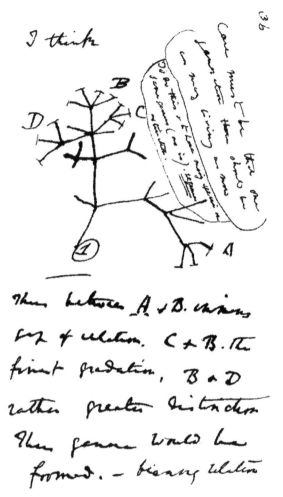

Photo 8.1 Darwin's tree of life

- **Conversations** – with yourself and others, gaining others' points of view on the issues you're considering, and adding these opinions into the "stimulus soup" you're creating. "We benefit in proportion to how different the other person is from us," says Collett. "The more you expose yourself to different constellations of variables, the more you start to see patterns, and for the student of insight, heterogeneity always trumps homogeneity; it's always difference over sameness."

- And of course **becoming a student of body language**. "All of my work is about insight – the gestures we make, the facial tics and tells, how we're sitting, how we move, our tone of voice, the clothes we choose to wear (or not wear). All of these are clues about what's going on. Read them well and right and your understanding of others will be profound and insightful. You'll have got inside someone else's head and be able to predict how they might respond to fresh stimuli you may throw their way."

"Our brain is much brighter than we are," Collett concludes. "It's doing all sorts of computations and combinations all the time, acquiring new information and then generating all sorts of candidate mini-epiphanies. Not all of them are genuine, breakthrough insights, but some of them are. And those are the essential element of any real sense of progress – personal, corporate, commercial."

NOTES

1 There are a *lot* of different mindmapping software packages available, including MindManager (www.mindjet.com), X-Mind (good on a Mac http://bit.ly/2MI2PWh), and iMind (www.imindq.com/). They all have devotees and salespeople, but I'd only encourage you to invest in one if you truly invest the time in mastering to use them at least as quickly as pens and paper. Ideally, more quickly. On writing software, I was initially very attracted to Scrivener but found that the medium was interfering with the message. Word is just so familiar and so easy and everyday that I concluded that investing the time in mastering Scrivener would get in the way of actually writing. And there's no point in that.
2 Austin Kleon (2012). *Steal Like an Artist*, Workman Publishing, p. 36.
3 It's said that the term "tissue meeting" was created by Jay Chiat, the founder of ad agency Chiat/Day, the agency responsible for iconic "1984" ad that launched the Apple Macintosh computer in the same year. Not all advertising executives like the tissue meeting. Here's a debate about the pros and cons in the UK ad industry bible, *Campaign* http://bit.ly/2N5B0Wz
4 Albert Einstein (10 June 1933). *On the Method of Theoretical Physics*. The Herbert Spencer Lecture at Oxford.
5 Charles Darwin (1998 edition). *On the Origin of Species*, Wordsworth editions, p. 100.

9

HOW TO BE MORE INSIGHTFUL

> *"Nothing is so powerful as an insight into human nature . . . what compulsions drive a man, what instincts dominate his action . . . if you know these things about a man you can touch him at the core of his being."*
>
> Original 1940s "madman" of Madison Avenue,
> Bill Bernbach

BRINGING THIS ALL TOGETHER

So there we have it. We've explored what insight is (and what it isn't), its progress through history, and what psychology and particularly neuroscience can tell us about insight. With all that in place, we went all metacognitive and thought about thinking. This gave us a highly practical and actionable model that anyone – however uncreative they may mistakenly believe themselves to be – can use to make it more likely they'll have the breakthrough insights they need. And they need them so that they can solve the most intractable problems that their bosses, colleagues, and clients might throw at them. With the simple scaffolding of the STEP Prism of Insight, it is possible to build cathedrals of the mind. It gives us all – public, private, or third sector, and in any role – a more reliable way of unlocking the one true superpower that actually drives innovation.

Figure 9.1 The STEP Prism of Insight – just one more time

And it's all down to curiosity, distraction, enlightenment, and co-creation. Sweat, Timeout, Eureka, and Prove.

So, if – as I maintain, and as I trust I've convinced you – this straight-forward model can help you be insightful, this final chapter gives advice about how to be even more insightful. It goes beyond the exercises associated with each quadrant of the STEP Prism, exercises designed to encourage you to capture and channel what you intuitively do each step of the way and to bring them into a more formal way of working. And it gives you a further set of tools and techniques that should put you and your colleagues in the situation where your insights are genuine insights and you can use them to tackle the challenges that you face in your organisation.

ALIGN YOUR DATA, EVIDENCE, AND FACTS – BUT ONLY AS A STARTING POINT

If you've ever grown vegetables – and particularly on an allotment – you'll know how hard it can be to create a steady stream of produce to supplement or even replace the supply from your local greengrocer or supermarket. For most of the year, you return from the allotment with nothing – apart from dirty fingernails, a pathological hatred for weeds, and scratches from brambles that seem to have grown and spread like triffids in the week since you were there last. Many of your intended crops either fail altogether for no obvious reason – particularly carrots or sweetcorn – or are eaten by slugs or rabbits or birds before you can get to them.

But if you plant courgettes – and always remember you need at least two plants to produce baby zucchini – come late summer, you will be faced by what is technically known as The Glut. So many courgettes that you soon run out of recipes (ratatouille, courgetti spaghetti, courgette cake, zucchini fritti/fries/frittata). So much produce that you end up, at the dead of night, dumping bags of them on the doorsteps of neighbours who once said, "If you ever have anything you don't need. . . ."

Data in the modern knowledge economy is like The Glut. For businesses and charities, universities and governments. All types of organisations, right across the spectrum of employment, have more data than they can cope with. There's an ever-stronger imperative – mandated by bosses and the apparent advantage being seized by others – to put it to work to competitive advantage. And at the same time there's a dire dearth of analytical talent and bandwidth to do just that. Even now we're often at the point where even modest data analysts can charge football star salaries.

As I showed in *Narrative by Numbers*, the explosion in data means that organisations are faced with a delicious data paradox and the paradox is this: it has never been more challenging to make sense of the data that surrounds an organisation, and yet it has never been more possible to do so. The trouble is knowing – even approximately – where to look and what to look for in order to build powerful, purposeful stories that resonate with those individuals or groups that an organisation is looking to influence. The principal challenges with The Glut of data are how to find and use relevant data and the need to be wary of the false positives that are an inevitable consequence of throwing together more and bigger data sets.

In the case of generating insight – of developing a profound and deep understanding of someone or something – The Glut presents us with a somewhat different challenge. We have already established that in order to increase your chances of being more insightful, you need to be curious – and almost certainly more curious than you are today. Curiosity requires you to find out more, ask more questions, absorb more data, access more data sources, be more lateral and less linear in what you consume, and look for inspiration from the unexpected. If you want to give your subconscious chance to create a novel and insightful recombination of different bits of old stuff into something new – and this is the very stuff of innovation – it has to have raw material to work with. These days, new somethings are very rarely created from nothing. So much has been invented that very few people are inventors any more. But many more are improvers and innovators, and those jobs need insight.

For insight generation, we should be less worried about the direct *relevance* of the information we consume and absorb. Who knows when that exhibition brochure or podcast might throw up a tasty morsel which, when combined with a nugget of market research and what an influencer posted last Thursday, might click into place and give us the blinding flash we need? What's more, as insight generation is clearly not a linear process but is rather more random – what statisticians call stochastic – I'd discourage anyone looking to become more insightful to ask, "When will I have taken in sufficient new stimuli to feed my subconscious?" It's perfectly possible that the first three bits of information you absorb in your quest to develop a deeper understanding become killer when your subconscious gets to work on them. But as being insightful is not like filling up a car with fuel, as it's not rigorously predictable, "when", "how much", and "what sort" questions matter much less.

The challenge presented by The Glut of data and information sources to insight seekers is that it can create a sense of paralysis in the face of all the potential opportunities for interesting and relevant data. Rather than not knowing what to snack on, it's often more like, "Where should I start?" There are so many places to go and people to talk to and things to read and watch and listen to that The Glut can trigger a freeze response and make you give up before you've started. And feeling overwhelmed – and yet still needing to solve an insight problem – can make you play safe. Revert to type. Come up with strategies that have worked before (for you or for competitors). Go to familiar, trusted data sources right in the heart of your echo chamber. And that approach is likely to lead you to either reuse an insight that's been overtaken by events or history or to do something that's neither new nor innovative and therefore won't change anything.

Here's an analogy. An analogy that assumes that university life 50 years from now, in many aspects apart from available data sources, will be more or less unchanged from today. Or even from my own, first experience of university life in the late 1980s.

Imagine you are a modern history student in 2070 set the challenge of writing about the British Brexit Crisis 2015–2025. Say a particularly vindictive professor had asked you to identify and rank the five most important factors that had led the UK government to seek readmission to the EU in 2029. You have access to videos of every speech made by every politician of every political party, with and without milkshake accompaniments. A bold initiative from Apple enables you to correlate politicians' biometrics – including heart rate, levels of stress hormones, and emotions both displayed *and* felt – with the words they said; an amazing use of Apple Watch data. You have archives of all news outlets' content and analysis, every post on social media by politicians, journalists, and members of the public. The darker side of the web – including both targeted, illegal ads on Facebook as well as the hidden recesses of ultra-right-wing nationalist sites – have all been catalogued and categorised by three helpful PhD students at the University of Maastricht. Voting records and patterns are available right down to the individual address level under the 2050 Freedom of Voting Information Act.

Where do you start? Well, a good place might be the YouGov poll from June 2019 which revealed the price that paid-up members of the

Conservative Party would be prepared to pay for Brexit, as replicated in Figure 9.2. Alongside documentary footage of soldiers shooting themselves repeatedly in the foot, as lemmings hurl themselves from cliffs onto barns full of turkeys, voting for Christmas.

But moving on from the realms of farce and fantasy, how can you hope in one week to craft a meaningful 5,000-word assignment from this mess, let alone rank the factors in order? You might have DataMinerBot AI software installed across all your devices, but you missed the webinar lecture on blended data. Your inner talk track might go something like this: "She's joking, right? This is one of those wild goose chases they tell you about at Freshers' Week. An exercise in futility which is more about the process of learning and finding out about how to learn rather than the subject itself – surely. I think I'll go to the bar."

My father Kenneth had an early life of extreme privilege, born into and growing up in Edwardian affluence in the early 20th century, his bedroom overlooking Hyde Park – even if he was disinherited in the early 1930s. He went to school at Winchester College, one of the most elite of elite of British public (fee-paying) schools; think a more rarefied Hogwarts. Like all young Wykehamists, Kenneth was keen to make a good impression, obey the rules, look keen. After a couple of days, he

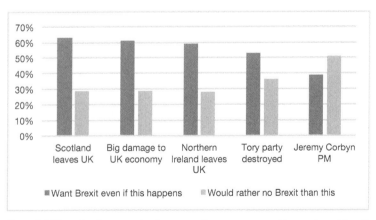

Figure 9.2 The price Conservative Party members are prepared to pay to get Brexit

was asked by one of the more senior boys, "So then, Knowles. Have you got your *pempe* yet?" Kenneth looked confused, paused, and stuttered. "Oh, you'd better go and see Howe about that . . ." said the senior boy, turning away in a flurry of coat tails, rushing off to Defence Against the Dark Arts.

So off he and many other new boys trotted, crossing paths, being sent hither and thither, blindly obeying orders to see this person, that under-gardener, this arts master, that prefect until finally . . . finally, under the pressure of this bizarre initiation ritual, he broke and asked whomever he'd been sent to most recently, "What is a *pempe*, sir?" If only he'd asked the first person who'd asked him, he'd have been told. "Why, it's nothing – and everything. *Pempe*. You read Greek, Knowles, don't you? *Pempe. Pempe moron proteron.* "Send the fool further." Your quest is at an end, but now write 1,000 words on what this means, and why, and have it with the headmaster by dawn tomorrow."

If you were that modern history student in 2070, you might feel like Kenneth. Come right back to your current job and consider the challenge you're facing, the seemingly intractable problem you need to solve, the insight into customer motivation you need to unlock. Does it all feel a bit *pempe*-ish? My advice – as a seasoned insight hunter with one or two things to say about insight – is to plunge in, right into the middle of things, and start absorbing. Start with the obvious – product data, market data, competitor behaviour, just to make sure there's nothing blindingly simple and straightforward that everyone's overlooked.

With the obvious out of the way, go broader, further afield, further leftfield. Look to the edges. Talk to people, look in places, visit environments that are not only not obvious but actually counter-intuitive. Want to know about the future of money and online banking? Then talk to people with neither money nor access to the internet, as Jem Fawcus suggested in Chapter 1. Talk to homeless people. Want to know about the next killer app for a smartphone? Engage with those who've never had a smartphone (admittedly an increasingly difficult tribe to identify and isolate). Try to learn what would make them reverse that ownership decision. What app would change their mind?

THE GAMES PEOPLE PLAY

Complete randomness of input may feel a bit too much like messing about and being random for randomness' sake. So, if that feels uncomfortable, be guided in your randomness. You could adopt the strategy of Luke Rhinehart, the nom de plume of the antihero of the cult 1971 novel *The Dice Man*. Set out a number of options (ideally six or 12) for where you could look next – whom you might consult next – and roll a di or two and "let the dice decide" for you.

Or buy a pack of *Oblique Strategies*, a set of 100 cards created by musician Brian Eno and artist Peter Schmidt in 1975. Each card features a challenging constraint designed to help break creative blocks.

Or use a set of Rory's Story Cubes – packs of nine dice, each covered with unusual icons or pictograms – which you roll and use to construct on-the-spot narratives. Interestingly, the concept started in 2004 when the eponymous Rory – a creativity trainer and coach – developed his first set of cubes as a creative problem-solving tool to help individuals and organisations look at problems in different ways. As the company has evolved over the past 15 years, it's found a huge market among children, and there are now Batman, Moomin, Looney Tunes, Scooby Doo, and Dr Who sets of cubes. Who knows where Batman or Bugs Bunny might take your next innovation and idea generation session. That really is looking to the edges, playing without constraints, and being properly childish.

Or work with an improvisational actor or troupe. It was Dan Pink in his book *To Sell Is Human* who first turned me on to the idea of improv. There are key lessons, including (i) saying "Yes, and . . ." not "No, but . . ."; (ii) seeing every new piece of information as an offer or an invitation (not something that will close down where you're going); and (iii) focusing on single ideas to keep performance scenes simple. These can all be incredibly powerful tools to force on-the-spot integration of old stuff into new stuff. And therefore of insight.

Or read and follow the advice of challenger brand guru Adam Morgan and Mark Barden in their book *A Beautiful Constraint*, or one of the myriad exercises set out by philosopher Daniel Dennett in his book *Intuition Pumps and Other Tools for Thinking*, from Occam's razor to the benefit of mistakes.

I love running workshops and most particularly for the games I get people to play – sorry, the exercises we run to stimulate insight and drive towards innovation. I'm no fan of the brainstorm. It's a technique that social psychology has definitively shown – particularly when done free form – encourages extraverts to show off and stifles contributions from introverts. I don't object to carefully choosing smaller, balanced groups of three or four, giving them each a role in their groups (chair, blue sky, voice of reason, scribe), and then having smaller groups report back their three best ideas to the bigger group. You see: a beautiful constraint.

One of my favourite and most productive exercises for short-term insight generation is an evolution of the psychological test known as Guildford's Alternate Uses.[1] The test was originally designed to reveal flexibility or fluidity of thinking – as detailed in Chapter 2. It asks subjects to think of as many possible uses of a simple, mundane object, such as a brick.

My adaptation of this test – perhaps it's more correct to say that it was inspired by this classic experiment – is called "If I was a . . ." Team members are asked to imagine their product, a competitor's product, a future product innovation, their company, their company's brand essence – the topic under consideration – as if it were something else entirely. "If my brand was . . ." a car, a holiday destination, a political party (careful), a celebrity, an alcoholic drink, a mode of transport, a genre of literature/film, a character in *Game of Thrones*, a food, an animal, a member of the Spice Girls, a sports personality, a sports team. Opportunities are only constrained by your imagination.

There's no end of tools and techniques that can set you off on the right path. What matters is that, to go on a voyage of discovery, you need to start. And not just for the current challenge that you face, but forever. Curiosity is a state of mind, a way of life, a forever commitment. If you want to be insightful, you have to be curious. You might need some guardrails – like Eno's or Morgan's or Dennett's – to get yourself going. But once you've practised and embraced curiosity one or two dozen times, it'll become second nature. As you'll see in the next section when we consider the Food Dudes programme.

PLEDGE YOUR ALLEGIANCE TO THE MODEL

Nike has been using its iconic "Just Do It" slogan since 1988. It was developed by Dan Wieden, the founder of ad agency Wieden+Kennedy. Perhaps surprisingly, Wieden was inspired by the last words of murderer Gary Gilmore, "Let's do it!"; Gilmore gained international notoriety in 1977 by insisting his death penalty be carried out for a double murder. Perplexing as Wieden's inspiration may be, "Just Do It" is a brilliantly pithy phrase that captures the insight underpinning Nike's purpose perfectly. This was first expressed by the company's co-founder, the legendary US track coach, Bill Bowerman, who said, "If you have a body, you are an athlete".

If you want to change your behaviour and do something different – for the long term – behavioural psychology tells us a three helpful and important things. The first is – to Gilmore, Wieden, and Bowerman's prescription – just to get on and do it. The more you do something you haven't habitually done, the more like the new you (and unlike the old you) it is. Your internal talk track becomes "I am the sort of person who goes running", "I am the sort of person who doesn't smoke", or "I am the sort of person who likes vegetables".

In part the act of doing transforms the individual, and your mental construct of yourself changes. The more often you observe yourself running or eating veg, the easier it is for you to accept yourself as a runner or a vegetable eater. And in part there's a process of what is known as systematic desensitisation. It's a technique that's used in cognitive therapeutic approaches to dealing with phobias, with progressive exposure to thoughts about and gradually the reality of the object of irrational fear. Like spiders, snakes, or – in my case – birds. This same technique is used to encourage schoolchildren to increase their consumption of fruits and vegetables, as in the Food Dudes programme pioneered by Professor Fergus Lowe and colleagues at Bangor University.[2] The more often children eat (and are rewarded for eating) novel foods, the less novel they become, and the more integrated they become into their eating repertoire; they become foods they choose to eat.

The second thing that behavioural psychology tells us about changing behaviour is that you're more likely to stick with a new behaviour if you make a public commitment or declaration of your intent to change. When I took up running in 2011 – initially as a joke, and to have something to write about – I started a blog about my experiences and shared it on social media, particularly Twitter. When it became clear to me, halfway through the Couch to 5K programme, that I'd stumbled upon something I loved, I upped my blogging and socialising game. I was making a virtual, repeated commitment to those in my circle that this was something I did – oh, and here's another one, another run. The blogs weren't really about running, they were about what I saw and thought about as I plodded round the roads and hills and fields of Sussex and beyond. But when I didn't blog for more than four or five days, I'd get messages on Twitter or via the blog asking if I was OK and if I was still running. This interactive, public commitment device of blog plus tweets inspired me to pull on my trainers and get out there again. At last count, there were 284 posts on https://firsttimerunner.wordpress.com.

And the third present from behavioural psychology is that, if you make a public commitment with a buddy who also makes commitments, you're that much more likely to succeed.

For all these reasons, now that you've gone through all the phases of the STEP Prism of Insight, I strongly recommend that you complete a pledge card for the four things you're going to do differently from now on, using the model.

- What's your **Sweat** – how will you make yourself more curious?
- What's your **Timeout** – how are you going to make sure that you're going to step away from the problem you're trying to solve, to allow your subconscious to do its marvellous and remarkable, recombinatorial thing?
- What's your **Eureka**? What are you going to do to be sure that you capture your breakthrough insight when it comes upon you? How will you recognise it?
- And what's your **Prove**? How are you going to share your insights – with colleagues, peers, or clients at just the right time? Early enough so that it's still fresh and not overworked, but late enough that it's been sufficiently developed and articulated.

I suggest that you fill in one new commitment in each of the four sections of the STEP Prism, under the following declaration: "Over the next three months, I pledge to start creating insights differently. I will do at least one thing new in each of the four quadrants of the STEP Prism of Insight – Sweat, Timeout, Eureka, and Prove." If you've done this exercise in a group, be sure to read your commitments to your colleagues and peers.

When I run training courses, I have these pledges produced and laminated on small cards (it makes them coffee-, beer-, and tear-proof). And then I send them back to the delegates as their own personal pledge cards – like those that Tony Blair and Peter Mandelson gave to all party members, candidates, and canvassers before the landslide 1997 and 2001 election victories by New Labour.

What's most gratifying for me is when I go back to train a new team in an client office where I've already run insight training and, as I walk past the desks of past delegates en route to the boardroom or wherever training is set to take place, they brandish their cards at me and say, "I'm still eating in a restaurant from a different country each month", "I'm still listening to and sharing new podcasts at our regular team meetings", or "I make sure I go to a museum or art gallery when I've filled my mind with stimulus but can't see the forest for the trees". Then I know that

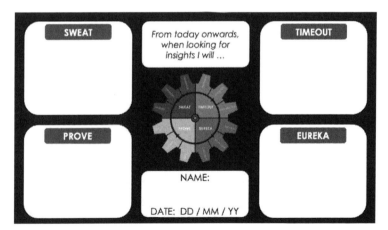

Figure 9.3 The STEP Prism of Insight pledge card

they're doing it for real, that their public commitment has stuck, and that making these commitments in front of peers and colleagues has worked its magic.

IT'S YOUR TURN

Copy the template from the page above or print a STEP Prism pledge card from www.howtobeinsightful.com/pledgecard and complete your own version. You'll be amazed how sticky it makes your commitment. Even better if you and other colleagues who've read the book make commitments together.

WHEN TO DO INSIGHT WORK

The US business writer Dan Pink has recently published a compelling book called *When*, subtitled *The Scientific Secrets of Perfect Timing*. There are two lessons in *When* that are particularly relevant for being more insightful. The first is the amusingly named, surprisingly effective Nappuccino that we've already considered (see p. 135).[3]

The second is Pink's assessment – based on the scientific consensus – of when it's best to do particular types of work, including when it's best to tackle insight problems. Whether you're a lark (like me, up at 5.40am like clockwork), an owl, or what Pink calls a "third bird"[4] – neither lark nor owl but somewhere in between, like 80% of the population – there are times in everyone's daily cycle that are optimal for different tasks.

Pink shares the research evidence that shows when during the day larks should do different things; the framing works for owls and third birds, too, it just that the start times are different. Pink shows that many of us do the wrong things at the wrong time of day. For instance, in the ascent to the peak, the ever-present tyranny of email means that most people spend the period best suited to data analysis, writing reports, and going through strategy proposals instead to doing one of the most mundane (and unsuitable) tasks that modern business throws at us: email.

That, he shows, would be much better done during the trough after the peak, a period much better suited to routine, relatively mindless tasks.

The ever-present tyranny of email means that many people do dive into emails first thing in the morning. For those with fear of missing out and perhaps particularly those with clients or collaborators in different time zones, the temptation to find out what's been going on while you've been asleep can mean that the email app is the first one that many people open, as early as when they're in bed, walking to the bathroom, or sitting on the loo. The desire to answer emails – often replying to all, quite unnecessarily – can mean that the email application on a computer is open all day. The "ding" of an incoming email can generate a Pavlovian conditioned response to drop everything and answer the email, all in the name of client or customer service.

This approach is draining, diverting, and most likely diverting your creative abilities to mundane tasks at the wrong time of day. If this is your regular modus operandi, consider whether you might change it, by only opening your email application at fixed times of the day (or week) and so only dedicating attention to email when it's the right time in your working day for you to do so, not to be at clients' and colleagues' constant beck and call. Customers and bosses want your best work, not your worst. And remember the evidence that suggests it can take ten times as long as you spent attending to an email to get back into the flow of what you were doing before you were diverted. Fifteen seconds' diversion to delete a spam flyer = two-and-a-half minutes' disruption; tolerable, perhaps. Fifteen minutes spent answering an email = two-and-a-half hours before you're back in flow; worth it?[5]

While this is all interesting, from the point of view of the central thesis set out in this book, I find it most interesting that Pink identifies the recovery period – late afternoon and into the evening for larks (later yet for third birds, and into the small hours for owls) – as "good for insight problems". As we've seen already, while the STEP Prism does not – and cannot – specify a time at which insight will strike, the recovery period does seem like a good part of the day during which any species of bird could invest time in capturing, sharing, and discussing the insights they are developing (Eureka and Prove). It also suggests that the period in the ascent to the peak is ideally suited to creating and articulating any nascent insights (Eureka), as well as flexing those curiosity muscles (Sweat). Meantime, divert your mind on the challenge at hand (Timeout) during the trough by "doing your emails" and also completing expenses or (if your organisation forces them on you) timesheets.

In *Elastic*, Leonard Mlodinow reports evidence from a French study by Rémi Radel which supports Dan Pink's assertion of when it makes most sense to do insight work. He concludes,

> The lesson is that, though we expect our best thinking time to be when we are fresh, our **elastic** thinking [emphasis in original] capacity may be highest when we feel "burnt out". That's good to know when scheduling your tasks – you could be better at generating imaginative ideas if you do that kind of thinking after working on a chore that involves a period of tedious, focused effort that strains your powers of concentration.

(p. 209)

That "period of tedious, focused effort" sounds very much like the administrative work Pink recommends for the trough.

IT'S YOUR TURN

Establish whether you're an owl, a lark, or – like most people – a third bird. Without altering the pattern of your working week, record when during the day you undertake different types of work. Are you a morning (and often all-day) emailer? Are you using the peak, trough, and recovery periods of the working day to optimal effect? How should you change to enhance how you spend your time, with a particular focus on the insight, ideation, and innovation aspects of your job?

INSIGHT SPOTTING FRAMEWORK

The purpose of this book is to introduce you to a new model of insight generation that will make you more insightful in tackling the challenges you face. And beyond the model, I also want to introduce you to my

Insight Spotting Framework. I find this to be incredibly helpful in understanding an existing product or proposition, where it fits in its own competitive space, and therefore where we might focus energies and attention for innovation.

Because I work a lot in marketing, market research, and marketing services, the framework focuses on brand campaigns and insights that underpin particular campaigns. As you'll see, it works for business-to-consumer as well as business-to-business companies. It also works for not-for-profit, charity, government, and public health campaigns. And with just a little bit of modification – omitting or leaving blank the second and third cells in the framework (campaign and execution) – it can work when you want to get under the skin (and into the head) of an organisation.

What's more, the framework encourages those who use it – individually and collectively – to identify the enemy, the mission, and the product truth of the brand, product, or organisation, all of which can be linked together. In this way, it calls upon the same kind of thinking as my workshop favourite, the "If I was a ..." game. This automatically has you thinking and bringing in information and data from alien worlds, looking to the edges, and seeking inspiration from atypical sources.

Before providing three worked-through examples, let's just set the parameters of the type of content you should put in each of the cells.

CRITERION	CONTENT
Brand	
Campaign	
Execution	
Insight	
Purpose	
Enemy	
Mission	
Product truth	

Figure 9.4 The Insight Agents' Insight Spotting Framework

Brand – which brand, product, or organisation are we considering?

Campaign – is there a particular campaign we're focusing on? If so, specify and detail it. If the campaign has a microsite, YouTube channel, Facebook page, Instagram feed, Twitter account – capture the details here for ready reference.

Execution – provide a short description of a specific execution related to the campaign at question or – if you're not evaluating a particular campaign – either leave this blank or give details of a few previous, iconic campaigns the organisation has run.

Insight – if you've got this far in the book, this should be no problem for insight spotting experts like you. If you were intimately involved in the campaign development, you'll find it on an advertising or communications brief. If you weren't, talk to those in your organisation or the agency(ies) that developed the work. And if they're not accessible, see if you can't create a meaningful articulation of the insight. What you don't want to do is present just data or casual observations that fail the patented "insight sniff" test. And although it's not a universal structure for insights, you could do worse than using the formula detailed in Chapter 1. Remember, that was:

[STATEMENT 1] because of [STATEMENT 2] creates [USEFUL CONSEQUENCE]

The example we considered at the time for Dove's Campaign for Real Beauty was expressed like this: "Women don't like how they are depicted by the beauty industry" BECAUSE "most women don't have (size zero) figures like those that dominate the media" AND AS A RESULT "they suffer from low self-esteem".

Consider the work Procter & Gamble has done every two years since it became a top tier Olympic sponsor – corporately and with its consumer product brands – to activate its annual $100m sponsorship of the games. Its "Thank you, mum (mom)" campaign has been run in dozens of markets and with the help of hundreds of athletes giving thanks to the sacrifices made by their mothers – the unsung heroes of Olympic success – for most of the past decade.[6] For "Thank you, mum" the insight could read,

"The mothers of Olympians make enormous sacrifices as their children grow and develop as sporting giants" BECAUSE "motherhood is a selfless role that asks for no reward" AND AS A RESULT "we should celebrate everything they do for their children".

Purpose – what the brand, product, or organisational purpose is. I don't mean "it washes clothes" or "it manufactures motorcycles". I mean what is the reason why it exists, the motivating principle that gets its employees out of bed every morning, the contribution it makes to the world because of its very existence. Many companies, swept along by apparently millennial concerns, seek to attach a moral, ethical, or social purpose to their brands, but for me, purpose doesn't have to tick any of these boxes. If it can – and it can do so credibly – then fine. But if it's a forced fit as it was with Pepsi and Kendall Jenner (see later) or there's even the slightest hint of greenwash or sanctimonious posturing that's entirely inappropriate and inauthentic for the brand, steer clear.

All organisations have a purpose, and for all businesses this is more than just "making money", "turning a profit", or "maximising return on shareholder value". Those are consequences of being in business, whatever CFOs may claim about fiduciary duties. Purpose is higher order than simply revenue and profit. Purpose is more than a mission or vision statement; it's the why behind the what, and, in that sense, is an expression of the insight behind why the organisation was established and what it exists to do. I often say to those who try to attach morality to purpose: "Purpose isn't about saving the world: it's much more important than that".

Here are some examples. Environmentally savvy outdoor clothing company, **Patagonia**, describes its purpose as "To build the best products, cause no unnecessary harm, use business to inspire and implement solutions to the environmental crisis". Unilever's antibacterial soap brand **Lifebuoy**, in active partnership with UNICEF and the World Bank, aims "To bring health and hygiene to a billion people". **Apple**'s purpose has shifted and flexed over the years, from "To make technology our slave, not our master" and "To create the 20th-century bicycle" to "To make manuals a thing of the past". Meantime, the **Royal Society of Arts** in London has spent more than 265 years attempting "To enrich society through ideas and action", though it may not always have expressed it quite that cutely. The purpose of my corporate and brand storytelling business, **Insight Agents**, is "To help companies sound like people and talk human". No social or environmental benefit there, just as there isn't in the **Harley-Davidson Motor Company**'s purpose, "To fulfil dreams of personal freedom". Ride on, easy rider.

If it's your own business for which you're completing an Insight Spotting Framework, you should either know or be able to access your purpose easily. If it's a client or prospect, you can ask them. And as purpose is deemed to be increasingly important, if you don't know anyone in the business you're profiling, Googling "[ORGANISATION NAME] AND purpose" often returns just what you need.

Enemy – the last three categories are interconnected. When we talk about enemies, we're not – necessarily – talking about competitors or rival organisations, however irritated they might make us feel. Enemies are often higher level; the personal, societal, or technological issue that the organisation at question is fighting against. They are those factors that get in the way of those we want to work with living the lives they want to lead. For an innovative transportation business – say Uber or Lyft – it could be generations of underfunding in public transport infrastructure and a lack of ready availability of affordable alternatives. For a free trade think tank, it could be a combination of red tape, regulation, and excessive taxation. For the National Trust (UK) or the National Parks (USA), it could be excessive screen time.

Enemies provide a rallying cry against which organisations can campaign like a non-governmental organisation or a charity, a UNICEF or a Greenpeace. When Persil discovered the value of children getting outside and dirty for its "Dirt Is Good" proposition, it took on screen time, helicopter parenting, and the overhype of stranger danger. And Persil is just a laundry brand.

Mission – having clearly established an enemy or enemies, an organisation can then identify its mission. This is an expression of purpose, but it's not the same thing as purpose. A mission can be very much more pointed and focused on the specific activities an organisation needs to undertake if it's to deliver on its purpose, if it's to defeat its enemies, if it's to deliver a successful campaign.

Product truth – this is what gives an organisation legitimacy and skin in the game to fight its enemies and even have its mission as its mission. If Persil as a brand were unable to remove grass stains, paint, and all varieties of food, it wouldn't be able to address its enemies or go on its mission. The laundry industry had made mothers (almost exclusively) feel like worse parents since the advent of soap opera as an advertising vehicle in the 1920s. "Whiter than whiteness" became synonymous with good parenting, and muddy knees the reverse.

Persil upended the category norms by declaring that "Dirt Is Good" in the mid-2000s, liberating parents to encourage kids to lead a life out loud, with fewer limits and no concern for muddy knees. Yet if the product couldn't be depended on – in the background – to deliver against its functional promise, the campaign would have fallen flat. What goes in this box of the Insight Spotting Framework needs to be a truth, after all.

Here are three, worked-through examples of the framework so you can see how it works and to inspire you to create one for your own organisation, for a client, or for a prospective client or partner you want to understand better – ideally with insight, with profound or deep understanding. They are for Sport England's "This Girl Can" campaign (2018), Pepsi's disastrous 2017 campaign, "Live for Now", and Nike's "Believe in Something" with Colin Kaepernick (also 2018). As you'll see, this framework can help identify failures as well as successes, including if you apply it at the planning stage and not just post hoc (or post mortem in the case of Pepsi).

Sport England – "This Girl Can"

"Fit Got Real" was the third in the series of films produced and distributed – largely without cost, on social media and not in paid-for spots online, on TV, or in cinema – by Sport England since the This Girl Can campaign began. What is so impressive about the campaign is that it has increased the number of women who regularly exercise by more than 1.6 million. More than 250,000 UK women now exercise every week who never exercised before the first execution broke. And this behaviour change and closing of the gender exercise gap appears to be permanent.

CRITERION	CONTENT
Brand	Sport England
Campaign	This Girl Can
Execution	Fit Got Real (2018) – https://www.youtube.com/user/thisgirlcanuk
Insight	Fitting exercise into busy lifestyles is challenging BECAUSE gyms are intimidating places where others judge you AND SO many girls and women don't take regular exercise
Purpose	To change perceptions of the benefits of exercise and close the gender exercise gap
Enemy	Worrying what others think, perceived barriers to exercise
Mission	To give women the confidence to take up exercise, sustainably
Product truth	Showing real women really exercising in real-life situations

Figure 9.5 Insight Spotting Framework for "This Girl Can"

Pepsi – "Live for Now"

When a brand strays into irrelevant, untenable territory, the results are often messy. In our always-on world, mistakes are not easily forgiven or ever forgotten because of the elephant-like memory of the internet. However much a brand might want to forget what it's said and done – and delete all official posts about that – traditional, digital, and social media commentary have an almost indefinite half-life. Pepsi discovered this to its cost with an ad that claimed its carbonated, caffeinated beverages could bring about, well, world peace.

In a high-production-values ad, produced by Pepsi's in-house Creative League Studio, we see young creative American citizens of different ethnic origins – a cellist, a photographer, a model (Kendall Jenner as herself), a guitarist, and dancers. All these creative types are near to a non-specific protest (lots of placards, but no evident cause). The protest appears to be growing to a crescendo when Jenner steps out of her photoshoot, pulls off her blonde wig, wipes her lipstick off with the back of her hand, and walks to the front of the protest. She picks up a can of ice-cold Pepsi and hands it to a police officer facing the protestors. He opens it, takes a swig, smiles, and the tension dissipates.

CRITERION	CONTENT
Brand	Pepsi
Campaign	Live for Now
Execution	Kendall Jenner – https://www.youtube.com/watch?v=dA5Yq1DLSmQ
Insight	People get really hot and bothered on protest marches BECAUSE there are significant differences between us AND SO why not cool them off with an ice-cold soda
Purpose	To bring people of different cultures together in the spirit of harmony
Enemy	Protests with insufficient, poor quality soft drinks; oh, and racial tension
Mission	To alleviate tensions with our refreshing products
Product truth	Carbonated soda really can cut through your thirst on a hot day

Figure 9.6 Insight Spotting Framework for "Live for Now" (sarcastically completed)

The ad has the end line: "Live bolder – Live louder – Live for now". It was released in the wake and context of a series of angry confrontations between the Black Lives Matter movement and US police. The ad incited an immediate and powerful backlash against Pepsi, which at first defended the campaign, saying that is was "a global ad that reflects people from different walks of life coming together in the spirit of harmony and we think that's an important message to convey". Kind of like the 1971 Coke ad with the soundtrack of "I'd Like to Teach the World to Sing" only in much more politicised and radically aggravated times.

The campaign was pulled in the wake of the backlash and was followed by a consumer boycott. The satirical TV programme *Saturday Night Live* included a sketch in which the imagined director of the ad summed up public reaction well by voicing the line, "We're just kind of using it to sell soda". In the spoof, the director tries to explain and justify the ad to family and friends on the phone by saying, "We stop the police from shooting black people by giving them a Pepsi".[7] Mmm-hmm.

It's unfair to tarnish all in-house production facilities with the Pepsi brush – and I know for a fact that PepsiCo is taking purpose much more seriously these days – but it seems unlikely that an external agency would ever have been sufficiently blinkered, unworldly, and fundamentally lacking in insight to bring this ad forward for Pepsi's consideration. They had – in the industry vernacular – been "smoking their own dope and drinking their own Kool Aid" (though Kool Aid is made by Mondelēz and not PepsiCo, of course).

Nike – "Dream Crazy"

American football star Colin Kaepernick, an African-American, refused to stand – and instead "took the knee" or kneeled – during the National Anthem before San Francisco 49ers games in 2016 and 2017. His protest was against racial injustice and systematic oppression in the USA. His action spawned a protest movement, with other players of diverse racial origin, following his lead. The campaign intensified when US President Trump called on National Football League teams to fire any player who protested as Kaepernick and others had. Kaepernick left the 49ers at the end of the 2017 season, became a free agent, but has not been signed since.

In the Nike ad, Kaepernick was the narrator – and subject – of a two-minute film telling the real stories of a large number of courageous athletes who have taken a stand against the odds stacked against them.

CRITERION	CONTENT
Brand	Nike
Campaign	Just Do It – 30th anniversary
Execution	Dream Crazy – https://www.youtube.com/watch?v=E48hHS-5HyM
Insight	We limit our aspirations for ourselves BECAUSE society tells us there's only so far we can go AND that stifles opportunity
Purpose	To ensure we consider and act on the campaign mantra: "Don't ask if your dreams are crazy. Ask if they're crazy enough."
Enemy	Society, conventions, norms, rules, politicians
Mission	To encourage everyone to "Just Do It" and realise world-beating potential
Product truth	Nike supports the craziest dreamers in sport, determined to take on prejudice, tragedy, seemingly insurmountable challenges – and become the world's best. Including the voice of a generation, Colin Kaepernick

Figure 9.7 Insight Spotting Framework for "Believe in Something".

Nike made the film to celebrate 30 years of encouraging athletes to "Just Do It", although Kaepernick's front-page and back-page news made him the most high-profile, controversial figure of all featured. The campaign caused a backlash against Nike, first from marketing commentators who predicted Nike's demise and then from white (often ultra-right-wing) Americans burning their Nikes, encouraging a boycott, and declaring they'd never buy from Nike again.

Despite the backlash, Nike sales improved immediately and sustainably, and its share price rocketed. Perhaps most satisfyingly of all, a sports store owner in Colorado who chose to boycott Nike products in the wake of the campaign and surrounding furore, went out of business after 21 years.[8] What's more, many of the social media posts of angry Americans burning their Nikes under the hashtag #JustBurnIt turned out to have been posted from IP addresses or accounts registered in Russia, as detailed in a report on *Wired*.[9] The very same bot farms responsible for reposting ads from the Trump and Leave.EU campaigns. This a campaign and topic that I and my fellow presenters addressed more than once on the Small Data Forum (www.smalldataforum.com), the monthly podcast focused on the uses and abuses of data big and small in media, politics, and public life that I co-founded in 2016 and continue to co-host.

IT'S YOUR TURN

With the framework explained in detail and two good (and one awful) campaigns detailed in the section above, now it's your turn to apply it to a brand, company, or organisation that you know well. It can be your own, a client, or a prospective client or partner. Be as honest and as clear as you can. If you're working in a team, make sure you all go through this section of the book, then complete the framework individually. Then come together to produce a definitive version of the framework that incorporates as many points and points of view as possible. And be sure that the insight is a genuine, data-driven insight that provides profound and deep understanding.

If you can fill all of the boxes in the Insight Spotting Framework, if you know your organisation's purpose, its enemies, the mission it's on, and the truths inherent in its offer – products, services, or ideas – and if you didn't earlier but now have a clear sense of the insight that underpins it, it should be straightforward to articulate it now.

THE LAST WORD

This framework, taken with the other tools and techniques outlined in this chapter and the channelled way of thinking about thinking revealed in the STEP Prism of Insight, should conspire to make you, your colleagues, and your organisation very much more insightful. In this way, you'll be able to live up to the promise held out in the quote from Bill Bernbach at the start of this chapter and you'll be able to "touch [a man] at the core of his being". And a woman. And whomever you're looking to influence of whatever gender, wherever they're from.

And because I'm always learning and always curious to find out others' experiences of insight and how to be insightful, track me down on Twitter or LinkedIn – I'm very discoverable – @samknowles and @insightagents and in the community we're looking to grow at www.howtobeinsightful. com. Come and say hi, and do let me know how you get on in your quest to unlock the superpower that drives innovation.

NOTES

1 The original paper is here R.C. Wilson, J.P. Guilford, P.R. Christensen, & D.J. Lewis (1954). A Factor-Analytic Study of Creative-Thinking Abilities. *Psychometrika*, 19, 297–311 http://dx.doi.org/10.1007/BF02289230
2 Professor Fergus Walsh: "The Food Dudes programme: Changing children's eating for life", http://caer.bangor.ac.uk/research/food-dudes.php.en
3 Dan Pink: "Nappuccino: A Scientific 5-Step Guide to the Perfect Nap", http://bit.ly/2VI1EXY
4 Despite running through more than 5,000 birds' names, Pink couldn't settle on a new, avian descriptor of 80% of the population. So he chose the enigmatic "third bird".
5 David Burkus (2016). How Email Made You Less Productive. *Forbes* http://bit.ly/2YJHLI3

6 P&G's campaigns have always been tearjerkers. Here's a recent example about mums helping their athlete children overcome bias and prejudice – as well as getting them to training on time, making them costumes, feeding them, caring for them more generally – ahead of the 2018 Winter Olympics: www.youtube.com/watch?v=sUg6s-ulp1w

7 The (imagined) writer-director of the Kendall Jenner Pepsi ad shares his concepts with friends and family just before the shoot – with thanks to *Saturday Night Live* www.youtube.com/watch?v=Pn8pwoNWseM

8 Adrian Horton (14 February 2019). Sports Store That Boycotted Nike over Colin Kaepernick Ads Forced to Close. *The Guardian* http://bit.ly/2wgYNLs

9 Matt Burgess (27 September 2018). Here's Proof That Russian-Backed Accounts Pushed the Nike Boycott. *Wired* http://bit.ly/2Hy8KKA

WHERE TO FIND OUT MORE

Here are some of the books and writers who inspired me directly in my personal odyssey towards insight. There are some TED talks and other stuff too, in a few pages, but mostly it's about good old-fashioned treeware. Ah the glory of books!

BOOKS

Adams, Douglas (1982). *Life, the Universe and Everything*. Pan.

Beahm, George (2011). *I, Steve: Steve Jobs in His Own Words*. Agate B2.

Blackmore, Susan (2000). *The Meme Machine*. Oxford University Press.

Briggs, Asa (2011). *Secret Days: Codebreaking in Bletchley Park: A Memoir of Hut Six and the Enigma Machine*. Frontline Books.

Chater, Nick (2018). *The Mind Is Flat: The Illusion of Mental Depth and the Improvised Mind*. Allen Lane.

Dennett, Daniel C. (2013). *Intuition Pumps and Other Tools for Thinking*. Penguin.

Earls, Mark (2015). *Copy, Copy, Copy: How to Do Smarter Marketing by Using Other People's Ideas*. John Wiley & Sons.

Foster, Richard (2001). *Creative Destruction: Why Companies That Are Built to Last Underperform the Market: And How to Successfully Transform Them*. Crown Business.

Gallop, Angela (2019). *When the Dogs Don't Bark*. Hodder & Stoughton.

Gladwell, Malcolm (2009). *Outliers: The Story of Success*. Penguin.

Grayling, Anthony Clifford (2019). *The History of Philosophy*. Viking.

Greenfield, Baroness Susan (2015). *Mind Change: How Digital Technologies Are Leaving Their Mark on Our Brains*. Rider.

Griffiths, John & Tracy Follows (2016). *98% Pure Potato*. Unbound.

Harari, Yuval Noah (2015). *Sapiens*. Vintage.

Hofstadter, Douglas R. (1979). *Gödel, Escher, Bach: An Eternal Golden Braid: A Metaphorical Fugue of Minds and Machines in the Spirit of Lewes Carroll*. Penguin.

Innocent Drinks (2009). *A Book about Innocent: Our Story and Some Things We've Learned*. Michael Joseph.

Johnson, Steven (2011). *Where Good Ideas Come From*. Penguin.

Judkins, Rod (2015). *The Art of Creative Thinking*. Sceptre.

Judkins, Rod (2017). *Ideas Are Your Only Currency*. Sceptre.

Kahneman, Daniel (2011). *Thinking, Fast and Slow*. Penguin.

Kaufman, Scott Barry & Carolyn Gregoire (2015). *Wired to Create*. Penguin Random House.

Klein, Gary (2013). *Seeing What Others Don't: The Remarkable Ways We Gain Insights*. Nicholas Brealey Publishing.

Kleon, Austin (2012). *Steal Like an Artist: 10 Things Nobody Told You about Being Creative*. Workman Publishing.

Kleon, Austin (2019). *Keep Going: 10 Ways to Stay Creative in Good Times and Bad*. Workman Publishing.

Knight, Phil (2016). *Shoe Dog: A Memoir by the Creator of Nike*. Scribner.

Knowles, Kenneth (1952). *Strikes: A Study in Industrial Conflict*. Basil Blackwell, Oxford.

Knowles, Sam (2018). *Narrative by Numbers: How to Tell Powerful and Purposeful Stories with Data*. Routledge.

Koestler, Arthur (1964). *The Act of Creation*. Hutchinson.

Kounios, John & Mark Beeman (2015). *The Eureka Factor: Creative Insights and the Brain*. Windmill Books.

Lee, Harper (1960). *To Kill a Mockingbird*. Arrow. 50th anniversary edition published in 2010.

Lewis, Michael (2016). *The Undoing Project*. Allen Lane.

Liddell, Henry George & Robert Scott (1940). *A Greek-English Lexicon*. Clarendon Press. New (ninth) edition.

Marsh, Henry (2014). *Do No Harm*. W&N.

Marsh, Henry (2018). *Admissions*. W&N.

Mlodinow, Leonard (2018). *Elastic: Flexible Thinking in a Constantly Changing World*. Allen Lane.

Morgan, Adam & Mark Barden (2015). *A Beautiful Constraint: How to Transform Your Limitations into Advantages and Why It's Everyone's Business*. John Wiley & Sons.

O'Brien, James (2018). *How to be Right . . . in a World Gone Wrong*. WH Allen.

Ogilvy, David (1985). *Ogilvy on Advertising*. Vintage.

Packard, Vance (1956). *The Hidden Persuaders*. Penguin.

Pink, Dan (2014). *To Sell Is Human*. Canongate Books.

Pink, Dan (2018). *When: The Scientific Secrets of Perfect Timing*. Riverhead Books.

Pinker, Steven (1999). *How the Mind Works*. Penguin.

Pinker, Steven (2007). *The Stuff of Thought: Language as a Window into Human Nature*. Penguin.

Poincaré, Henri (1914). *The Foundations of Science: Science and Hypothesis, the Value of Science, Science and Method*. Thomas Nelson & Sons. Complete text, http://bit.ly/2w7lt0z

Poynton, Robert (2019). *Do: Pause*. Do Book Co.

Rhinehart, Luke (George Cockcroft) (1971). *The Dice Man*. William Morrow/Talmy Franklin.

Rosling, Hans, Ola Rosling, & Anna Rosling Rönnlund (2018). *Factfulness*. Sceptre.

Sharma, Robin (2004). *The Monk Who Sold His Ferrari*. HarperCollins.

Silver, Nate (2012). *The Signal and the Noise: Why So Many Predictions Fail — But Some Don't*. Penguin.

Spiegelhalter, David (2019). *The Art of Statistics: Learning from Data*. Pelican.

Sullivan, Luke (1998). *Hey Whipple, Squeeze This: A Guide to Creating Great Ads*. John Wiley & Sons.

Syed, Matthew (2015). *Black Box Thinking*. John Murray.

Tasgal, Anthony (2018). *The Inspiratorium: A Space for the Curious*. LID Publishing.

Trott, Dave (2015). *One Plus One Equals Three*. Macmillan.

Walker, Matthew (2017). *Why We Sleep: The New Science of Sleep and Dreams*. Penguin.

Wallas, Graham (1926). *The Art of Thought*. Reprinted 2014 by Solis Press.

Webster, Richard (2005). *Why Freud Was Wrong*. The Orwell Press.

Young, James Webb (1940). *A Technique for Producing Ideas*. Reprinted 2003 by McGraw Hill Education.

Zaki, Jamil (2019). *The War for Kindness: Building Empathy in a Fractured World*. Crown (an imprint of Random House).

TED TALKS AND OTHER VIDEOS

Brené Brown on Empathy – and the differences between empathy and sympathy. Excellent short animation from the Royal Society of Arts, http://bit.ly/2FjDe1x and thanks to Saskia for the tip.

Creamer, Alastair (October 2012). The revolution looks like this (on why everyone is creative), TEDxOlso, www.youtube.com/watch?v=EUzSR45i8oE

Gordon-Levitt, Joseph (April 2019). How craving attention makes you less creative, TED2019, http://bit.ly/2ZyILMU

Kounios, John (2016). The Eureka Factor: Aha moments, creative insight, and the brain, http://bit.ly/2H2YdGU

Oppezzo, Marily (April 2017). Want to be creative? Go for a walk, TEDxStanford, http://bit.ly/2Zx0qk6

TED talk playlist on "Where do ideas come from?" http://bit.ly/2QczrHy, including:

- Johnson, Steve (July 2010). Where good ideas come from, TEDGlobal2010, http://bit.ly/2NAUowM
- Grant, Adam (February 2016). The surprising habits of original thinkers, TED2016, http://bit.ly/2L0UyLS
- Ridley, Matt (July 2010). When ideas have sex, TEDGlobal2010, http://bit.ly/3432lk8

OTHER STUFF

Rory's Story Cubes (2004). www.storycubes.com

Schmidt, Peter & Brian Eno (1975). *Oblique Strategies*. Available as randomly generated suggestions, http://stoney.sb.org/eno/oblique.html or to buy as cards at www.enoshop.co.uk

INDEX

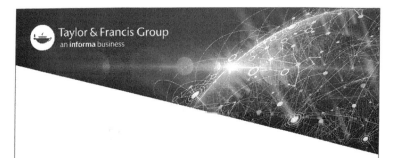